THE DYNAMICS
OF DISCUSSION

THE DYNAMICS
OF DISCUSSION
Communication
in Small Groups

SECOND EDITION

Stanley E. Jones
University of Colorado, Boulder

Dean C. Barnlund
San Francisco State University

Franklyn S. Haiman
Northwestern University

HARPER & ROW, PUBLISHERS, New York
Cambridge, Hagerstown, Philadelphia, San Francisco,
London, Mexico City, São Paulo, Sydney

1817

Sponsoring Editor: Alan M. Spiegel
Production Manager: Jeanie Berke
Compositor: TriStar Graphics

Art Studio: Vantage Art Inc.

THE DYNAMICS OF DISCUSSION
Communication in Small Groups,
Second Edition

Library of Congress Cataloging in Publication Data
Jones, Stanley E.   1935–
    The dynamics of discussion.
    Edition for 1960 by D. C. Barnlund and F. S.
Haiman.
    Bibliography: p.
    Includes index.
    1. Small groups. 2. Decision-making, Group.
3. Discussion. I. Barnlund Dean C., joint author.
II. Haiman, Franklyn S., joint author. III. Title.
HM133.J65   1980   301.18′5   79–23412
ISBN 0-06-380438-7

CONTENTS

v

PREFACE

The first edition of *The Dynamics of Discussion* by Dean C. Barnlund and Franklyn S. Haiman was a leading book in the field of small-group communication for over a decade. I joined Barnlund and Haiman in writing this second edition. So that I have no "hidden agenda," I should point out that a major purpose of this preface is to show how sound and challenging the first edition of the book was in its basic conception as well as how new thinking and research have caused us to reexamine some of the topics and positions of that text.

At first, we had a rather simple revision and update in mind. But after our initial discussions, there were so many ideas we wanted to develop that we were soon planning a number of new chapters and substantial revisions of old chapters. We felt that the major strength of the first edition was that it had a consistent, coherent perspective, which we wished to retain as the foundation of the present edition. In the following section I will describe that perspective, and, in the succeeding section, I will present the new features of the second edition.

A POINT OF VIEW

Barnlund and Haiman brought together two currents of thinking which continue to provide the basis for present-day conceptions of the nature of groups and discussion. The first of these currents was begun in the 1920s by John Dewey and his associates—applied scientists who concerned themselves with the ways ideas are generated and tested. The second current was initiated by Kurt Lewin, who developed a psychological theory of groups in the 1930s and 1940s. The many others who followed him continued to develop this theory through laboratory and field investigations.

The synthesis of these approaches which Barnlund and Haiman sought had certain features. First, it called attention to the fact that many of the problems and potentials of group action were shared by all democratic institutions. Second, it stressed the idea of "dynamics"—that behavior in groups is determined by a multiplicity of variables, including choices made by the participants. With this perspective, it was not surprising that the authors did not believe there were any discussion techniques that would work in all situations. A third feature of their synthesis was a consistent but open-ended treatment of the subject of group discussion. This means that while the entire book was based on certain philosophical assumptions (described in Chapter 1 of this edition), the advantages and disadvantages of *various* approaches to group discussion were often described, leaving it to readers to make choices among the available alternatives.

As a consequence of this point of view, the authors developed a number of distinctive orientations to specific topics in the first edition which we have retained in this book. Some of these are as follows: (1) "Leadership" was seen as a function of groups which could potentially be shared by all group members and which was not likely to be invested successfully in any one person. (2) "Norms" were not discussed simply as invisible standards to which a group aspired (as they are in some other treatments of this topic), but rather they were linked to tangible phenomena—patterns of behavior—which can be observed and predicted. (3) Discussion was considered as more than "cooperative" behavior. The notion that confrontation and dissension are frequent and essential aspects of group discussion was developed in one of the first treatments of the topic of "conflict" in the field of communication. (4) Relationships among various types of groups were stressed through the concept of "the continuum of discussion groups." While primary emphasis was given to decision making, other purposes were also examined, including those of "cathartic" and "learning" groups.

MAJOR ADDITIONS AND CHANGES IN THE PRESENT EDITION

While the philosophical and psychological currents of thought begun by Dewey and Lewin continue to influence our thinking, we have also been influenced strongly in this edition by a relatively new current coming from the maturing field of communication theory and research. Recent developments have caused us to re-think our positions on three key issues.

A New Look at Discussion Skills

We reaffirm the position that insight into and awareness of complex factors affecting group discussion are more important to effective participation than are specific techniques. However, in this edition we do call attention to what Michael Argyle has called "social skills"—complex acts required for maintaining the flow of conversation or for "reading" the responses of others. Many of these skills are concerned with the "nonverbal" aspects of communication, although most involve a combination of verbal and nonverbal messages. Such skills are not taught, we are confident, by prescriptions found in books. They are acquired mostly, we believe, through *awareness* and *imitation* of models. To this end, we have included some descriptions of such behaviors in order to create awareness as a basis for imitative behavior.

Renewed Emphasis on Communicative Acts and Processes

In this edition, we have tried to strengthen the amount of attention given to the role of *message exchanges* in group functioning. There are no separate chapters on "communication" because the entire book focuses on how groups are made to work (or fail) by the process of communication. For example, we are concerned not only with the effect of "cohesiveness" on group productivity, but also with the exchanges among people which tend to create or negate the development of feelings of attraction to the group and the messages which signal the growth or decline of such feelings. Such topics as "nonverbal communication," "the use of language," and "communication networks" (who talks to whom), which will be discussed at some length in the book, are considered under broader topics such as group norms and social pressure, leadership, and cohesiveness.

Treatment of Conflict as a Potentially Positive or Negative Phenomenon

Although conflict was recognized as a normal and necessary part of discussion in the first edition, it was also treated primarily as something to be overcome or resolved. Although we hold that conflict often stems from misunderstandings of the motives of others and mistaken assumptions of individuals about threats to their interests, we also recognize that conflict can come about because of genuine clashes of interest. In this edition, we more strongly stress the positive aspects of conflict. We note, for example, that expressions of conflict may often be signs of healthy functioning in a group. The fact that group members confront one another suggests, in most cases, that they trust others and themselves well enough to bring differences into the open and to struggle for change, and we recognize that often conflict should be encouraged as a means of promoting needed changes.

ORGANIZATION OF THIS BOOK

This edition has five major sections. Part I, The Role of Discussion in Human Affairs, examines those processes which are basic to all groups and introduces concepts which are used throughout the book. The next two parts are based on the idea that each group has both a socioemotional, or interpersonal, dimension as well as a task or problem-solving dimension. Part II, Interpersonal Relations in Groups, examines factors which influence the way discussants feel about the group, other individuals, and their own roles. Part III, Problem Solving in Groups, focuses on task accomplishment. Conflict management and descriptive and prescriptive approaches to the process of decision making are examined here. Part IV, Leadership in Groups, deals with processes which cut across the socioemotional and task dimensions since groups need leadership in each of these areas. In the final part, Implications of the Discussion Process, the impact of groups on individuals and the values of group discussion are assessed.

ACKNOWLEDGEMENTS

So many people have influenced the first and second editions of this book that it would not be possible to list them all. However, the authors would like to acknowledge the help of Diane Jones, Thomas Frentz, and Elaine Yarbrough, who read portions of the manuscript and gave advice at various points in its preparation. We would also like to thank Mrs. Goldie Graham and Mrs. Beth Crary of the staff of the Department of Communication at the University of Colorado, Boulder, for the typing of the manuscript.

STANLEY E. JONES

Part I
THE ROLE OF DISCUSSION IN HUMAN AFFAIRS

Chapter 1
A Perspective on Discussion

There is a curious contradiction in the myths that are nurtured by a democratic society such as ours. On the one hand, we tell ourselves that every individual makes a difference—that every vote counts, that any child may grow up to be president, that great events of history are frequently shaped by the influence of one person. Yet we also extol the supreme virtues of group efforts—from ball team to space team, from Junior Achievement to Senior Citizens, from the town meeting to the state and national legislature. "Be yourself," says one set of voices. "Be a good team player," says another.

The realities of our culture are no less contradictory than are the myths in their pressures upon us. Individual achievement is, in fact, often handsomely rewarded with money, power, and prestige. We look for celebrities in the worlds of politics, journalism, entertainment, and sports, and concentrate upon them the almost incessant attention of the mass media. Yet behind these personalities is a vast, usually invisible, network of organized effort that makes their stardom possible. One can, with little difficulty, recite the names of "movers and shakers" of the recent past such as Billy Graham, Martin Luther King, Jr., John Gardner, to mention but a few, who would have been nothing without well-run organizations behind them. Even Ralph Nader, who, perhaps more than any other person on the contemporary American scene, came to public prominence as a "loner," soon began functioning as part of a cohesive and highly effective team. It is clear that only through organizing the combined energies of many people does anyone make a lasting impact on a society as vast and complex as the one in which we live.

It is not only those seeking to change society who must engage in group interaction to achieve their ends. At every stage of our lives all of us function as participants in small groups. Most of us start out as members of a family and as students in a classroom. Those who become employed are involved in work groups of one kind or another. The majority of us find our recreational outlets with other people—in social groups, hobby groups, sports groups, music groups, and other associations based on common interests. Community organizations, service clubs, religious activities, and political endeavors also attract the participation of large numbers of people. In all of these associations we interact with others as we seek to achieve whatever personal goals we may have. Interaction in large measure means group discussion, for it is primarily through the process of oral communication that members of groups share their feelings, coordinate their activities, and make their decisions.

DISCUSSION AND DEMOCRACY

Where there is discussion, there is also the possibility of mutual influence, for when people are made aware of the needs and views of others, they may adjust their own thoughts and behavior accordingly. Where there is mutual influence, there is what we call a "democratic process," for the essence of that process is the exchange of information and attitudes among people for the purpose of arriving at group decisions in which all have had an equal opportunity to participate.

As the number and variety of group efforts in our society have multiplied and as the amount of discussion taking place has correspondingly expanded, the pressure for communication to be mutually influential, or democratic, has also increased. An understanding of the causes of that pressure will help us to see why some people have optimistically proclaimed that democracy in group interaction is "inevitable" (Slater and Bennis, 1964, pp. 51–59). Others, meanwhile, have called attention to counterforces which serve to inhibit the development of democratic processes.

The first and most obvious reason for the increase in mutuality of influence that has occurred in many kinds of groups was already alluded to when we noted the growth in the size and complexity of our institutions and of our problems. With greater size and complexity has come greater specialization of knowledge, followed by greater dependence of one person upon another. One can no longer be a rugged individualist in the frontier sense of the word. The old-fashioned business tycoon, for example, who was familiar with every detail of a company and could make decisions single-handedly, must now turn to lawyers and accountants to help with tax problems, engineers to help with automation, and psychological consultants to advise on personnel matters. Whether a problem be a matter of family concern or a high-level decision about government economic or foreign policy, the insights and knowledge of all who are affected by that problem are essential to finding adequate solutions.

Although the factors of size and complexity can account for much of the collaborative action that now takes place, they do not by themselves explain the extent to which it has been carried, for leaders and coordinators could still collect the information they need from individual specialists and make the final decisions themselves. This is, in fact, done in many instances. There would seem to be still other reasons why government administrators, businesspeople, teachers, and organization leaders have moved so strongly in the direction of group discussion as a means of conducting their affairs.

Another cause appears to be the growing realization that, as a result of having the opportunity to exert influence, the members of a group are better informed and more loyal than had they not had a share in the decision-making processes. In the case of educational groups, participation in free discussion seems not only to increase a student's interest in learning but also to enable the student to assimilate material more thoroughly. In the case of groups whose purpose is to make policies, it has been found that participation in that process increases a member's willingness to work for the implementation of whatever actions are agreed upon. In both instances, the opportunity to be influential leads to a greater sense of identification with the group and intensified attraction to its goals.

But this insight has been known to wise people for centuries, so that although the realization of it may be catching on in wider circles, it is difficult to believe that this factor alone would account for a large share in the growth of democratic processes. As far back as the Renaissance, the political philosopher Marsiglio of Padua recognized the validity of this principle—at least on a society-wide basis if not explicitly with respect to small groups:

> A law is useless if not obeyed. . . . Since that law is better observed by any one of the citizens which he seems to have imposed upon himself, the best law is made by the deliberation and command of the multitude of citizens. . . . This cannot be if a single man or a few make law by their own authority. . . . In such case the remainder of the citizens, perhaps the majority, would endure such a law, however good, with impatience or not at all, and bearing contempt toward the law would contend that not having been invited to

share in its creation they would in no wise observe it. On the other hand, any citizen will endure and obey a law however irksome, that is made from the deliberation and consent of the whole multitude, because he himself seems to have imposed it upon himself and, therefore, cannot complain against it (Marsiglio of Padua, in Coker, 1938, pp. 250–251).

We may find a fuller explanation for the increasing acceptance and use of collaborative group communication if we examine two other important and interrelated cultural developments which have had their impact at both the societal and small-group levels—the breakdown of traditional authority and the demand by large numbers of previously deprived individuals that they be accorded the rights and respect that are given to other people.

The breakdown of traditional authority is not a phenomenon that is unique to our times, much as those who decry its occurrence would like us to believe. Challenges to dogmas and decrees of those in authority, whether on questions of government, religion, the physical environment, social custom, or sexual mores, have occurred wherever and whenever inquiring and scientific minds have raised questions and sought empirical answers—and that has been going on for all of recorded history. What is different in our day is that more questions are being asked in more areas by more people, as the answers from the past seem less relevant to our problems and as the authorities who propound them seem less credible. When questions are asked and scientific methods of inquiry are employed in an attempt to answer them, open discussion necessarily ensues.

As long as a field is governed by an authoritarian philosophy there is no need to discuss any questions that arise. The answers given by the authorities, whether they be church leaders, tribal chiefs, great books of the past, or the customs and traditions of the society, are accepted without dispute. To the extent that mysticism may be a dominant philosophy, there is again no room for discussion. Beliefs that are derived from hearing "inner voices" or from seeing visions cannot very well be checked out by others. Such beliefs can only be asserted and then accepted or rejected on the basis of the credibility of the source. Although probably all of us at one time or another individually operate on the basis of intuition—and justifiably so—most of us nowadays would agree that a more verifiable method of understanding is preferable as a basis for group action.

When one bases an approach to problems on the philosophies of empiricism, rationalism, and pragmatism, that is, on observation, logical deduction, and testing out possible solutions in action—in short, on scientific methods—one is virtually compelled to engage in discussion with others, for a scientific observer is aware that as a human being one's perception of objects and events is influenced by personal biases; that try as one may to be objective, the process of perceiving is a selective activity governed by one's own needs and experiences. Hence we have to check and discuss our observations with others, in order to arrive at a more complete and accurate picture of situations. Likewise the processes of logical deduction are often too tricky and intricate for a person to place exclusive trust in his or her own reasoning powers. We need to expose our chains of logic to others whose intelligence we respect in order to discover any fallacies we may have committed or any other ways of interpreting the data which we may have overlooked. Finally, in the testing-out phase of problem solving, scientifically minded people are eager to exchange experiences, to find out how a particular hypothesis, solution, or course of action worked when tried by others; to compare notes on successes and failures. It is through processes such as these—essentially democratic in the mutual influence they exhibit—that modern medicine has replaced witchcraft, irrigation and conservation have supplanted worship of the weather gods, and economic planning has superseded the myth of the free market.

Closely linked to the questioning of the traditional doctrines of society's leadership is the rising self-respect of ordinary men and women. Far more aggressively in our time than ever before in history, individuals and groups of people who have heretofore been excluded from the mainstream of society's decision making have demanded a share in that process. Beginning with the labor movement, which sought not only more money for workers but also a greater voice in the management of working conditions, and followed by the civil rights and black power movements, the student rights and youth counterculture movements, the women's movement, the Native American movement, and gay liberation—one group after another has sought to participate more fully in controlling its own destiny and the destiny of the nation of which it is a part. With the increased recognition and power they have achieved, and are still seeking, these groups and their members are able to make collaborative dialogue occur.

When one or a few people in an institution or society possess all the power, and the others are relatively weak and helpless, optimum conditions for discussion, mutual influence, and democracy do not exist. Discussion in such circumstances exists only at the sufferance of the powerful, and, generous as these people may sometimes be, they are not likely to abdicate their power voluntarily when vital interests are at stake. To be sure, one can cite instances in which powerful individuals or groups have seen that it was in their enlightened self-interest to accept influence freely from others who were in no position to force it on them. A number of benevolent dictators in history have, on their own initiative, attempted to institute democratic processes in their countries before revolutionists had to come along and fight for them. Some enlightened businesspeople provided decent wages and working conditions for employees before unions came on the scene. But these are tenuous grounds upon which to base democracy, for the fact of life remains that the biggest ones in the gang can bring discussion to a screeching halt the moment they take a notion to do so. "A democracy can be such in fact," said Theodore Roosevelt, "only if . . . we are all of about the same size."

The most solid and enduring basis for democratic interaction exists when the participants possess relative equality of power. Mutually influential discussion is assured only when those desiring discussion—usually those who are dissatisfied with the way things are—have sufficient power to make those in control of the situation listen to them. The biggest hurdle which advocates of change usually confront is to gain the concession from those in power that a topic is at least discussable. Admitting a subject to discussion is admitting the possibility of change.

The correlation between power and democratic interaction can be seen clearly in the family. As children grow older and gain the physical strength, and sometimes the financial independence, with which to fight back, their parents are forced to become less arbitrary with them and to discuss issues that may arise, relying on reason and persuasion rather than coercion. But, since children have always grown older and more independent, it may be asked, why is there more give and take in the family today than formerly? We have already identified some of the answers to that question—children know more, adult views are less certain and definitive, and many parents have come to recognize the morale-boosting advantages of persuasion over coercion. But in terms of sheer power, children have also made significant gains. They are more mobile and, hence, less easily controlled. Furthermore, they have access to the resources of peer groups and the mass media to offset the previously more exclusive domination of parental influence on their thinking.

In the field of labor-management relations the shifting balance of power and the resultant growth of discussion and democracy is even clearer. In those industries where unionization has been most successful, labor has attained a tremendous increase in strength and, as a result, has been able to demand a larger share of the profits as well as a greater voice in many of the decisions affecting day-to-day operations. Bosses are now forced to discuss questions which they used to regard as no one else's business. (The expression "a greater voice" is in itself an indication of the close relationship between power and open discussion.) The relative power of workers and management varies, of course, with the ups and downs of general economic conditions, since a worker's independence is directly affected by the opportunities that exist for alternative employment.

In national affairs we often discover to our amazement that individuals who are thought of as having great authority—even the president of the United States—must be sensitive to all sorts of interests and must ordinarily confer and consult with many others before making major decisions. And surely this is more true of countries such as the Western democracies, where there is a substantial distribution of wealth, than of countries like most of those in the Middle East, where the wealth that exists is concentrated in the hands of a few. It is no accident that those nations which we think of as having the most purely democratic forms of government, such as in Scandinavia, are also the countries that have achieved the greatest equality in distribution of resources, whereas those nations with a highly unequal distribution of wealth, such as in South America, are the most authoritarian.

Perhaps the clearest example of the relationship between power and mutually influential discussion is seen in international politics. Now that the nations of the world have become so interdependent that none is able to "go it alone," the necessity for working problems out through discussion has become evident. Though warfare still breaks out occasionally in one place or another, the overall balance of power is such that force is not usually capable of resolving differences. The conference table then becomes the only alternative, not because the participants so altruistically believe in peaceful accommodation, but because they recognize that they cannot impose their will through the exercise of military power.

Having now examined some of the major forces that are at work to produce an ever-increasing amount of mutually influential discussion, we must also take note of counterpressures that are operating to undermine that development. One of these is the very size of the institutions that we cited at the outset as a primary cause of specialization, interdependence, and democratic interaction. Because the democratic discussion of problems requires a great deal of time to find out how large numbers of people feel, followed by much effort and ingenuity to draw out a consensus from the many conflicting views that are expressed, the process sometimes bogs down in indecision and inaction. Because power detests a vacuum, there are always those who are ready to move in to fill the gap. Thus we often find that while discussion rambles on, people of action have grabbed the ball and run with it. This problem is endemic to almost all institutions that are supposedly governed by a democratic decision-making body which has an executive arm to implement its policies—the U.S. Congress and the presidency, a city council in a city manager form of government, a school board and school superintendent, the board of directors and the full-time operating head of a voluntary community organization, a private educational institution, or a corporation. The body with the formal authority to make policy is, in the first place, overly dependent on the executive for information and suggestions, which can be selectively presented to suit the latter's own purposes. Beyond that, the best the whole group may be able to do by way of policy formulation is to adopt such broad resolutions that the executive, at the implementation stage, actually makes most of the critical decisions. Thus we may have the appearance, without the reality, of democratic interaction.

Another kind of appearance without reality occurs in those situations where clever leaders—parents, teachers, employers, or public officials—knowing that participation improves morale, invite discussion and pretend to be open to influence, but only do exactly what they intended to do before the discussion ever took place. That kind of duplicity, carefully executed, is sometimes successful for surprisingly long periods of time. One likes to think that it is eventually unmasked and that those who have been duped will be less gullible another time.

Despite the difficulties in making collaborative participation work in large and complex institutions and despite the occasional sham that occurs, the fact remains that mutual influence through group discussion has grown dramatically in our time and shows every indication of continuing that growth. The major barrier that stands in the way is the continued concentration of power and information in the hands of a few, although the apathy and lack of skill which sometimes characterizes those to whom collaborative opportunity is offered may also present a problem. To the extent that such imbalances of power continue to crumble and ordinary people are willing to accept responsibility and prepare themselves for participation, we can expect discussion to play an ever larger part in our lives.

Thus far, we have explained what we see as the major forces at work in our society which tend to increase the use of discussion and thereby increase mutual influence or democracy. We have also examined some of the counterforces which tend to undercut this trend. And yet, in our attempt to describe we have already implied a certain way of looking at things. Our most basic assumption can be summed up as follows: *For the most part, democratic group processes are both more desirable and more effective as a means of solving problems than autocratic processes.* Virtually any generalization such as this one, however, is subject to scrutiny and qualification. For example, it could be argued that autocratic procedures are sometimes justified because of a need for immediate action, or because, in some cases, one person must take ultimate responsibility for a decision. We could reply that emergency situations are often manufactured by leaders who have failed to inform others of impending decisions and that complete responsibility need not be assumed by a person who acts as a representative for a group. But an assumption must be recognized as such before it can be subjected to such analysis

SOME UNDERLYING ASSUMPTIONS

Readers will better understand the perspective we have taken if we identify our starting points. We have found it beneficial to our thinking to draw out these assumptions in the form of propositions about the nature of discussion, training in discussion, and the value of discussion. We feel a responsibility to state these assumptions so that the reader may examine them rather than to leave them covert and unstated. We also hope that these ideas will stimulate others to examine their own assumptions about the nature and uses of discussion.

The Nature of Discussion

PROPOSITION 1
The face-to-face group is both a microcosm of larger groups and a distinct entity in itself.

We believe that in many ways the problems faced by all groups are similar, regardless of their size: (1) All groups need leadership. (2) All groups develop characteristic patterns of dealing with new information and with one another. (3) All groups must strike some balance between the attention given to emotional relations and that given to adaptation of the group to the environment (usually in the form of a "task" which the group chooses for itself or which is assigned to it).

Therefore, whether we are concerned with a private organization, a community government, a committee which forms spontaneously to deal with a problem, or an entire society, features such as those named above will be present. For this reason, learning about discussion also means learning about the *basic* features of all groups.

But groups also have problems and ways of functioning that are specific to face-to-face situations involving relatively few people. Perhaps the major differences are that small groups, where people come into contact with one another directly, allow for greater *speed* in the transmission of messages and greater *potential* for participation of each member. Thus, there are certain special features of discussion groups: (1) Responses can be read immediately. In fact, responses often accompany the sending of messages. So, as a person is expressing an idea, he or she may know how other group members are responding even before the sentence is completed. (2) Compared to other groups in which members are in one another's presence less frequently, there is little that can be hidden. Unless people are careful to mask reactions, others who are alert and perceptive will see and perhaps hear how communicators feel about what they are saying and about what others are saying. (3) Because of its size, the small group can be much more flexible in its functioning than is possible for larger groups. For example, division of labor need not always be formalized when the business of the group is carried on in a face-to-face situation.

Throughout this book readers will find that we make analogies to larger groups, especially to American society as a whole, while talking about the small group. However, when we come to those problems and ways of behaving that are specific to the face-to-face situation, we will temporarily abandon the "microcosm" notion to focus on the unique features of small-group discussion.

PROPOSITION 2
The principles of group discussion are highly variant from culture to culture.

Communication behavior is largely culture-bound. The authors have chosen to describe group discussion phenomena as they occur in a major segment of one society, and most of what is written in this book could carry a qualifying statement: "This holds true for the dominant culture in the United States." This is not to say that we are insensitive to the particular problems and pleasures of international and interracial communication and to the differences in the way discussion is conducted in varying cultures within and outside the United States. Rather, we have simply found it necessary to limit our scope to those group situations which are most numerous in American society. Regardless of his or her cultural background, the reader may find it helpful to think of this volume as a sort of "handbook" for small-group phenomena in a certain part of a certain society.

By saying that discussion is "highly variant" from culture to culture, we are implying that there may be some cultural universals in group-discussion behavior despite the many differences. We have already said that there are some problems which characterize all groups regardless of size. We could extend this generalization to state that there are certain features of groups which are likely to apply across cultures. If we were to adapt this book for another culture, many of the headings found in the Contents might well remain the same. We presume, for example, that a group in any society will possess some degree of cohesiveness, some type of leadership, and some forms of decision making. Each chapter would have to be extensively rewritten, however. For instance, in many cultures it is common for a status hierarchy with one clear leader to be acknowledged by group members when they first meet. Such hierarchies also exist in American groups, but it is comparatively more common for groups in this culture to begin with less well-defined levels of status and for leadership to emerge from the discussion. Thus, the general topics considered in this book might be employed as a basis for comparing group phenomena in different cultures, but the details about each topic would vary considerably according to the culture.

PROPOSITION 3
Discussion is a dynamic, ever-changing process involving many causal factors.

In any group, there will be various "outside factors," not entirely within the control of the group members, which will influence actions. A family may move from one city to another because of a change in the job assignment of one member; a social agency may be transferred to another region; a local factory in a manufacturing firm may receive a new set of orders; a nation may be confronted with a change in policy of a foreign power.

There are also "inside" or "internal factors" which affect behavior. Even in a group "confined to quarters," where outside influences are held to a minimum, there will be changes in the way people deal with one another over time. For example, in Altman and Haythorn's (1967) experiments with simulated submarine isolation, roommates went through stages in their relations. Progressively, they used the same central area of their enclosure less and less as they began to establish separate territories on each side of the room.

In almost every situation, these outside and inside forces intersect and mutually affect one another. The sensitive group member is one who is aware of these influences as they come to shape the activities of the group in important ways. What is needed, then, to prepare people for group action is a philosophy and method of understanding groups that is consistent with the complexity of the phenomena.

Training for Discussion

PROPOSITION 4
Effective training in discussion involves making the learner aware of group process and the choices available to the individual, and then encouraging experimentation with various approaches.

If the idea that discussion is influenced by many factors in a fluid situation is accepted, then it follows that there are no principles or pieces of advice that will hold true for all circumstances. It is our conviction that education is not the giving of answers, but rather the providing of a framework and a stimulus for the student's own problem solving. In view of this philosophy some may wonder at our occasional use of the word "training," a concept which may imply to some a process of drilling certain skills or techniques into a person, much as one thinks of training a dog. We wish to make clear that we disavow such connotations when we use the term in this book. We feel it is possible to think of the word as being synonymous with "education," and it is in this sense that we use it. In fact, we take an extremely dim view of any process in this field—be it labeled training or education—where the aim is primarily or exclusively that of teaching people a set of skills and techniques.

We assume that the best we can do in training a person for more effective group communication is to help him or her learn how to solve problems, rather than giving answers. This involves essentially four kinds of experiences:

1. People must learn to become infinitely more sensitive than most people to what is going on in any given discussion. They must learn why people behave in their interpersonal relationships as they do and must be aware of as many of the factors operating in the situation as they can possibly discover. A large share of the information presented in this book is intended to fulfill these needs.

2. People must develop a basic set of criteria or values by which they can judge and choose among the many possible courses of action which may be taken in a given situation. In other words, they must have some goals clearly in mind before deciding what to say or not say, what to do or not do. Much more will be said of this in the remainder of the book.

3. They should know about different ways of dealing with situations, so that when they are faced with a concrete problem of group communication they will have a variety of alternatives to draw upon and will be able to choose among them in accordance with the requirements of the particular situation and in line with the values by which they are operating. Again, this book will try to acquaint the reader with many possible alternatives.

4. Finally, learners must adopt an experimental attitude toward participation in discussion; that is, once people have assessed the conditions which appear to be operating at any one time, they must be willing to try out behaviors which seem likely to bring the desired results. To attempt to influence others always involves some risk, especially if something is being tried which is, for that person, new or unusual. Here learners are pretty much on their own. At least there is little that this book can do to bring about this experiential kind of learning, except to offer encouragement and to provide suggestions for activities which involve the learner in trying out new communication behaviors. This we do in the chapters which follow.

The Value of Discussion

We believe it is not sufficient to describe the nature of the group process and to explain how one should go about learning to discuss. We must also take a stand on what we believe is desirable. The remaining basic premise upon which this book is built concerns the ultimate value of discussion as we see it.

PROPOSITION 5
Group action is a means of achieving the ends of those individuals who participate in discussion and should never become an end in itself.

We assume that when people act in concert it is because they feel they can achieve goals for themselves with the help of others that they cannot attain alone. Although there may be times when the problems which a group confronts may be so taxing that individuals must subordinate their personal interests to those of the other members of the group, we take these to be conditions which are tolerated only because they contribute eventually to the benefit of the members.

In selecting the enhancement of the individual as the ultimate value of discussion, we are placing ourselves in opposition to those group situations where individual members unwillingly subvert their needs to the majority. The most extreme example of this phenomenon would be brainwashing as it has been practiced in prisoner-of-war camps and in other kinds of political detention centers. A less extreme example may be found in some encounter-group situations where individuals who refuse to meet group expectations are exposed to strong psychological stress through scapegoating and other types of pressure. One need not look to groups which have the expressed purpose of changing people for examples, however. Any time a group member is subtly or overtly coerced to abandon his or her goals and appear to agree in order to avoid group dissolution or sanctions from other members, the same general principle applies. These circumstances could occur in an organization, a committee, or a family.

This proposition should not be taken as an endorsement of rugged individualism. There are situations where group solidarity can provide greater gains for the individual than could be achieved by pressing for the satisfaction of personal needs within the group or going it alone. Minority groups provide an example. One writer on race relations, Alvin Poussaint, has made the following observations with regard to the situation faced by blacks:

> The acceptance by the Negro of . . . [the] idea of individual merit has worked to his detriment, for it has operated to sustain a delusion in the face of a contradicting reality. It would perhaps be more realistic for black people to develop and orient themselves in terms of overcoming barriers to them as a group. Only then will acceptance or rejection as *individuals* follow. Achievement of this group freedom, however, requires . . . expending greater group assertiveness . . . and adopting a positive and proud stance toward themselves and others (Poussaint, 1970, p. 26).

This summary of the assumptions underlying this book, presented as a series of propositions above, is not intended as a complete statement of the outlook of the book. However, these are the assumptions which we regard as most comprehensive. They underlie the entire argument of *The Dynamics of Discussion, second edition.* Hopefully, by stating them here, the rest of what we say will become clearer.

The reader may feel that the assumptions we have discussed here are "obvious." We would not at all be dismayed by this reaction if it means that we have been able to state in concise terms some generalizations about the extremely complex topic of discussion which are applicable to a wide variety of circumstances. At the same time, we must also comment that these assumptions have not always seemed obvious to people writing or teaching about discussion. On the other hand, the reader may wish to challenge, question, or search for exceptions to our propositions. Whether he or she comes eventually to agree or disagree with these assumptions, we feel this would be a worthwhile exercise in the process of becoming aware of and testing underlying notions about discussion. But the reader should be alerted to the fact that much of what we say in the rest of this book is predicated on the thinking that we have presented here.

SUMMARY AND CONCLUSIONS

Certain trends in our society have influenced the rise of discussion, mutual influence, and democracy. The size and complexity of modern society and, therefore, the need for specialization have made interaction necessary. Partly because of a breakdown in traditional authority and demands for respect by ordinary people, our leaders have had to rediscover the old principle that people are better informed and more loyal when they have a chance to discuss and help decide on the issues which affect their lives. In addition, the use of the scientific method as a way of solving problems, as opposed to the intuition of authorities, has encouraged discussion (although occasionally scientists behave like intuitive authoritarians). While the powerful seldom give up control voluntarily, the actions of organized labor, minorities, and other interest groups have brought about a greater equalization of social and economic power. Working against all of these democratizing influences is the tendency of centralized authority to seize power in times of crisis or in periods when democratic institutions fail to act and the occasional deceptive use of discussion as a manipulative tool.

Underlying the approach of this book is the idea that, in most cases, democratic processes are both more effective and more desirable than autocratic procedures as a means of solving problems. Certain other related assumptions of our perspective can also be seen. The functioning of democratic government on the societal level is related to face-to-face interaction because small groups tend to be microcosms of the larger groups which surround them. Thus, the principles we discuss in this book apply most directly to the predominantly middle-class American culture. The complexity of the interplay of influences coming from larger groups with the specific characteristics unique to each small group makes it virtually impossible for us to give simple prescriptions for participation in discussion. Rather, we suggest that people learn about discussion best by becoming aware of these complex factors and by experimenting with ways of behaving in actual group situations. Finally, while we advocate that people join with others in discussion as a way of bringing about change by democratic means, we believe that the group should never be all-important and that the ultimate value of this activity depends on the benefits which it affords the individual.

STUDY SUGGESTIONS

1. Does the assertion that family decision-making processes in our society have become or are becoming increasingly democratic conform to your experience? Are you aware of any trends or forces working in the opposite direction?
2. Do you agree with the proposition that scientific methods of problem solving inherently are conducive to mutual influence processes? How can that view be reconciled with the often-stated proposition that in an increasingly technological and specialized society ordinary people are more and more at the mercy of the experts?
3. If it is true that mutual influence is only possible to the degree that there is relative equality of physical, economic, and/or intellectual power, is it realistic to believe that democracy is a viable mode of operation in classrooms, in corporations, or even as a system of government?
4. Try to identify places in society, or on campus, or at work, where decisions are made by a single person and involve consultation with no one. Identify those in which some collaboration is required—an input of information, approval of the decision, instructions on implementation. Then identify some in which there is consistent and total collaboration among all people involved.
5. Study the decision-making processes of your own organization or your own department: What types of problems are left to experts? What types of problems involve instruction and persuasion? When must competing interests confront each other and decisions be voted or arbitrated? When is there consistent, cooperative decision making? When are these methods of solving problems appropriate and when are the wrong methods employed? Why?
6. Trace the various stages in the solution of a specific problem in an organization with which you are familiar. For example, how did the problem become recognized? How was it given priority? Who initiated action on it? How was the problem solved? Who participated in its solution? How was it, or is it to be, implemented?
7. What examples can you find of the principle that small groups are microcosms of the larger groups of which they are a part? For example, can you think of any organizations in which face-to-face groups tend to adopt standards of behavior or ways of operating (autocratically or democratically) which are found throughout the organization? Can you cite exceptions to the microcosm principle, where groups function in ways fundamentally different from those of the surrounding organization, community, or society? Are these groups considered "deviant" by members of the larger society? Or, are there other explanations for their differences?
8. Does the idea make sense to you that knowledge of group theory—of the many factors which affect interaction—coupled with experimentation provides the best approach to learning about how to discuss? Can you think of any principles or assumptions about the practice of discussion in groups that you try

to follow regardless of the situation? Can you think of exceptions to the principle or principles?

9. In what situations would you be willing to say that the needs of the group are more important than the needs of individual members?

Chapter 2
Group Communication: Transactions Within Systems

Imagine we have just entered a room in which people are sitting in a circle. A drawing has been placed in the center of the group. Everyone has been asked to examine the drawing and then to consider the following questions: What is this? What do you see in it? What does it mean to you? Looking over their shoulders we see this picture:

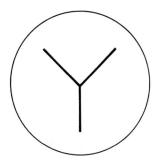

At once someone says, "It's the letter 'Y'." From the opposite side of the circle another person argues, "It looks like the peace symbol to me." "To a ceramicist," someone adds, "it's the support we use under plates when they're fired in a kiln." Other voices join the conversation, adding different interpretations—"a branding iron," "sign of an approaching fork in the road," "a button," "hubcap design on a car wheel," "stick figure of a person walking," "a rifle sight." Another voice suggests, "It's a trivet, the iron thing you put under hot casseroles when they come out of the oven." Someone else adds, "It reminds me of the device we use at the cafeteria for slicing pies and cakes into equal portions."

Imagine what would happen if, instead of this simple diagram, an abstraction had been placed in the center of the circle—a word, a thought, a problem, an opinion. What would we then predict about the meanings it might elicit? And if that abstraction referred to a controversial topic of our day—abortion, nuclear energy, sex roles, existentialism, extrasensory perception—the meanings would undoubtedly be still more varied and the intensity of feeling even deeper. We might be faced with seemingly irreconcilable arguments, emotions, convictions.

PERSONS

To understand human communication one must begin by exploring the process by which meaning comes about. If we consider the preceding episode, we can identify two critical features of communication. First, notice that communication began not between members of the group, but within each person. Communication, in its broadest sense, is intrapersonal.

Like all objects and events, the diagram has no meaning. If it did, all competent observers would be led by the same evidence to the same conclusion. In that case there would be no need to communicate interpersonally; any intelligent person would be able to perceive the meaning of every event without discussing it with anybody. While we often talk as if the world *has* meaning, every experience contradicts this assumption. The world simply exists. Our experiences only provide resources from which meanings can be created to satisfy our shifting needs and motives.

Second, communication not only begins within each person, but is an active, creative process rather than a passive, reactive one. (Some of the feelings of helplessness and victimization of our day arise from this false notion of the world coercing and manipulating us.) People, not events, mean. For an event to acquire significance it must be given it through some interpretation. And this requires an interpreter. This is true even when the event consists of a symbolic act by a person—a speech, a casual comment, or a gesture. Objects and events acquire meaning only after observers assign meaning to them. How else can we account for the diverse meanings attached to the diagram?

Given that interpretations are individual, we may search for the sources of differing perceptions, although it may not be possible to discover all of them. In the case of the diagram, one reason for the varying meanings is that it was viewed from different physical perspectives. From one position in the circle the diagram was a "Y"; from the opposite side it appeared to be the "peace symbol." In addition, there is clearly a psychological and sociological dimension to the meanings given to this diagram. Experience on a ranch, in a cafeteria, in a ceramics factory undoubtedly contributed to seeing the picture as a branding iron, pie slicer, or ceramic support. The issue, of course, is not which observer was right or which was wrong. All these ways of construing the diagram are perfectly reasonable.

And yet, although there may be numerous factors which lead to different interpretations, the potential meanings may be narrowed somewhat by the nature of the object of perception itself. The diagram looks more like a hubcap, for example, than a clothes hanger—although an addition of certain details might make the latter perception more probable than the former. In short, events—including symbolic events—place *constraints* upon meanings, but do not determine them.

It has been suggested that people relate to the world not merely by acquiescing to it, or even by interacting with it, but by "transacting" with it (Barnlund, 1970). That is, every person is born with different potentials and into a different family; each is rewarded and punished for different behaviors; each creates a unique personal identity and hierarchy of impulses and values. These facts, attitudes, habits, motives—as well as the data of the event itself—combine to make the situation intelligible. *Every experience acquires its meaning out of a creative transaction between what the person brings to the situation and chooses to select or reject of what can be found there.*

Although we do not stand at the center of our physical universe, we do, in effect, stand at the center of our experiential universe. All meanings originate within us. They reflect an imaginative integration of past and present to derive meanings relevant to the future. Events do not arouse identical meanings for any two people because they neither approach nor see them from the same perspective. Student and teacher do not discuss the "same" grade, nor farmer and developer the "same" land, nor doctor and patient the "same" operation, nor buyer and seller the "same" price, for none of these can be the "same" for people viewing them from different vantage points. Meanings are not found outside us in the world of objects and events, but inside the mind of the interpreter. Rarely do events support identical meanings for two people, and what similarity does occur often reflects similarity in their past or present circumstances.

If all knowledge of the world is inescapably subjective, a product of the perspective from which events are viewed and the motives we bring to them, there are deep implications in this for human communication. It suggests that when we talk, it is the perceived world—not the real world—that we talk about, cry about, fight about. As Walter Lippmann once suggested, it is not the world "out there" that is the focus of our conversations, but the "pictures in our heads." There are no facts except those arising out of personal observation, no arguments free of personal assumption, no convictions unrelated to personal values. In short, there is no way to perceive the world without a perceiver. And no perceiver can interpret it except through the lens of his or her experience.

SMALL GROUPS

Communication, however, is not simply an internal process, concerned only with the evolution of meanings within solitary human beings. It is concerned also with the way meanings evolve through an exchange of messages between people and with the factors that facilitate or complicate that process. It is because the experience of every person is unique, fragmentary, and subjective that communication is necessary; a world in which everyone saw alike and thought alike would require no communication at all.

Interaction is necessary to compensate for limitations that are inherent in our personal views of the world. It is a way of counteracting the subjective and provincial nature of a singular view of anything. While there may seldom be one correct way to view an event or one perfect and elegant solution to a problem, interaction can help people to discover which perceptions are less useful than others. When we recognize the limits of our subjective vision of the world, we seek to collaborate with others; when we fail to recognize such limits, when we become arrogant about our personal truths, we dismiss or sabotage such collaboration. On a university campus, one set of architects designing a new building may confer with students, faculty, secretaries, administrators, and custodians in order to appreciate the needs of those who will use the structure. Another group of architects, assuming that their own expertise is sufficient, may design another building that cannot be used without extensive and expensive reconstruction because they have failed to consult with the persons involved.

However, communication is not merely a way of compensating for shortcomings in human perception, but it is also a way of expanding and enriching the meaning possibilities of any experience. Creativity itself seems closely linked to the capacity for considering a variety of perspectives on a problem, and this condition is a unique property of any collaborative group. Studies comparing decisions reached by individuals working alone and those by collaborative groups show the immense potential of communication for improving the quality and originality of decisions (Kelley & Thibaut, 1969). That consensus or fresh solutions do not always appear—that confrontation may produce only hostility, that differences may provoke defensiveness, and that patience can wear thin in the face of complexity—does not eradicate the potential of such groups, but testifies to the difficulties in realizing that potential. The advantages of collaboration are not automatic, but depend on the sensitivity, talent and commitment of the group in realizing this promise.

The potential advantages of interaction, of course, require that people have some basis for common understanding from which they can work in narrowing individual interpretations of any event. This means that some shared perceptions and a shared code of verbal and nonverbal messages must exist. It is mainly culture which provides this—a point we will examine later in this chapter. But relationships themselves also serve this end. The more people are together, the more their behaviors become predictable and understandable to one another. This is the reason why people who know one another well can often interpret the meaning of one another's behavior more accurately than they can that of a stranger. A word, a facial expression, or a certain action all may have a special meaning among people who have interacted for some time. Thus, the combination of cultural and relational codes provides a starting point for mutual understanding.

Of course, human interaction takes many forms. People eat together, travel together, work together, attend lectures together, participate in demonstrations together. All involve some form of communication. But the form, that is, the context of the communication and the manner of interacting, differs in many respects from one to the other. At one extreme lies face-to-face conversation between two people—the *dyad*. Here the communication is interpersonal. The interaction is usually highly informal, spontaneous, unstructured, rather unpredictable, and satisfies human needs for attention, appreciation, support, and intimacy. At the opposite extreme lie collective or public forms of communication. Here tnere is much greater control; hundreds or even thousands listen to an address or watch a performer. Messages are usually calculated and rehearsed, and the role of speaker and listener are sharply defined and enforced. Collective forms of communication permit large numbers of people to be informed, entertained, aroused to action, and these seem to be most effectively realized by reducing active participation in the process.

Between these two extremes lies the discussion group. It is communication in this setting that will be our focus here, but what exactly is meant by such a group? The question seems trivial and the answer obvious, but they are not. For example, how shall we differentiate between 10 or 20 people standing in an elevator, waiting in a theater lobby, or riding in a commuter bus and the members of a decision-making committee, participants in a class discussion, or clients in a therapy group?

It is not enough for several people simply to be together in the same place at the same time. They must be linked psychologically as well as physically. There must be some feeling of mutual involvement and a recognition of their common fate. According to Robert Bales, each member must also have a clear enough perception of the others to be able to recognize or recall their presence as members of the group (Bales, 1950). To do this one cannot merely observe others, but must interact with them. The number of people capable of such face-to-face interaction, without subdividing into smaller groups, is probably no greater than 25. Groups, too, have a sense of their own boundaries, often distinguishing sharply between those who "belong" and those who are "outsiders." Further, there is a tendency for groups to persist over time, to survive the loss and replacement of some of their members.

The small discussion group incorporates some of the informality and spontaneity of dyadic communication and, at the same time, borrows some of the task orientation and sharper focus of the collective communicative setting. Within even the smallest group there will be some specialization of roles and functions, and an emergence of norms to regulate how members communicate with each other. Nearly all of the preceding qualities would also apply to jazz groups, basketball teams, chamber quartets, and construction crews. But in the discussion group, speech is the dominant form of interaction, although various other communicative signals also play a part. The group exists to share ideas and feelings, and these are expressed through verbal and nonverbal means. *Thus the small discussion group consists of 3–25 people who perceive each other as participants in a common activity, who interact with each other dynamically in a face-to-face setting, and who share information and attitudes through verbal and nonverbal systems of codification.*

There is another kind of group that is closely related to the face-to-face discussion—the organization. Members of both small groups and organizations have a sense of belonging and sharing a common activity, but the greater size and duration of the organization distinguishes it as a separate entity. In addition, much of the communication in organizations is not direct, as it would be in a small group. For example, the initiator of an idea in a corporation may pass it on to a department head, who elaborates on the idea and sends it to a division head, who then changes and relays the message to the president or board of directors; that is, in order for the entire organization to function as a unit, information must travel through channels. However, there is a close relationship since most small discussion groups operate within this larger group, and much of the business of the organization is carried out in face-to-face groups. The organization often serves as an intermediary between the small group and the culture.

CULTURES

The meanings which people place on events are influenced not only by the nature of the events themselves and by interaction in dyads, small groups, and organizations, but also by the largest groups of all—cultures. Cultures exist for many reasons, but paramount among them is the need to create a "universe of discourse" for their members (Barnlund, 1975). Without some common way of codifying sensations or of symbolizing meanings, each person would be condemned to solitary confinement within his or her own experiential world. Cultures arise out of the necessity of establishing processes through which people can preserve contact with one another, carry on cooperative activities, and provide for their own growth and survival.

Cultures train us to select what is critical to our existence. Even the perception of color and form have been shown to be influenced by culture. Segall, Campbell, and Herskovitz (1966) found that people living in "carpentered" environments, where straight lines, sharp angles, and rectangular forms prevail, differed in their vision from people who grew up in noncarpentered environments. Any infant born into any culture is quite capable of cultivating the ways of seeing, hearing, smelling, and tasting that are unique to that culture. But having done so, it is difficult—and, some argue, impossible—to acquire equal facility for perceiving the world exactly as members of other cultures do. Some hint of the difficulty in shifting from the cultural biases of one culture to another is suggested in the simple frustration we experience in doing ordinary tasks with the hand opposite the one we normally use.

Cultures exert an even greater influence over interpretations of what is perceived. Even when members of different cultures see the same physical form, such as the swastika, it is unlikely to give rise to the same connotations for a Jew, a Buddhist, or a Navajo, for the associations each brings to its interpretation are highly discrepant. The concept of *cultural relativity*, long associated with the names of anthropologists such as Margaret Mead and Ruth Benedict, suggests that every culture creates unique frames of association and hierarchies of values out of which members of a culture create their meanings. Some cultures value facts, others feelings; in some countries time means little, in others it is treated as a limited resource; individuality is valued in some societies, but is feared in others. One can imagine the depth of misunderstanding and of disagreement in communication between cultures occupying the opposite ends of these polarities. Although all societies permit some latitude in interpretations of reality, the extent and kind of differences tolerated have a profound effect upon the content and form of interaction within a society.

Perhaps nowhere is the impact of cultures as profound or as evident as in the communicative styles they promote. Cultures encourage not only ways of seeing and of meaning, but also certain ways of relating to others. Comparative studies of communicative styles reveal that cultures influence what can be talked about, who should talk to whom, and the specific forms of communication that are favored (Barnlund, 1975). Every society develops its own conversational agenda, encouraging talk about some topics and discouraging the exploration of others. Members of some societies find it comfortable to discuss politics, but not sexual behavior; others feel religious matters are private, but financial questions can be aired in public. The sharing of ideas is preferred in some places, and the sharing of feelings in others. Some cultures reverberate with noisy argument, and others seek to avoid direct confrontations between their members. How conversations should begin, and how they should end, is subject to cultural influence. There is often a proper time and place for interpersonal conversations in many societies, but the times and places are not always the same. Encounters between members of some cultures are highly ritualized, and in others highly spontaneous. Human interaction is used primarily as a means of communal celebration here, a vehicle for creating cohesiveness there, and a way of solving problems elsewhere.

Cultures, by favoring certain human relationships over others, also open and close certain channels of interpersonal influence. Every culture—and every group—has a social structure of some kind. It may be an elaborate vertical one in which every person is superior or subordinate to someone else, or it may be one in which status distinctions of any kind are denied. Some cultures make it easy to communicate within sex boundaries, but discourage interaction across them. In other social systems sex differences are less important than age, power, race, wealth, or education in directing the flow of communication. As a social structure changes, the number and capacity of channels for conveying information also change. Rarely are social structures alike for different cultures, and, hence, a single message can provoke diverse interpretations when communicants do not share the same culture. In short, all messages acquire some of their significance from the person who authors the message and from the person for whom it is intended.

Most important of all, cultures create the symbolic codes that comprise the messages in these channels. Every person would be isolated from every other person unless signals with common meanings could be devised with which to express and interpret experience. The hundreds of languages—Russian, Tagalog, Swahili, Spanish, etc.—constitute distinctive and elaborate systems for sharing meanings within the same community. But to regard human communication as synonymous with words is to suffer from a severe case of interactional myopia. People do not interact through a single code such as language, but through a multitude of signaling systems.

The presence or absence of a person "communicates" and is often one of the most eloquent expressions of approval or disapproval. Where people choose to sit may reveal something of their motives and may affect interpretations of their remarks by others. A slight change of posture can signal a shift of mood or thought, a desire to speak or to stop speaking. Facial expressions, gestures, eye glances all become critical ways of articulating meanings. And while all of these nonverbal behaviors are found around the world, the interpretations placed on each behavior in combination with other messages vary widely from culture to culture.

The meanings we create and wish to share with others are invented by us, but not entirely by us. Cultures, through what is sometimes called "world view"—perceptual biases, value systems, and social structures— and through their verbal and nonverbal codes, provide much of the raw material out of which unique personalities and meanings arise.

DETERMINED AND SPONTANEOUS SYSTEMS

All human communication occurs within a system, but not all systems involve human communication. Broadly defined, a system is anything which functions by means of interdependent parts. For example, an automobile motor is a mechanical system. If all parts operate well, the motor runs efficiently; if one part is defective, the motor may cease functioning, or else eventually other parts may deteriorate. The natural environment may also be viewed as a system; the destruction of any element—a species of animals, the quality of the air, a source of water—may have a significant impact on the rest of the environment. Likewise, persons, dyads, groups, organizations, and cultures are all examples of systems, but they operate in ways distinctively different from nonhuman systems.

A notable shift has occurred in the way we think about human personality and human institutions in this century. There are many ways of labeling this philosophical and scientific shift in perspective: It is a shift from viewing human beings and social systems as "static" to viewing them as "dynamic," from regarding them as "reactive" to regarding them as "transactive," from approaching them as "closed" systems to treating them as "open" systems. In the classical approach of behavorial science, people were regarded, as were the materials studied by physical scientists, largely as objects. Human action could be accounted for and explained by correctly identifying the critical elements in the environment that caused it—behavior was simply a "response" to a "stimulus." Changes in the stimulus produced more or less automatic changes in the response. Objects carried their own meanings, and these were assumed similar for all "objective" observers. Any differences in meaning were attributed to "errors" or "distortions" on the part of the perceiver. Personality consisted of the stable traits of a person that persisted, as do the qualities of iron, from one setting to another. People were seen as the slaves of circumstance, trapped by external forces into inevitable reactions. The vocabulary used today for describing human behavior still reflects this view with terms such as "response," "reaction," "recognition" far outnumbering the proactive terms that imply people are also "initiating," "spontaneous," "actualizing"—active as well as reactive toward their environment (Allport, 1960).

The traditional view of communication reflects a similar point of view. For some time, communication has been regarded as a sharply bounded, discrete event. It began when someone said something; it ceased when talking stopped. People still refer to the "need to communicate more" as if it were something quantitative, something one chooses or chooses not to do. Communication required a speaker, a message, and a listener. All were bound together in a linear, causal sequence: Someone put a meaning into words, and these, in turn, accounted for the effects produced in someone who heard them. The speaker was active, supplying the "stimulus"; the listener was passive, merely "responding" to the dictates of the message. Messages, like physical elements, could be analyzed apart from their context and their inherent effectiveness evaluated. Listeners, whether consumers, students, or citizens, were at the mercy of those who controlled the media of meaning.

Useful as these models were in accounting for some aspects of human behavior, their limitations soon became apparent. Events were given different and equally valid interpretations by different competent observers. People were not only influenced by circumstances, but were themselves the inventors of those circumstances; they acted as well as reacted. Senders of messages had to be almost equally preoccupied with interpreting the behavior of receivers in order to gauge what should be sent; receivers similarly were rarely passive, even though silent, but were actively sending their own messages. No message had a fixed meaning, for it changed with the motives attributed to the sender, the context in which it appeared, and the orientations of those who heard it.

Gradually it was recognized that determined and spontaneous phenomena do not operate according to the same principles. As physical scientists came to favor more relativistic, circumstantial, and probabilistic models, so social scientists, too, began to question their deterministic models of human behavior. A rigidly determined model, if it actually fit human behavior, would make it far easier to describe and predict human events, but such models developed serious shortcomings. Human perception could not be explained adequately by examining the stimulus alone (nor even the perceiver alone), for it provoked too many different reactions. What was seen was obviously affected not only by eyesight, but by the emotional state, cognitive style, and cultural background of the observer. Similar environments often gave rise to strikingly different personalities, and different environments sometimes produced strikingly similar personalities. People, unlike objects and machines, seem to display not merely greater complexity but greater flexibility of action.

Deterministic systems consist of a limited number of stable elements or parts that have been given an inner structure and have been wired to operate according to a prescribed program. Some, like an ordinary clock, do little beyond repeating built-in sequences in endless succession. Others, like a thermostat, can react to external conditions. Some, like a steam generator, can make internal adjustments to keep the system from destroying itself. But all can be described as deriving their integrity from the constancy of their inner structure. It is accurate to refer to such devices as "reacting" and "responding," for they operate in automatic and predictable ways. They can be taken apart, their elements examined, and then reassembled. They are at the mercy of external forces and their own internal organization. They do not elaborate or transcend their own limits.

Spontaneous systems, or "open systems" as they are often called, differ in many ways from determined systems. For the most part, they are highly complicated. They consist less of an assembly of parts than of a fluid mosaic of variables. They operate more or less continuously, moving from one condition to another without clearly defined boundaries between them. Spontaneous systems are less dependent on external conditions, are even capable of revamping their own potentials, for their limits are less precisely fixed and can change over time. They not only draw upon the world about them, but are themselves instrumental in shaping the world they inhabit. This elusive quality is suggested in such phrases as "we got precisely what we deserved" and "we have met the enemy and they are us." As George Leonard (1970) suggests, the most critical problems of our age—racism, violence, pollution, population—are not something "out there" that we can act on so much as something "in here" that we must change. Solutions to such problems lie neither outside us nor inside us, but in the interaction of the two (p. 140). The boundary between organism and environment is more accurately defined by a hyphen than a conjunction.

PERSONS AS SYSTEMS

There is more than a superficial connection between what has been said about the nature of communication and the nature of systems. Communication is the process which makes systems, particularly spontaneous systems, possible. It is the flow of information both within and without the organism which triggers growth, adjustment, or decline. In his classic work, *The Wisdom of the Body*, Walter Canon speaks of the body not as a physical object, but as a "fluid matrix," a self-balancing, self-correcting system. Through richly interrelated organs the body maintains its physical integrity in the face of threatening environmental conditions by continual adjustment in metabolism, temperature, blood sugar level, and heartbeat. To Sigmund Freud, psychic integrity was similarly protected by a system of dynamic and compensating inner defenses. But physical survival and psychic defense are not the only qualities that distinguish the human species. There is need also to expand and grow, to transcend previous levels of expectation and performance. One specialist refers to the endless "effort after meaning" revealed in every human act; another emphasizes the "ceaseless symbolization" by which people turn raw sensations into significant meanings. Symbolizing appears to be the "species-specific" and "species-differentiating" potential that enables human beings to create cultures, sciences, arts, philosophies.

It is quite accurate to refer to the simplest level of communication as an intrapersonal system. A person is not a mechanical device, assembled and permanently wired to respond to some master plan, but is a complex system of interlocking processes used to comprehend *and* create the context in which one lives. To preserve and enhance the system, people must remain sensitive to sensory cues within and outside the body. As events transpire, details will be selected, meanings attributed to them, motives linked to these meanings, consequences imagined, and decisions reached. As a result of experience, the inner structure of the organism is modified; no person is the same after an experience as before it. Every experience leaves some trace and thereby becomes part of the context of every subsequent event. Any disturbance in these processes, such as sensory deprivation or denial of one's own feelings, converts an open system into one that is more closed, more fully determined. This decreases its flexibility and, if continued long enough, leads to deterioration or death.

SMALL GROUPS AS SYSTEMS

If the individual constitutes a primary communication system, small groups constitute a secondary communication system. Individuals seek not merely to give meaning to their own experiences, but to share them with others. These interpersonal exchanges provide some way of comparing experiences, of obtaining new perspective on them, of exploring their consequences. In addition, interpersonal and group affiliations expand our capacity to solve problems, to employ a wider variety of talents, and to secure commitment to changes in beliefs or actions. Just as people form a concept of the self—a physical and psychological entity bounded by their own skin—so do groups create a similar sense of identity and belonging through the boundaries of membership they maintain. As people join groups, an internal structure evolves, special skills are recognized, roles become identifiable, and certain ways of communicating are favored. As problems are identified, information shared, opinions expressed, differences explored, and decisions reached, an internal process comes into being that gives every group a distinctive "character."

While it is necessary that the group develop its own ways of functioning internally, it is also necessary that the group keep in contact with and adjust to its environment. The environment consists mainly of the larger systems which surround the group—the organization, the community, the culture. Should information from the environment fail to reach the group, or should members fail to evaluate their own processes, survival is threatened because the group system declines in its spontaneity. The maxim that lack of growth leads to stagnation and decline applies to both individual and group systems, and growth requires internal change and external exposure.

CULTURES AS SYSTEMS

Beyond the individual and the group lies the large organization and, finally, culture itself. As environmental problems multiply in number and expand in space and time, the resources of more people must be mobilized to meet them. Here, too, the concept of an open system seems to apply. Social systems are not mechanical monsters, permanently programmed, set in operation, and destined to unwind to inevitable ends. They are the creations of people who find them useful in protecting and enhancing the potentialities of the individual as well as those of the group.

Like persons and groups, cultures also create boundaries. Some are geographical (as the borders of sovereign nations), and others are psychological (as in ethnic identifications within a social system). Within these borders complex social structures arise to integrate the talents and to widen the opportunities of members of that society. Channels are created so that social problems can be identified, specialized information can be transmitted to where it is needed, technical skills and resources brought into play, and policies articulated and enforced.

To accomplish this mobilization and utilization of information and talent, there must not only exist channels of interpersonal influence but appropriate sorts of messages as well. A critical cultural function, therefore, is the maintenance of languages—conventionalized systems of verbal and nonverbal cues—for articulating ideas, negotiating differences, sharing feelings, and executing decisions. The dominant values of a culture, shaping its view of reality and of the institutions it creates, are diffused throughout the society not only through speech, but through other codes as well—painting, ritual, dance, music. As with each of the other open systems we have described, cultures are prone to decline and collapse. The failure to recognize environmental threats, or the inability to adapt institutions and social processes to respond to them, makes social systems vulnerable to defeat or decay.

WHEELS WITHIN WHEELS

The continued existence of any open system, then, requires that it maintain its integrity. To endure requires a certain capacity for stability, for what in systems terms is called "homeostasis"; that is, systems must adapt to disturbances from within and without in such a way as to reestablish equilibrium or homeostasis. Persons, groups, and cultures all have their tolerances, and no system can exceed its own tolerance for long without risking its own destruction. A person may go without water, without sleep, without dealing with negative feelings about self, but not for long. A group may disregard critical problems, may refuse to admit inadequacies in their procedures, may deny developing strains in interpersonal relations, but not for long. A culture may block the flow of vital information, may refuse to admit mounting antagonisms within the body politic, may refuse to reexamine its institutions or policies, but not for long.

Open systems are distinguished from closed ones not merely by their greater capacity for homeostasis, but also by their capacity for elaboration and growth over time. In fact, open systems are rarely static, or even homeostatic; they are evolutionary. They do not merely survive crises, but can convert them into occasions for learning and growth. The infant matures into a child, into an adolescent, into an adult, but these represent not merely changes in physical form but changes in capacity for unique, rich, and complex behaviors. Groups, too, often display a remarkable evolution over time, moving from a loose collection of isolated strangers into a cohesive and creative unit. As any student of history knows, cultures as well exhibit patterns of growth and expansion as they respond to the challenges of time and space.

To say that an open system is spontaneous or evolutionary simply means it does not have to repeat the same adaptive techniques in coping with challenges to it. It can invent new and more adequate ways of handling problems. The evolutionary direction, of course, may be positive—toward more flexible and mature responses—or it may be negative—toward more rigid and stereotypic responses. Whether the direction is toward growth or defense seems to depend on the capacity of the system to remain open and internally responsive. Failure in open systems seems to arise from one of two sources: (1) the system becomes insensitive to changes in the external environment that threaten its continuation (the system has become closed), or (2) internal processes have lost their flexibility (the system has become rigid). To realize their full potential, individuals, groups, and cultures must transact with the outer world and revise inner processes in the light of their success or failure.

One of the fascinating consequences of viewing persons, groups, and cultures as systems is to recognize how they relate to each other. There is no sharp line that divides person-group-culture. Each person stands at the center of his or her own universe but, as Figure 1 suggests, at the same time is a part of many interactional systems and remains a part of them, in one way or another, at all times. These multiple existences are expressed by Thornton Wilder in *Our Town* when Rebecca Gibb reads an address from an envelope: "Jane Crofut; the Crofut Farm; Grover's Corners; Sutton County; New Hampshire; United States of America; Continent of North America; Western Hemisphere; the Earth; the Solar System;

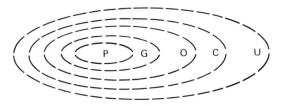

P = Person G = Group O = Organization C = Culture U = Universe

Figure 1 The larger interactional system of communication.

the Universe; the Mind of God." (Since every event and person exists in time as well as space, she might also have added as part of the address: "this age, this century, this year, this month, this day, this moment.") We are born into a physical world, a specific culture, a given community, a particular family, and all at the same moment. All people carry on a process of communication within themselves, but at the same time interact with other persons, groups, organizations, and cultures. All coexist within the larger frame of the physical universe. Each system simply provides another perspective from which to examine the processes of communication and to reflect on their adequacies and inadequacies.

Furthermore, one can see that none of the systems is independent of the others. No system operates in a vacuum. Each exists in and creates the context of the others. This is easier to appreciate as one moves inward from the physical universe, but is equally true as one moves outward from the solitary person. The universe sets limits on the nature of cultures; cultures, in turn, form the context of social institutions; the latter, in turn, limit the variety and complexion of groups; primary groupings, like the family and neighborhood, supply the milieu for the emergence of distinct human beings. But it is also true that each individual forms the social environment in which other people define themselves, that the character of groups influences the character of larger organizations, and that these, in turn, shape the values of the culture.

Thus it is important to remember that the border of one system is simultaneously the border of adjoining ones. And, because of this fact, each influences the others. Every system is born out of the womb of surrounding systems, and each creates opportunities and places limits on the others. Without culture there would be no music, no science, no technology, no art, no language, in short, no means by which individuals could create distinctive personalities. The Greeks could write no symphonies, nor build skyscrapers, nor correct heart defects, not because some quality was lacking in their individual citizens, but because the principles and techniques that make such activities possible had not yet been created by society. One cannot express a meaning in jazz until the musical form and instruments exist to make such expression possible. As John Gardner (1968) wisely reminds us, too many believe "that the only effect society can have on the individual is a destructive one" (p. 149). Without the nourishment of a surrounding culture, people would be without the materials and means of expression. Ignorance is the most oppressive of prisons.

Yet the nurturant role of society should not obscure the fact that culture can stifle creative impulses as well. The need for stability, for homeostasis in the face of challenge, may prompt reliance on traditional practices that stamp out fresh ways of meeting human needs. Through insistence on social norms, or through application of social pressure against deviance, individuals may be manipulated into preserving cultural forms that have lost their meaning or effectiveness for them. From this perspective it is accurate to speak of individuals being victimized by the social system to which they belong.

It is a mistake, however, to assume that influence passes only in one direction between individual, group, and culture. There is continual traffic back and forth across the boundaries of systems. As has been noted, "individual and society are antecedent and consequent of each other; every person is at once a creator of society and its most obvious product. Individual acts are framed within a cultural imperative, but cultures derive their imperatives from the acts of individuals" (Barnlund, 1975, p. vii). Any change in a single person, if emulated by others, is capable of diffusing throughout groups, organizations, and society. Every act of every person endorses or deviates from existing patterns of behavior.

SUMMARY AND CONCLUSIONS

The foregoing concepts concerning transactions and systems will provide a basis for much of what follows in the remaining chapters of this book. The following key ideas should be kept in mind:

1. Communication does not involve a simple transference of meanings from one person to another. Rather, any communication event involves a *transaction*, an exchange in which the perceiver and the perceived each contribute to the outcome—the meaning. This can be viewed in two ways: (a) At the *intra*personal level, the private experiences of people come into play as they assign meanings to events. The meanings of individuals are seldom—if ever—exactly the same. (b) On the *inter*personal level, where two or more persons interact, people exchange symbols in an effort to share meanings. These ideas may seem obvious once stated, but people often fail to recognize the transactional nature of communication. When people do not realize that meanings are in people and assume there is only *one* way to view a situation, conflict between persons, groups, and nations is almost inevitable.

2. Understanding between people is always incomplete, but no degree of understanding would be possible if it were not for the fact that *systems provide a basis for the sharing of meanings*. It is largely culture which satisfies this need by maintaining a way of viewing the world as

well as verbal and nonverbal codes to be used for communication. When members of the same culture come together, they have a means of achieving some commonality of meanings. When persons of different cultures come together, they must learn something of the perceptions and language of the other. But organizations and groups may also develop common frames of reference and "in-group languages" which may supplement the broader, culturally shared world view and language. Within the small group, certain acts and phrases may come to have special meanings. For example, if a family habitually assembles in the kitchen as they arrive home, when one person goes straight to his or her room, other members of the family are likely to share an interpretation: "Something is wrong."

3. All communication takes place not within just one system, but within a context of systems. While the focus of this book is on discussion groups, you will find that we often cross boundaries into other systems in our analysis and then return again to the small group. For example, we will examine the effects which culture has on the role relationships which people establish in groups. Even in a culture such as ours, where equality of the sexes is valued in word if not always in deed, it is common to find that a woman, and not a man, is appointed to the position of "secretary" in a small group. We will also point out, however, that the process can work in reverse. A woman who refuses to accept a subservient position, who points out the sex bias in the ways she is treated, may be able to change the ways a group functions. Or, a small group which insists upon equal treatment for women in such matters as hiring and promotion can affect the larger organization of which it is a part. The cumulative effect of many such acts may be to change the culture.

This is a theme to which we will return often. Groups set standards for the behavior of individuals; organizations prescribe tasks and working conditions for groups; and cultures affect the priorities of organizations. But individuals, groups, and organizations need not become the passive recipients of "orders" from above, although they are always influenced by larger systems. That persons and groups so often accept with silence conditions which they find abusive, despite democratic ideals, is evidence that the open and spontaneous nature of human communication systems is not widely understood.

STUDY SUGGESTIONS

1. If one accepts the premise that there are wide variations from culture to culture in the modes of behavior that tend to characterize small group processes, does it necessarily follow that one can make no value judgments asserting that some modes are better than others?
2. Is there a contradiction between the propositions presented in this chapter: (1) that meaning is in people and (2) that culture is a system of shared meanings? How can these two assertions be reconciled?

3. List some "systems" that you are familiar with that seem "deterministic" or "spontaneous." What are the essential differences between them? Can deterministic systems become spontaneous? Can spontaneous systems become deterministic?

4. Identify an event—simple or complex—that occurred in the past day or so. It is probably easy to recall because of the significance it had for you. Try, then, to identify as many of the factors that gave it this significance: your past experience, values, motives, expectations. What alternative meanings might it have had for other people in the same circumstances? What are a number of different ways you might communicate your intrapersonal meaning interpersonally?

Chapter 3
Individual Motives and
Group Goals

The number of groups which make up the fabric of human society is incalculable. Chester Barnard once estimated that "the number of formal organizations in the United States is many millions, and it is possible that the number is greater than that of the total population" (Barnard, 1948, p. 4). When the number of casual and accidental associations is added to this figure, there is no doubt that there are many more groups than individuals, at least in this society.

Some idea of the broad scope of human associations may be obtained by examining the groups cited by one college student in a profile of his memberships:

St. Paul's Choir
Marching Band
Alumnus of
   Wilson High School
Family
Swimming Team
Sunday School Class
Film Society
Spanish Drill Section

Dormitory Council
Seminar in Sociology
"C" Skow Fleet
Jazz Combo
Representative at Model U.N.
Chicago Auto Club
Staff Member of Summer
   Camp for Handicapped
   Children

Of course, not all of the above associations are discussion groups as defined in Chapter 2. The Chicago Auto Club is not really a club but a business organization which provides service to stranded motorists. The swimming team and jazz combo meet face-to-face (or, rather, "side-by-side" in the case of the swimming team), but do not spend much time in conversation. Membership as a high school alumnus does not involve discussion, except perhaps at a class reunion or at an informal meeting of friends home for the holidays. But at some time, most of the groups listed above engage in discussion, and it is the primary activity of a number of them. And if the student were to include the various combinations of people with whom he relaxes and socializes from time to time, the list of discussion groups would be very large.

Why do Americans join so many groups? Partly, the answer has been suggested in earlier chapters. A democratic form of government should, and does, promote diversity in groups as a means of involving individuals in collective decisions. In addition, the American culture also encourages "joining" by valuing change and problem solving and by permitting a wide variety of personal contacts through its social structure.

More specifically, why do people pick the particular associations that they do? It is essential to deal with this question in order to have a full understanding of the complexities of discussion. One of the major problems faced is that there are seldom two people who bring to a group exactly the same kinds or intensities of purposes. Out of the mixture of these individual motives must emerge the group goals if meaningful communication is to occur.

INDIVIDUAL MOTIVES

The first and most obvious reason for people to join with others in discussion is an interest in the publicly stated goals of the group. If they want to learn something about international affairs, they sign up for an adult education course in world politics. If women want to work for antisexist causes, they may join a local chapter of N.O.W. (National Organization of Women). If people want to fight against legalized abortion, they join a right to life group. If such adherence to the publicly avowed goals of a group were the sole motivating force behind participation in an organization, students of the discussion process would have a much easier time of it than they do. But their study might also be rather dull.

Although it is likely that most of the members of any organization will share, to some extent, at least, the publicly stated purpose of the group, it is just as likely that they will have private goals which are variations of it. Many are also apt to be motivated by purposes which are additions to, or even substitutions for, the publicly stated objectives. Let us look first at how the variations of a group's goals might operate.

Variations on the Public Purpose

In many neighborhoods in large cities across the country, there have come into existence in recent years organizations which are variously known as block clubs, neighborhood improvement organizations, or home owner's associations. Their major purpose is to stem the tide of deterioration of homes and property in the area. To achieve this end, residents of the neighborhood come together in meetings to talk over common problems and to work out courses of action. Even granting that all share the same major goal—the prevention of blight—we find in these groups a number of variations on this central theme. One home owner, for example, is primarily interested in preserving a clean and wholesome environment in which his children may play and grow. Another, who is planning to move in two or three years, is primarily interested in protecting the market value of her house. The personnel director of a large business enterprise in the area is concerned only that the neighborhood be safe enough so that employees will not hesitate to accept jobs there. An old-time resident feels that the neighborhood can be kept from deteriorating only if blacks are prevented from moving in, whereas a young college professor who lives there thinks a racially integrated and well-maintained area would serve as a fine example to other communities that integration does not have to result in a loss of property values. One can see immediately that the task of arriving at satisfactory decisions in such a group is going to be much more complicated than it would be if there were greater similarity in the motives which brought the members of the group together.

The Group as a Means to Private Ends

Illustrations of the use of groups as means to the private ends of their members abound in any gathering or collection of people. There is the college student who joins a fraternity or sorority as a means of getting ahead in campus politics; the business or professional man who joins the Lions, Rotary, or Kiwanis club in order to make contacts which will lead to customers or clients; the person who participates in charity fund-raising campaigns in order to move up the social ladder; and church members who attend services to meet friends and show off their clothing as well as to worship—these are all instances of the use of groups as means to private ends. There is no reason why such private goals need conflict with the publicly avowed purpose of the group or why people should feel guilty about them, but these motives will certainly have an effect on the nature of the individual's participation in the group. For example, a woman who is involved in a drive to raise funds for cancer research because she has lost a child to the disease is more likely to disagree with some questionable campaign idea proposed by the committee's chairperson than is another member who, in addition to raising money, is also eager to be invited to join the chairperson's country club.

Group Interaction as an End in Itself

Group membership may also be an end in itself. An individual may value so highly the friendship of the other members of a group that she participates in their discussions not only for the purpose of solving some common problem but also for the sheer pleasure of being with people whose companionship she needs and enjoys. This person's behavior will be considerably different from that of another member who obtains his primary social satisfactions elsewhere and whose only motivation with regard to this particular group is to accomplish the task to which the members have publicly committed themselves. The latter individual, for example, is more likely to desire an orderly procedure and be less inclined to "waste time" than the former member. Since we know that the human being is a social animal with strong needs for companionship and an aversion to long stretches of loneliness, it is safe to assume that participation in most groups is, to some degree and for most members, an end in itself.

Conflicting Public and Private Purposes

We have seen now that the participants in a group may possess different degrees of interest in the publicly stated purposes of the group, that they may be committed to many private variations of the public goal, and that they may be motivated by additional goals which lie within or beyond the group. We have also seen that these variations and additions, although increasing the complexity of the group's operations, may be entirely compatible with shared public objectives. However, there are instances, and they are not uncommon, where private goals may conflict with the group's avowed purposes. The most extreme example of this would be the FBI agent who, incognito, joins a radical political group in order to keep tabs on its activities, or the foreign agent who works her way into a vital defense agency in order to collect secret data or to sabotage its policies. In everyday life, however, there are less extreme and less conscious instances of group subversion.

One common illustration is the business official who is assigned by his boss to a committee whose task he regards as unimportant or useless. Such an individual may feel that the hours spent in discussion with the other members of the committee may either result in a policy recommendation which their superior will file in the wastebasket, or culminate in such a microscopic change as to make effort seem fruitless. Such an attitude on the part of one or more committee members, whether justified or not, will obviously have an influence, either overt or indirect, on the course of the discussions.

Misunderstandings About Motives

Frequently a conflict in motives is more apparent than real. Some group members may *assume* that their motivations are different from those of others when actually they are the same. For example, students frequently assume that teachers are more interested in *evaluating* class participation than in promoting the learning of the students, while the students see themselves as being interested mainly in learning. Thus, a student may be reluctant to ask a question which reveals ignorance, whereas, if the teacher is interested in evaluating participation at all, he or she may be more impressed by students who show an eagerness to learn than by students who ask questions only when they are quite sure of themselves. In turn, the teacher may assume that students are mainly concerned with grades, whereas the teacher sees himself or herself as being interested in promoting learning.

It is easy to see how such expectations can be self-fulfilling. The teacher may see the students' failure to ask questions as a confirmation of the expectation that students don't really want to learn. The teacher may discontinue efforts to encourage students to ask questions about things they don't understand, and the students may see this as revealing that the teacher really doesn't want to hear such questions. In the end, both teacher and students may come to accept evaluation rather than learning as the main goal of class discussions, thus taking on the motivations assumed about them by others.

Of course, some assumptions about disagreement between one's own goals and those of others are accurate. When such conflict does exist, the participant may be reluctant to reveal the difference in motives. Occasionally, there is good reason for participants who suspect that their motives are deviant to be cautious about revealing private goals. The individual in an organization who volunteers to be in charge of a committee in order to gain prestige to help in his or her campaign for a higher elective office the following year may well be correct that it would be risky to admit the reasons behind acceptance of the chairperson's position.

On the other hand, people often regard their own motives as socially unacceptable and, hence, avoid revealing them, when in actuality there is no good reason for such reticence. The employee who attends a meeting because the boss desires it or the student who takes a course out of a need for a particular number of credit hours in that field should not automatically assume that these facts must be kept secret, particularly when there is no conflict between the individual's private motivations and the purposes of the group. The fact that the employee may participate in a discussion under compulsion need not prevent that person from becoming a useful contributor. Many students become interested in and learn a great deal from courses in which they enrolled originally for other reasons. In short, were people franker with themselves and others about the variety of motivations which bring them to a group, many of the enigmas of the discussion process might be dissipated.

Unconscious Motivations and Hidden Agenda

There is, however, another reason why these private goals may not be revealed: The individuals themselves can be unconscious of their own motivations. For example, the college freshman who joins a fraternity may not actually be doing so because of any reasons he could state, but primarily because he feels socially insecure in the strange new university environment in which he finds himself and desires the aid, comfort, and protection of belonging to some clique or in-group. The businessman who devotes tremendous amounts of energy to his company, and is one of the most forceful and vocal members of its inner councils, may not fully realize how much of his behavior is a compensation for his basic feelings of inferiority. And a teacher, leading a classroom discussion, may be completely oblivious to the way in which she exploits the group to satisfy her own ego needs.

Indeed, a vast amount of the interaction that takes place in a discussion is motivated by unconscious determinants such as these. If we are to understand the process fully, we must not be so naive as to believe that all the remarks of participants can be interpreted solely as attempts to reach the publicly stated common objectives of the group. Rather, it must be assumed that the contributions made to a discussion are motivated by a variety of objectives, some conscious and some unconscious, some relevant to the common goals of the group and some to the private purposes of the individual members. Thus, when Jack disagrees vehemently with Jill's proposal, it may be that he really thinks it is a poor idea, or it may be that he is trying to put Jill in her place because he feels she has been having things too much her own way lately. It may also be that unconsciously he is competing with Jill for the group's leadership. Or he may fear that if Jill's proposal were adopted, the group might finish its work and disband sooner than he would like it to.

Whenever a situation exists where there are a significant number of private motives, either conscious or unconscious, lurking beneath the surface and influencing the course of the discussion in subtle, indirect ways, we refer to the group as having "hidden agenda." In other words, there may be items of "business"—a rebellion against the leader, for example— which some or many members of the group are unaware of or which, for one reason or another, are not talked about openly. Although it is probable that every group, even the most frank and intimate, has some hidden agenda, the problem becomes serious only when the nature of the items on the hidden agendum is such as to interfere with the effective pursuit of the group's avowed purposes. We will have more to say about hidden agenda in Chapter 8, where we discuss the role of conflict in decision making.

GROUP GOALS

When the complexities of individual motives are taken into consideration, it is easy to see why groups sometimes have trouble deciding on their purposes and have difficulty in accomplishing such purposes once they have been acknowledged. Conflicting motives, assumptions of conflict when none exists, and conscious and unconscious hidden agenda all make it difficult for the group to develop a single thrust. It may become like the horseback rider who "galloped off madly in all directions." Failure to arrive at some agreement on the primary aim and function of the group is likely to undermine later efforts to collaborate effectively.

It is not necessary for every group to eliminate all differences in motivations. Some are complementary and can be accomplished simultaneously. Some degree of conflict in purposes can be tolerated. But in order for the group to satisfy rather than frustrate the needs of as many members as possible, there must be at least enough agreement so that two issues are settled: (1) How much emphasis will be placed on individual needs as opposed to group goals? (2) What would constitute an effective outcome for the discussion, an accomplishment of its primary function? Another way of saying this is that the group members must acknowledge, overtly or covertly, that they constitute a certain *type* of discussion group as classified by its general purpose.

On the continuum in Figure 2 five representative types of discussion groups have been placed. As a beginning we can note that the groups on the left-hand side of the continuum, in general, exist to satisfy personal needs. To participate in them is an end in itself. They meet our need to be recognized as unique personalities. Through them we preserve our contact with other people. They provide security and support for us in times of stress, or they may simply establish communication lines for the sharing of

Casual   Cathartic   Learning   Policy–Making   Action
Groups   Groups   Groups   Groups   Groups

Figure 2 Types of discussion groups.

experiences. To say that membership in these groups is an end in itself is to say that these groups need not accomplish anything beyond maintaining satisfying human relationships.

Interaction in the groups on the right-hand side of the continuum usually is a means to an end rather than an end in itself. Environmental rather than personal pressures account for the formation of these groups. Citizens, concerned about the medical care facilities in their community, may form a committee to investigate the problem; executives meet to confer with each other about company policy. Practical decisions must be forthcoming from groups of this type if they are to fulfill their purpose. It should be kept in mind, however, that these groups are situated on a continuum, and each has some of the characteristics of the other. Most groups must create reasonably satisfying human relationships and make some progress toward accomplishing their tasks. It is only the balance between personal and social goals that shifts as one moves from the left to the right across this diagram.

Casual Groups

Let us begin by studying the conditions of discussion in each of these groups. The casual group is probably the most familiar type of discussion group known. Within a day most of us are in dozens of spontaneous discussions with friends and acquaintances. Conversational groups form anywhere—on a street corner, over a cup of coffee, among the members of a car pool. On occasions the group is thrown together by social accident; at other times people will go to great lengths to participate in a particular kaffee klatsch or bull session. Here, as Malinowski termed it, *phatic communion* prevails, that is, communication carried on for the purpose of establishing warm human relationships, laying the groundwork for more practical communications at other times, or simply overcoming silence. In a brief exchange, or at the beginning of a conversation, the topics may be predictable and mundane—the weather, sports, news of the day—but, as an interaction progresses, talk may flow in many directions in a free associative manner. The statements one makes in conversation are normally not subjected to rigorous examination or critical testing; personal experiences need not lead to documented conclusions.

This should not be interpreted to mean that casual groups are unimportant. They are the main link between us and our society. As early as 1902, Cooley called the attention of sociologists to the vital role they play in forming the personality of the individual. It has only been recently, however, that scientific studies have been devised to show the impact of social groups on self-concept.

Another area of research which has been neglected until recently concerns close observational studies of the actual patterns of behavior in casual groups. Among those involved with this subject is the sociologist Erving Goffman, who has devoted a major part of his career to attempting to decipher the informal rules which govern our casual everyday contacts (see Goffman, 1967). For example, he suggests that once a person has projected an image of himself or herself in a group, others tend to avoid challenging this impression if at all possible in order to prevent an incident which will prove embarrassing to all concerned. The strategies which people employ to avoid such threats to the social situation, as well as the ways in which they deal with a challenge when it does occur, are intricate and involved. Although Goffman's analysis of the structure of casual encounters tells us a great deal about how people define and maintain social encounters, we must turn to others for the details of such daily activities as greeting behavior (Kendon and Ferber, 1967), initial conversational topics (Berger and Calabrese, 1975), and good-byes (Knapp, et. al. 1973).

From time to time in this book we will borrow ideas from sociologists such as Goffman as well as cite studies by communication scholars of the patterns of messages employed in casual conversation, in order to show in general how relationships are formed. However, we will not focus very often on casual groups *per se* for two reasons. In the first place, all groups contain some elements of casual exchanges. For example, one of the patterns to which we have referred consists of signals that are used by individuals to show when they want to get into the conversation or when they are ready for others to begin talking, and these messages will operate in much the same way regardless of the objective of the group. It is usually not necessary to single out the casual group because most of the principles which we could cite will also apply to other kinds of groups.

A second reason is that when we go beyond those principles which apply to all groups, it is very difficult to predict what will happen in a casual group. What is distinctive about them is the relative freedom in the flow of topics which is allowed and the lack of a prescribed agenda. This may be the source of the casual group's attraction for us, and it is doubtful if we will ever be able to predict the directions which such conversations take with much scientific precision. The charm of these groups is captured very well in one of William Hazlitt's essays:

> The best kind of conversation is that which may be called *thinking aloud*. I like very well to speak my mind on any subject (or to hear another do so) and to go into the question according to the degree of interest it naturally inspires, but not to have to get up a thesis upon every topic. . . . You thus lose the two great ends of conversation, which are to learn the sentiments of others, and see what they think of yours (1930, p. 217).

Cathartic Groups

Another reason for discussing matters with other people is that it gives one an opportunity to express and explore emotions. At times, everyone has a real need to share positive feelings. For example, one's family or roommates may serve as a cathartic group when one has good news to tell. A victory celebration of an athletic team is an occasion which permits the boisterous and uninhibited expression of joyous emotions. Probably the more common purpose of cathartic groups, however, is to provide an outlet for the accumulated tensions and irritations of everyday life.

The venting of negative feelings may serve an especially important function since, according to some observers of this culture, Americans tend to see happiness as the absence of pain and, thus, work at talking away unpleasant feelings. They seldom enjoy a poignantly sad moment as might a Latin American. The student union of an American university will be filled with people satisfying their need for emotional release immediately following an examination period. Employees will be found in earnest conversation around the water coolers, the coffeepot, or in the corridors, discussing shifts in company policy and, perhaps unconsciously, getting rid of some of the anxieties that each decision creates. To a degree, even the traditional Thank-God-It's-Friday drink with friends may serve this function, although the purpose here may be more to get rid of general feelings of tension than to deal with specific sources of annoyance.

Sometimes this need is institutionalized, and people have been amazingly ingenious in forming groups to help each other in periods of personal crisis. Alcoholics Anonymous is a notable example. Organizations often use cathartic groups as a way of satisfying personal needs while working on problems at the same time. Labor grievance meetings and other kinds of organized gripe sessions recognize the need for discharging the accumulated hostility that lurks in all of us, as well as provide forums where changes in conditions can be initiated.

In everyday situations, the line separating the casual group and the cathartic group is not a sharp one. While conversation may flow rather freely from topic to topic in a casual group, the members of cathartic groups are more likely to focus their remarks on the irritation which provokes their hostility or depression. As we move across the continuum, then, we find there is a greater awareness of the specific issue that brings people together and a sharper sense of direction. Perhaps this is true to a lesser extent of groups where predominantly positive feelings are expressed than of those where negative feelings are released, but, even in the former situation, the group is likely to discuss primarily the events which have created their good feelings.

The distinction between the casual group and the cathartic group becomes clearer in certain special kinds of situations which we can broadly label "experiential groups." Such groups permit people not only to give vent to their emotions, but also to learn something about themselves. This, in effect, moves us closer to the learning group.

The goals pursued in various types of experiential groups may be somewhat different. Probably the best known are therapy groups and sensitivity training or encounter groups. Therapy groups tend to meet on a regular basis over an extended period of time and concentrate on getting individuals to understand underlying motives that produce conflicts and tensions in their lives. Encounter groups, on the other hand, tend to meet for long hours on consecutive days and are more likely to be concerned with getting people to become aware of their own feelings as well as those of others, rather than dealing with underlying motives. Either type of group might go in both directions, however. What such groups have in common is that a full range of emotions, both positive and negative, are likely to be expressed, and, in a properly conducted group, a trained and experienced leader will be present.

Learning about one's self does not have to be a deep psychological experience in which the specific problems of the individual are examined. "Theme-centered" discussions may be concerned with broad sociological problems, such as racial prejudice or discrimination against women, which touch individuals in very personal ways. A consciousness-raising group, for example, may consider such specific topics as sexual bias in hiring or problems of role relationships in marriage, while also giving people an opportunity to express feelings about the circumstances of their private lives. This kind of experience actually involves an amalgam of the cathartic group and the next category which we will discuss.

Learning Groups

We join groups, also, to learn more about the world around us. Discussion is widely used in our schools—in seminars, quiz sections, laboratories, and in the classroom generally—to help people assimilate information, to teach them to evaluate ideas critically, and to stimulate original thinking. Adult education programs permit those beyond school age to satisfy their curiosity about world politics, science, or literature. Businesspeople, teachers, scientists, and professionals also find it useful to meet regularly at conventions, seminars, or workshops to exchange ideas, compare new methods, and talk over common problems. A group of neighbors who agree to get together, not just to chat, but to explore thoughtfully some aspect of child rearing, may transform a casual group into a learning group. If such a discussion does not inform group members or produce new insights, it is regarded as a failure or a "waste of time" by those who joined in the conversation.

The question of how deeply members should become personally involved in a learning-type discussion is a controversial issue. Some say that learning groups, particularly in the classroom, should be as objective as possible, that the scientific posture is best for learning. This view—one would be tempted to call it the "cerebral" school of thought—emphasizes the "intellectual" side of learning and aims primarily at the accumulation and objective testing of facts. This view is strongly urged by Mortimer Adler:

> Emotions should have no place in the classroom or in discussion. We must distinguish between the heart-to-heart talk (such as between lovers) where emotions are the whole of it, and the mind-to-mind talk which is discussion. *Emotions should have no place in mind-to-mind talk* (italics ours) (Adler, 1954, p. 11).

However, Adler does not rule out the *possibility* of emotions forcing their way into the discussion, but cautions that they should be avoided wherever possible, for they interfere with the objective consideration of ideas.

> We have feelings about our thoughts and so emotions will enter. The point is not to suppose that you can be emotionless but rather to watch what emotions do, for they can disturb discussion. Anger, all the forms of personal aggression, personal antagonism, impatience, all these things will interfere with discussion (1954, p. 11).

On the other hand, the "gut school of learning" holds that learning must be visceral—it must affect the bloodstream and the nervous system of the person doing the learning. If the feelings of participants are not affected, then what is assimilated will be only skin deep and will have little effect on the subsequent behavior of those in the group. As evidence, the proponents of this school would cite how few of us are changed in any pervasive way by the facts we read in our papers and textbooks compared to the fundamental changes in personality produced by psychiatric sessions where feelings are not excluded.

To extricate ourselves from this dilemma, we would hold that both views need to be combined. Attractive as Mr. Adler's metaphor is, his "mind-to-mind" and "heart-to-heart" distinction has no scientific validity. One cannot partition the human personality, and attempts to do so only lead to distortions which add to the immaturity of the individual. For this reason we have placed the learning group in the middle of our continuum, because to us it seems a compromise between the highly personal experience of the cathartic group and the more immediate goal orientation of policy-making and action groups. One does not merely *feel* about school bussing; there are also facts to be learned. But facts alone do not tell us what should be done (the policy-making function) or how to go about doing it (the action function).

The learning group is likely to benefit also from having some plan for its meeting. It is difficult to conduct a coherent discussion if people are constantly changing the subject. At the same time, too faithful a commitment to an intricate and inflexible agenda may stifle original ideas. As we move along this continuum to the right, then, we find that groups have a clearer view of their problems and are able to determine more sharply the relevance of their remarks.

Policy-Making Groups

Perhaps the most common image to arise in peoples' minds whenever the word "discussion" is mentioned is a committee consisting of a group of people appointed to make decisions about matters of policy. Corporations, universities, religious and fraternal organizations all rely heavily upon them for conducting their affairs. The committee has become such an integral part of our way of life that some observers describe democracy as "government by committee."

Policy-making groups usually are formed because something goes wrong in the environment—schools become overcrowded, labor-management relations deteriorate, foreign powers complain about trade agreements, communities want to rehabilitate slum areas. They may also come about because of a desire to change already acceptable conditions—a corporation seeks to increase its profits, a faculty decides to improve its methods of teacher evaluation. Groups of this type assume, or are given from a higher administrative unit, authority over a particular problem. They may be asked simply to investigate the conditions leading to the problem, or they may be charged with discovering and evaluating possible courses of action. Most important of all, policy-making groups are expected to develop carefully worked out recommendations that will elicit the support of those vitally affected by the problem.

The complexity of the problems considered by deliberative groups of this type will change the character of their discussion. As problems become more complicated and well defined, members may feel that some organization is necessary. An agenda is one way to insure that all vital aspects of the problem receive appropriate attention and that the group will move systematically from issue to issue.

External restraints also are often placed on policy-making groups: (1) They are normally given a target date by which to complete their investigation—a week, a month, or longer. (2) They are expected to produce decisions that are practical as well as theoretically sound. These restraints may give group members a greater sense of responsibility for what they say in their meetings and affect how critically they appraise the ideas that are exchanged. After all, a military strategy or a new fiscal policy has to be lived with for a long time. And the consequences of a wrong decision sometimes may be fatal. We should remember that discussions in learning groups, while they may not culminate in any sort of mutual agreement, may also result in individual members making personal decisions about future actions. A discussion of foreign policy by the League of Women Voters, though academic in one sense of the word, may well change the way individuals in the League vote in the next election. In general, discussion in the policy-making group, however, tends to be more objective and more structured, while preserving much of the spontaneity and informality of the previous groups we have described.

Action Groups

The last group on our continuum is the action group. The reason for considering the policy-making and action groups separately lies in the nature of the tasks they are assigned. Policy-making groups, for the most part, take up issues that are intricate and require serious and lengthy investigation. The decisions that are reached will commit an organization to a relatively permanent course of action. Action groups, on the other hand, are created to determine how and when policies will be carried out. The administration of policies, in contrast to the formulation of them, involves making dozens of practical decisions, each one of which is relatively insignificant in itself. Consider a university about to change its admissions policy or a large corporation weighing the merits of diversifying its line of products. Who is to be admitted to the university, that is, what shall be the new criteria of admission, is a matter of policy. So is the question of whether or not to manufacture a new line of products. But once these broad questions have been answered, many other committees will be needed to execute the decisions. Admissions officers and members of the faculty will have to decide the fate of hundreds of applicants in the light of the standards they have been given. Within the corporation, heads of departments will have to confer about new materials and changes in production schedules.

Our characterization of the action group should be qualified to some extent. Not all action groups simply carry out policies made by others. Some are policy-making groups first; they carry out their own ideas. Some radical action groups which throw themselves in front of bulldozers, picket against bussing for school integration, or even kidnap an heiress for political purposes may be interested in the efficiency of their operation, but they certainly aren't interested in production schedules. They're looking for *action*, in a different sense of the term. Discussion will undoubtedly be a part of their planning phase, but later this gives way to physical action.

No other discussion group works under the pressure that the action group encounters. There is usually no time to attend to the personal needs of committee members. Severe limitations are often imposed, either because policies carry with them deadlines or because what happens in one action group has to be coordinated with decisions made by committees working on other aspects of the same problem. As a result, digressions from the central purpose are likely to be frowned on as interfering with the job of the group. On the whole, most effective action groups will place greater emphasis on a fairly strict agenda and on efficiency in general.

Overlapping Group Purposes

We believe there is a social reality in the distinctions among types of groups that we have made here; that is, the types can be recognized as different basic functions served by groups in this culture. One would ordinarily realize that the general purpose of interaction had changed if he or she went from one type of group to another. It is important, however, to avoid classifying discussion groups too rigidly and thus stereotyping our reactions to them. The concept of a continuum is used to emphasize that the differences are significant but sometimes subtle. On certain occasions it may be difficult to decide whether a group is forming to pass the time of day or to release tensions, whether emotional expression carries with it learning about human nature, or whether a committee is dealing with a matter of policy or action.

Some groups pursue a single objective over a long period of time. A group of neighbors may meet socially for a lifetime without ever engaging in anything more serious than casual conversation. The members of a board of directors may have virtually no social contact with each other and meet only when they have to decide practical questions of management. Some groups become institutionalized, that is to say, they acquire a long-term set of goals and a permanent organizational structure to go with those goals. A chapter of The John Birch Society or of Alcoholics Anonymous may become identified in people's minds with only one of the purposes described.

However, many groups change their purposes from meeting to meeting, or even within a single meeting. A group of students chatting together over coffee may find they share very strong feelings about a campus issue and use the group to vent their feelings as well as simply to make friends. A policy-making committee, finding its way blocked by intense prejudices or personal animosities, may have to provide time for "clearing the air" before any constructive analysis of a problem can be started. Sometimes groups run the gamut of the continuum: They start out casually, even accidentally, and then go on to investigate, to formulate policy, and to carry out their decisions. When a problem requires that a group cover all of the basic purposes in this way, the continuum can be used as an agenda for discussion, as we will show in a later chapter on prescriptive approaches to the decision-making process.

To describe the operation of every sort of group from a kaffee klatsch to a summit meeting is an unmanageable undertaking in a book of this length. Some lines of demarcation have to be drawn. In this book we have chosen to concentrate mainly on the conduct of those groups in the middle range of the continuum, especially learning and policy-making groups.

Each of the groups we have mentioned, however, throws light on some aspect of the discussion process and each will help to explain some of the problems of discussion. From examining how casual and cathartic groups operate, we will learn something about the interpersonal relationships that are conducive to effective cooperation. If we want to know more about accomplishing tasks quickly and efficiently, we will get some clues from the way action groups function.

SOCIOEMOTIONAL AND TASK FUNCTIONS OF GROUPS

We have stressed the point that there may be elements of each type of group in all the other types. Another way of looking at the continuum of discussion groups is to note that they vary in their relative emphasis on socioemotional and task functions. This is an important distinction, and most of the rest of this book is organized around these two concepts.

Traditionally, theory about groups has been divided into two interrelated processes, each of which is identified by several names, all referring to the same basic concepts. One process is variously called "the maintenance function," "the socioemotional dimension," or "interpersonal relations." The common idea in these phrases is that all groups must "maintain themselves" (stay together) by managing social feelings (emotional responses to one another) through skillful handling of person-to-person ("interpersonal") relations. The other process is called "the adaptive function," "the problem-solving dimension," or "the task process"; that is, the group "adapts" to the demands of the environment by finding solutions to difficulties or problems through a process of accomplishing a task.

Theorists differ on the degree to which they consider this distinction to be "real" or merely convenient as a way of talking about groups. Bales (1950) saw the two processes as very real in that they constituted the primary issues which every group must confront. What is more, he saw these two functions as being in conflict. In his view, to the degree that the group focuses on interpersonal relations, it must neglect the task, and vice versa. Thus, he pictured every group alternating between emphasis either on task or on interpersonal relations. Others have found the distinction to be no more than a useful way of analyzing group behavior, but have not been as sure as Bales that each act which occurs in a group can be categorized as relating primarily to one dimension or the other.

We are inclined toward the latter point of view, although we see value in this distinction. Sometimes it is quite clear that group members are focusing on one or the other: When ideas are being discussed or decisions being made in a rather unemotional and highly businesslike manner, clearly the task process is predominant. When group members' feelings about one another are being aired openly, the socioemotional dimension is clearly predominant. Much of the time, however, both processes play an important part in the way people communicate. Usually, what people say has more to do with the task at hand, but *how* they say it, especially their nonverbal behavior, has more to do with interpersonal relations.

Readers will see that the following parts of the book are concerned with each of these dimensions of group discussion. Part II, which immediately follows, treats the subject of interpersonal relations, while Part III deals with problem solving. Part IV, on leadership, applies to each dimension since groups need both socioemotional and task leadership.

If one looks back on the continuum of types of discussion groups, it can be seen that the next part of the book is especially applicable to groups toward the left of the continuum, since interpersonal relations are especially critical in casual and cathartic groups, and certain kinds of learning groups as well. On the other hand, Part III applies somewhat more to groups on the right side of the continuum, since task processes assume special importance in policy-making and action groups. This division is by no means absolute, because all groups have both a socioemotional and task function. Regardless of the type of group, the attitudes of the group members toward one another will ordinarily come into play. Not all groups, however, have a task or produce a "product." Since the feelings people have for one another almost always affect the way they work together, we will start our analysis in the next section with a consideration of socioemotional processes.

SUMMARY AND CONCLUSIONS

People seldom have goals exactly the same as those of their fellow group members. Although the publicly stated purpose of the group provides a common ground, some members may perceive this central theme in ways different from others. In addition, some may see the group primarily as a means to private ends; others may be mainly interested in the interaction as an end in itself; and still others, in a few cases, may have the objective of sabotaging the purposes of the group. Discussion group members sometimes assume wrongly that their private motivations will be unacceptable to others and, thus, do not get their needs met as effectively as they might. The untold purposes, or "hidden agenda," of discussion participants constitute a barrier to communication, although they usually cause major problems only when they are in sharp contrast to the group's avowed purposes.

While it is not necessary for group members to eliminate all differences in motivations, it is necessary that they agree on the *type* of purpose they are pursuing. Going along a continuum from the most individual-oriented to the most group-oriented forms of interaction, we have examined the differing natures of casual, cathartic, learning, policy-making, and action groups. It is obvious that no rules can be laid down which will apply with equal validity to all of these kinds of groups. Almost any prescription will be right for some group at some time and wrong for another group at another time. Rigid control of the conversation in casual groups is as inconsistent with its purpose as no control of irrelevant talk is in an action group. However, this survey of the uses of discussion will give us a basis for answering many technical questions about practices and procedures. Knowing what kind of a group we are dealing with will allow us to decide more intelligently such questions as what kind of leadership is required, what sort of agenda if any, may prove helpful, and what degree of objectivity will help to fulfill the group's purpose.

In spite of social critics who have expressed alarm about the dangers of creating "organization men," the question we face in the twentieth century is not *if* we should participate in groups. That has already been answered for us. The question to ask is what *conditions* should prevail within the groups we belong to so that they will yield the maximum social benefit without sacrificing human individuality. In other chapters of this book we shall explore some of these conditions of group life and try to arrive at ways of accomplishing both these ends.

STUDY SUGGESTIONS

1. Is a group (e.g., a family or a college fraternity or sorority) that functions sometimes as a casual group, sometimes as a cathartic group, sometimes as a learning group, sometimes as a policy-making group, and sometimes as an action group more likely to elicit a strong emotional commitment from its members than is a group (e.g., an encounter group, a philosophy seminar, the cast of a play, or a construction crew) that functions at only one point along the continuum of types of groups? Why or why not?
2. Of all the small groups in which you have been a participant, which one stands out as having group goals that were the most congruent with your individual goals? Which one stands out as having group goals that were the least congruent with your personal goals? Can you think of any group of which you have been a member where the attainment of your personal goals came partly from the achievement of group goals and partly aside from, or even in spite of, the group goals? How, if at all, did the nature of your participation differ from one to another of these groups?

Part II
INTERPERSONAL RELATIONS IN GROUPS

Part II

INTERPERSONAL

RELATIONS

Chapter 4
The Social Context of Discussion

When a group meets for the first time, it has no history, but, almost paradoxically, it does have a "character." Almost everyone has been in a group which seemed doomed from the start. It might have been a class which met for a number of months, a committee which worked together on a task for several weeks, or a party which lasted only a few hours. People simply did not seem to get along with one another, and all efforts to change relationships seemed to fail. But the opposite is just as likely. Some groups seem to be compatible from the beginning, and maintaining this momentum requires very little effort.

Such extreme situations are probably unusual. Because groups are open, spontaneous systems, they also take on aspects of character which are of their own doing, which grow out of their interaction. Nevertheless, the way the group members relate to one another—the emotional atmosphere, the sense of comradeship—is influenced by the "input" or initial states of the system. In short, every group operates within a *social context* which includes the way its task has been structured, the group size, the personalities of the members, and the setting in which the meetings take place.

TASK STRUCTURE

It frequently happens that the task of a learning, policy-making, or action group will be assigned by a teacher, a supervisor, or a department or division head. The assignment will probably include a statement of the group's specific goal (what it is supposed to accomplish) and often a deadline for its accomplishment. The mandate may also structure the task by indicating how the members are supposed to work together or how they will be evaluated.

There are many kinds of task structure. In some situations, group members are told they may get together at a time of their choosing. In others, they are told to meet at certain times. Some task structures specify strict procedures which the group must follow, while others provide little or no procedural direction. Some groups are supervised closely and others loosely. Some evaluations are based on the entire group's product, and others on individual contributions to that product.

Task structure almost always influences to some extent the way group members exchange ideas and make decisions. What is perhaps less obvious is that it may also influence their morale and the way they feel about one another. Research studies have shown that one aspect of task structure has particularly strong effects on interpersonal relations in groups: *cooperation versus competition*. In a cooperative situation, the group is evaluated as a unit: If the group succeeds, everyone is rewarded; if it fails, everyone fails. In a competitive situation, group members are evaluated separately and in competition with one another: To the degree that each person succeeds, others must fail.

In one study by Deutsch (1949), for example, students from a psychology class in a university were placed in five-person problem-solving groups. Cooperative groups were told that they would be compared with other groups and that all members of the best group would automatically receive the highest possible grade in the course. Competitive groups were told that only the person who did the best in the group would automatically receive the high grade. As might be expected, these conditions affected greatly the quality of the group products. The group members in the competitive situation brought up more good ideas than those in the cooperative situation, but apparently they were unable to get together on the ideas, because the cooperative groups produced better group solutions. What is more, the socioemotional climate was also influenced. Cooperative groups expressed more friendliness toward one another during the discussion and were more satisfied with their outcome.

It is interesting that cooperatively structured tasks cause people to get along better with one another, but not at the expense of the task, since such structures also promote better decisions. And yet, those who set tasks for groups often ignore this principle. Employers sometimes pit employees against one another by stating—or implying covertly—that they are look-ing to see which members of a work group will "shape up" and which will be fired. Administrations in academic institutions often require de-partments to rank-order their members at the end of each year and to dis-tribute salary increases accordingly. While such actions may be justified in the name of rewarding individual achievement, they may also serve to reduce group morale—and group productivity as well.

Even in those situations where a certain amount of personal alien-ation may be present before a group meets, the use of cooperative task structures can be used to improve relations. For example, Weigel, Wiser, and Cook (1977) placed students in interracial groups, each of which was graded as a unit. The result was an increase in liking for individuals of other races and a lessening of interracial tension.

Of course, task structure is not all-powerful. If the group members have a long history of hostility toward one another, the structuring of a task in such a way as to encourage cooperation may not be sufficient to reverse this trend; among people who have close and warm relationships, even a competitive situation may not be enough to force them apart. Task structure is an important element in the social context, but it interacts with other factors, including the numbers and kinds of people who are placed together in a group.

GROUP COMPOSITION

Suppose for a moment you have the job of appointing people to a com-mittee. Immediately, there are two questions to resolve: *How many* peo-ple should there be in the group? What *kinds* of people should make up the group?

Group Size

Many studies have been conducted with the purpose of trying to discover the "ideal" size for a group. It has sometimes been suggested that five members is a particularly good number, especially for decision-making groups, because it permits all participants to be involved as much as they wish, provides sufficient diversity of information and expertise, and allows the breaking of ties in voting because of the odd number. However, we are inclined to answer this question by saying, "It depends on the situa-tion." The maximally effective group size depends on the needs of the group, which are in turn affected by a host of factors. In a policy-making group, for example, size may be governed by how many specialized skills are required to solve a given problem and how much diversity is needed to have all conflicting points of view represented. In an action group, it may depend on how many people are required to perform a task or on how many individual jobs must be assigned. The usual size for an experiential group, where personal growth is the aim, is about ten people. The reasoning is that a larger group will not provide enough time to get around to the emotional needs of each group member with enough frequency to keep everyone involved. On the other hand, fewer than this number might mean that there will not be sufficient diversity within the group to promote the kinds of supporting and challenging behaviors needed.

Although it is impossible to specify an ideal number of members for all types of groups, there are some principles which should be kept in mind when group size is being determined. First, as the membership exceeds an optimum number, participation becomes centralized (Bales, et. al, 1951); that is, the larger the group, the greater the likelihood that a few people will monopolize the discussion. Second, as participation becomes lopsided, active participants will become more satisfied while inactive members will grow less satisfied with the group. There may be some people who would prefer to be ignored (Berkowitz, 1956), but they are probably exceptions to the rule. Third, consensus is ordinarily more difficult to achieve in larger groups. There will be more diversity of opinions as group size increases, and the decreasing satisfaction of some members may cause them to express more disagreement.

As a general rule, we suggest that the nature of the task should be a guiding consideration in the determination of group size. But where the satisfaction of each and every member is of paramount importance, where consensus must be reached quickly, where practical difficulties in getting the group together present a problem, the group should be as small as it can while still affording sufficient diversity to accomplish the task.

Personality Characteristics of Group Members

One of the most commonly held beliefs about groups is that the personalities of the participants will determine the final outcome. Certainly, there is some truth in the belief. In fact, the term "personality trait" is usually defined as "a *general* tendency to respond similarly in a variety of situations." It is on this basis that we characterize people as "introverts" or "extroverts," "dominant" or "submissive," and "adjusted" or "neurotic." If we accept the idea that there are personality traits or tendencies, it follows that if we know certain people well enough to see them in varied circumstances or if we have had an opportunity to observe their answers to a battery of personality tests, we will be able to make some predictions about their behavior. In turn, this information could be used to create a productive and compatible group.

Probably the faith that many people have in the predictive power of personality is overdrawn for the reason that people not only have general response tendencies, but they also have "situational personalities" which are specific to given contexts. A professor who is shy and retiring at a party may be expansive and extroverted in the classroom. The rampaging fullback on the football field may be a reluctant participant in class discussions. The permissive psychotherapist in the office may be a strict parent in the home. Nevertheless, research does suggest that personalities influence socioemotional relations in groups.

PERSONALITY AND INDIVIDUAL PARTICIPATION

Certain kinds of people tend to be especially helpful in the development of group climate, while others tend to hinder it. For example, "authoritarian" people are those who believe it is good that some people be in power and that others stay in subservient positions. As a consequence, the authoritarian tends to be bossy and demanding of other group members (Haythorn, et al., 1956). When faced by a strong leader or a united majority, this kind of person tends to give in more readily than a nonauthoritarian. In other words, such a person wants—and actually feels a strong need for—someone to be firmly in charge. Obviously, such a person is likely to be seen as "hard to get along with" by less authoritarian group members, especially if they are trying to operate on democratic principles—encouraging widespread participation and influence.

At the same time, however, the authoritarian group member should not be condemned outright. There are some situations where democratic principles do not apply, at least in the short run. Group members may be very happy to have a well-qualified authoritarian in their midst in circumstances involving an extreme emergency. Likewise, in some action groups, including certain kinds of military units and athletic teams, an authoritarian may be liked and respected. Vince Lombardi, the late coach of the Green Bay Packers, comes readily to mind as an example. We must keep in mind that each principle we state with regard to effective discussion may be altered depending on the total group context. Authoritarians are *usually*, but *not always*, detrimental in their effects on socioemotional relations.

Certain kinds of personalities tend to be especially helpful to democratic groups. Perhaps surprisingly, there are people who are "assertive" or "dominant" but not necessarily authoritarian. They like to solve problems, to meet challenges, to collaborate with others, and, as a consequence, they tend to participate heavily. Although they are not highly oriented toward power or status, they may, nevertheless, assume leadership. Their overall effect is to contribute to feelings of group unity (Borg, 1960; Haythorn, 1953). As Shaw has pointed out, however, those dominant people who promote good relations are probably only moderately high in ascendant tendencies and are not extremely dominating (Shaw, 1976, p. 191). Another general personality type, characterized as "sociable," likes to be with people and tends to promote positive feelings in groups. Others, who tend toward being "unsociable" and who are inclined to be suspicious and jealous of others, produce the opposite effects (Haythorn, 1953).

The personality traits we have described seldom account for the expected effects with anything like 100 percent accuracy. It is more common that the traits contribute 30 or 40 percent to the individual's behavior or to his or her effects on others. In short, personality tendencies may be an important factor influencing the actions of people in a group, but they by no means account for everything the individual does. Other factors in the group situation must account for the remaining 60 or 70 percent. In fact, certain elements in the experimental settings that produced these findings have probably accounted for the percentages being as high as they are. We would suggest that personality probably exerts the most influence on individual behavior when certain conditions exist:

1. Group members do not know each other prior to the meeting. Thus, they have not yet developed appropriate situational responses and have fallen back on their usual patterns of behavior.
2. Group members are placed in situations in which they must operate under restrictive time pressures. If there were more time, individuals might respond more spontaneously instead of relying on habitual reactions.
3. Group members do not anticipate working together in the future. Thus, they can "afford" to show underlying response tendencies without fear that later on they may suffer for their excesses.

Combinations of Personalities

From the information given thus far, we might conclude that the ideal group member for most situations should be assertive—but not too assertive—and highly sociable. If this were all that had to be considered, we could conclude that the greater the number of such people present in a group, the better everyone will get along. But the impact of each individual personality on the total group climate is limited even in the situations we have described above where general traits are likely to emerge. The reason for this is that groups are systems composed of interdependent elements—the whole is more than the sum of the parts. So we must also consider how the personalities of the group members "fit together." Summarizing the research on "compatibility," Shaw (1976) concludes that:

> ... when group members have personality attributes that predispose them to behave in compatible ways, the group atmosphere is congenial, the members are relaxed, and group functioning is more effective. On the other hand, where member attributes lead to incompatible behaviors, members are anxious, tense and/or dissatisfied, and group functioning is less effective (p. 219).

Two specific conclusions emerge from the studies which Shaw reviews. First, dominant people tend to get along with their opposites—people who do not have needs to be prominent—but not with other dominant individuals. Second, people who are either high or low on "affiliation"—the need to be with others—tend to get along best with their own kind. Assertiveness and sociability are "ideal" traits for a group member only when there are not too many assertive people, when other participants are similarly high in affiliational tendencies, and when task structure and other situational factors require people with these qualities.

Demographic Characteristics

There are a number of other ways people might be classified other than on the basis of personality types, and these characteristics might affect the way people participate in groups. A list of such factors would have to include sex, age, race, socioeconomic status, education, intelligence, and task-related abilities. Research shows that various combinations of such personal characteristics can produce different sorts of interpersonal relations.

Here we are often faced with a "trade-off." In general, people get along best with those who are similar in background and abilities (see Shaw, 1976 pp. 86–91, 163–175). And yet, diversity is often desirable in terms of task accomplishment. As an example, consider an advisory council to a school district in a poor neighborhood. Should such a group be composed only of those with the highest economic status, education, and intelligence when the needs of the community require the consideration of perspectives which may not be reflected by such a membership? The answer is not obvious. Often, it will depend on whether the situation calls for maximization of task productivity or compatibility within the group. Frequently, a compromise solution will be needed, so that the group will be composed in such a way as to secure some degree of compatibility in backgrounds while maintaining sufficient diversity of opinion to facilitate effective adaptation to the environment and the task demands.

The sex composition of a group is a special case in point. The research is rather consistent in showing that women, in comparison to men, are less aggressive and competitive (McGuire, 1973; Uesugi and Vinacke, 1963) and more conformist to majority opinion (Costanzo and Shaw, 1966). Here, similarity is not the only factor to be considered. The findings suggest that a group of all women is more likely to be more compatible than one composed entirely of men, although they do not tell us how mixed groups will compare with homogeneous female and male groups. Of course, the results of studies are likely to change as the role of women changes in the culture. But even assuming some validity to the findings, it would not be realistic to conclude that all groups should be composed entirely of women. Perhaps the clearest implication is that most—but not all—groups should have mixed populations, since the aggressive tendencies of the males may be balanced by the cooperative tendencies of the females (see Baird, 1976). Again, a trade-off is suggested: Aggressive responses may have certain advantages in terms of task accomplishment, while passive qualities may contribute to group maintenance.

SETTINGS FOR DISCUSSION

Once the task and composition of a group are determined, a place and time for meeting must also be decided. In a general sense, everyone knows that settings affect feelings, but such influences tend to operate on the periphery of awareness for most people, so this aspect of context is often overlooked.

Alternative Locations

If there is more than one place where a group might meet, some possibilities may be eliminated in favor of others. The location of a meeting may be significant. One of the authors recalls an incident at a large weekend encounter group conference in which some black students were offended by the fact that their living quarters were located in an isolated part of the facilities, distant from the conference headquarters. The location was interpreted by the black students as a covert message from those who arranged the meetings about the importance of their participation.

Location may also have significant effects on the group according to *whose territory* is occupied for the meeting. When the principal of a school calls a group of students into his or her office for a conference, the role relationships are reinforced by the choice of locale. Similarly, if a group member has volunteered his or her home for a meeting, the other participants may feel some reluctance about directly confronting their host in that environment. For this reason, a "neutral" location may be more desirable for any discussion which is likely to involve conflict and where equal status is sought for all discussants. However, this factor must be balanced against the possible advantages to the group as a whole of selecting an environment which will be conducive to the desired group atmosphere, even if this involves meeting on one of the group member's "home ground."

The Physical Environment

There has been much informal theorizing about the effects that the size and decor of a room may have on the way people interact with one another. This subject was the exclusive domain of interior designers and architects for some time. But social scientists have also become involved in these issues. One of the earliest attempts at the development of a comprehensive theory of environmental influences is found in a book by Ruesch and Kees entitled *Nonverbal Communication*. In studying many photographs of homes, offices, and commercial stores, these authors found that rooms often carry rather clear messages, left there intentionally or unintentionally by those who arrange or use the environments. For example, an office with neatly upholstered chairs whose backs have been pushed snuggly against a polished table free of objects may say, in effect, "Sit down by invitation only." On the other hand, if the table has a rather rough, unfinished surface and the chairs are placed in casual disarray, with objects spread around randomly on the top, the message may be "Make yourself at home." Whether the general impression created by a room very often conveys such precise meanings may be questioned. But it does seem certain that environments affect the behavior of group discussants in some rather specific ways.

AESTHETIC EFFECTS OF THE ENVIRONMENT

Despite the intuitive sense in the notion that room decor influences how people feel in an environment, we know of only two studies where this effect has been systematically demonstrated. Maslow and Mintz (1956) had two examiners question people about the "pleasantness" and "well-being" that they saw in photographs of faces. Some people judged the faces while sitting in an "ugly" room, while others were in a "beautiful" room. The results showed that the faces seemed more pleasant and expressive of well-being in the more attractive surroundings. In a follow-up study, Mintz (1956) found that the examiners, who spent three weeks going back and forth between the rooms, reported increasing feelings of discomfort in the ugly room, and found themselves looking forward to their time in the beautiful room.

The implication of these findings is that the attractiveness of a room may affect how the members of a group will interpret the feeling states of others, and, in the long run, those feelings may become directly affected by the environment. It is not surprising, therefore, that people commonly report changes in the emotional climate of a group as a result of moving to more aesthetically satisfying surroundings.

We do not mean to say that a luxurious, psychologically warm, comfortable setting is always the best one for discussion. For example, one of the authors once taught a college course specifically concerned with the effects of environment on communication. As part of the activities of the class, meetings were held in a variety of settings, and on one occasion the group chose to meet in a graduate lounge, a richly decorated room with deep easy chairs and a thick carpet. Very little work was accomplished, and people became furious with each other because of their plodding discussion and lack of enthusiasm. Some people even fell asleep. In short, the suitability of an environment depends in part on the purpose of the group.

CUES ABOUT THE SOCIAL SITUATION

Almost any room will contain cues which point to broad cultural categories of social occasions that define appropriate behavior. We are so conditioned to these kinds of messages that we do not need to pause to decide how to respond. A blackboard, rows of desk chairs, and a single desk at the head of a room provide one with an immediate, obvious message: "This is a classroom." Certain ways of behaving are automatically implied in a given culture unless a point is made about exceptions. "Hold up your hand when you wish to speak," for example, is a rule known to all American students, and it is one which is generally followed, unless the teacher says explicitly, "Go ahead and talk without being recognized." By way of contrast, a room filled with Christmas decorations containing a punch bowl prominently displayed tells people that interaction will be informal and suggests that they should get into a "Christmas spirit." The living room of a house would be the usual setting for such an occasion, but even a classroom or an office can be readily transformed for this purpose by appropriate manipulations of the environment.

Of course, some of the objects and the way things are arranged in a room have a functional purpose. A blackboard, for example, allows members of a group to write in a place which can be viewed by others. But most features of a room also have symbolic meaning. There is no reason why a classroom *has* to look like a classroom, or why a living room must have a sofa and chairs instead of mats on the floor, *except* that in a given culture those objects and arrangements inform people about the nature of the social situation. In this way, the selection and arrangement of a physical environment for a meeting tells people, in part, how they should act and even how they should feel.

SEATING ARRANGEMENTS

Besides giving information about the general social situation, a physical environment may also contain cues which have rather specific implications for how people will relate to one another. The spatial configuration of seats in a room especially seems to have this function.

The shape of a meeting table will affect how people see the situation. A circular arrangement suggests the relative equality of each participant. A square table, on the other hand, may imply that the group will be divided into four equal factions. Unlike the circle or the square, a rectangular table does not imply equality of either individuals or factions but, rather, suggests the existence of one, or possibly two, "head" or "chair" positions at each end. According to a study by Strodtbeck and Hook (1961), a juror who sat at the end of the table during jury deliberations was more likely than others to be chosen as foreman. Even if there is no designated leader in a group, people who sit at the end positions, and also those who sit at the midpoint on the sides, are more likely to dominate the conversation (Hare and Bales, 1963). Thus, a status structure and a network of communication may be implied by the table shape.

How close or far away people sit in relation to one another may also influence interaction in a group. According to anthropologist Edward Hall, who has written extensively on the meaning of spatial arrangements (Hall, 1966), certain social situations go with certain interpersonal distances. Hall suggests that there are various "zones" for specific kinds of activities, at least among middle-class white Americans:

1. Intimate relations occur between the "zero" distance of a close embrace up to 1½ feet. Except for couples kissing on the street and people temporarily being pushed together in an over-crowded elevator or subway, intimate distance is almost never used in public. It is reserved primarily for relationships between people who are very close, like lovers and very good friends, and for private places, especially during conversations where deep feelings are being discussed.
2. Personal relationships call for a distance between 1½ and 4 feet. This zone is used primarily by friends during a casual conversation. The inner area of this zone might be used by rather good friends, and the outer area—"at arms length"—might be employed for a conversation among acquaintances.
3. Social relationships, as characterized by most meetings where business matters are discussed, are usually at 4–12 feet. A rather informal meeting might take place in the inner area up to about 7 feet, while a more formal discussion might occur within a radius from 7 to 12 feet.
4. Public relationships, as found in public speaking situations, would usually involve a distance of 12 or more feet. At this distance, it becomes difficult to carry on back-and-forth talk. A considerable distance of 25 feet or more makes conversation all but impossible. This amount of space would be used to isolate an extremely important person from a surrounding crowd.

Hall's theories suggest that the closer the distances, the greater the feelings of emotional involvement. Research studies support this idea; for example, people tend to sit closer to those they like than to those they dislike (Mehrabian, 1968). One possible implication of such findings is that a group which desires to maximize feelings of psychological closeness ought to sit as close together as the number of participants will allow. But this conclusion ought not be overgeneralized. Another aspect of Hall's theory is that there are appropriate distances for various kinds of activities, so the closest possible spacing might not fit all situations. Forcing a physical intimacy on people not yet ready for it may be like forcing personal verbal disclosures on people who do not yet trust one another.

The safest generalization would be that the spatial arrangements for a meeting ought not to restrict the group members to distances which will be alienating and make conversation difficult, as would be the case if a rather small group sat around a large table. At the same time, unwanted intimacy and a feeling of being crowded, as might be found if a large group met in a very small room, should also be avoided. This means that physical arrangements should permit most group discussions to occur within the "social zone" of 4–12 feet. The exact distances employed can then be regulated according to the desires of the group members for psychological closeness. Of course, the size of the group will also be a determinant of physical closeness, and this suggests another disadvantage of large groups of ten or more members: Not only does increasing size limit participation and thereby lessen the satisfaction of the less active discussants, but it also may decrease feelings of involvement of the group members with one another.

We have said that seating arrangements may be dictated, in part, by the physical environment of the room in which a meeting takes place, and that this may in turn affect the way people relate to one another. But we have also suggested that the participants in a discussion may make *choices* about how they will utilize the facilities provided them. They will decide (consciously or unconsciously) who to sit close to, whether they will occupy a central or "leader" position, and whether they will occupy the same or different seats at each meeting. These choices may be limited by the physical environment, but they are partially left up to the individual and are, therefore, indicative of how he or she feels about others in the group. For this reason, we will leave further consideration of spatial arrangements to the next chapter on "The Development of Group Cohesiveness."

In general, our examination of the setting for discussion suggests that whenever group members sense a discomfort stemming from their physical surroundings, they should find a more congenial place for interaction. However, they may also be able to reorganize their environment—even to the point of redecorating! Of course, too much preoccupation with setting could distract a group from its main purpose, and it might even become a welcome but unneeded escape from the difficulties facing the members. Our point is that it is necessary for participants to be aware of the potential effects of settings in order to make conscious choices.

CONTEXTUAL DYNAMICS

So far we have focused on certain contextual factors which influence the character of group interaction. We have examined mainly those conditions that are under the control of the people who have formed the group—the task, the setting, the personnel who comprise the group. But this may have left the impression that such factors, once decided, always remain the same. If this were the case, we would be dealing with a closed system, that is, with a deterministic system which continues to function according to its parameters once the elements are brought together. With human groups this is clearly not the case. Although the circumstances under which a group operates may be rather stable and their impact rather consistent, these influences are also subject to change over time. This change can come about in various ways.

First, there may be new input into the group once it has been formed. The problem which the group was set up to solve or the structure of the task may be altered by changes in the larger organization of which the group is a part. People may be transferred within a corporation, causing them to join or leave the group. The meeting place may be shifted because of factors outside the group's control.

Second, whether or not changes are introduced by outside forces, the group can alter the impact of the social context by the perceptions and actions of its members. The group may choose to ignore a competitively structured task and behave *as if* everyone were to receive an equal reward. Reticent individuals may discover that they are respected for their ideas and may participate more than they would ordinarily. Dominating individuals may learn to adjust their behavior as a result of feedback from others. Even the place of meeting may acquire a special emotional tone so that it carries a unique meaning for those who use it. The "ugly" room may soon seem "beautiful," or the "beautiful" room appear "ugly."

Finally, the group may affect the social context by influencing the surrounding system. Members may petition or bring pressure on the authorities in charge to change the nature of their task, their personnel, or their physical environment.

IMPLICATIONS FOR THE PRACTICE OF DISCUSSION

The fact that the socioemotional climate of a group is influenced by its context has certain implications for discussion participants. The first and most obvious of these is that awareness of the potential influence of task, group size, personality, physical environment, and other contextual elements may be helpful to a person who is in a position to determine the conditions under which a group will work. At times, these decisions may be largely matters of guesswork, since the variables are complex and complete knowledge is often not available. But there is no reason why intelligent choices should not be made with the knowledge that the success or failure of the group is not solely determined by initial conditions. Once the group is formed, however, there are ways that the members can make use of their awareness of the discussion context.

In most groups, it is probably desirable for people to get to know one another "as people"; that is, they should know something about how others carry on their lives outside the group, including those bases of motivation which brought them together in the first place. This kind of discussion can be distracting if the group has a definite task to accomplish and time is severely limited. But "social" discussion can be very useful, even if the group is formed for some purpose more definite than casual conversation. Group members can become more sensitive to their individual uniqueness and thus gain insight into the motivations of others. It also shows that "outside" matters are not irrelevant in the group.

Open verbalization about contextual influences may not always be appropriate, of course. This is especially true of comments about the personal traits of other group members. "You two are arguing because you're both authoritarians who can't stand to be challenged" is the sort of remark almost guaranteed to intensify animosity. However, an awareness of potential personality clashes can be helpful in the hands of a sensitive and tactful group member. When such conflict does exist, it might be more helpful if another member of the group were to express personal feelings about the argument or make comments designed to mollify the hostile feelings. Assigning blame to personality may very rightfully make the accused person feel that his or her individuality and capacity for being flexible are being denied.

Group members should also be aware that too much attention to outside factors can inhibit productive discussion. Instead of working toward achievement of group goals, members may fall into the habit of spending considerable amounts of time talking about what is happening to them as individuals outside the group or gossiping about the larger organization of which the group is a part. If this activity is mutually satisfying to the participants and if they have no obligation to achieve their original mission, such discussion presents no problem. But if the original assignment is important, something must be done to get the group back on the track. Outside factors may become an excuse for failing to cope with the group task. If individuals constantly plead that mitigating circumstances prevent their attending meetings or otherwise doing their jobs or if the group as a whole falls into a pattern of complaining about the limitations under which it is working but not doing anything about them, effective group action is jeopardized.

Assuming these potential excesses are avoided, when a group member shows awareness of the influence of contextual factors, it is usually a sign of sensitivity to the feelings of others (and perhaps to the group member's own feelings as well). For example, one author recalls an occasion where he and two other people met for the first time with a well-known psychiatrist whose research specialty was nonverbal communication. The meeting took place at an office in the psychiatrist's research laboratory. The three visitors were seated on a couch on one side of the room. Noting one visitor's half-joking comment that she felt as though she were "in a lineup," the psychiatrist suggested that the group move to another room, where the seating arrangement gave an equal position to each person. His responsiveness to the feelings of his guests created a relaxed atmosphere and thereby contributed to a productive and enjoyable meeting.

SUMMARY AND CONCLUSIONS

Social climate may be influenced by factors which are only partially within a group's control and which exert more-or-less enduring effects. External authorities may determine the purpose of the group and the way people are supposed to work together. Of the various elements in this "task structure," it is especially important whether the group has a cooperative orientation, where all members are judged as a unit, or a competitive structure, where individuals are evaluated against one another. Cooperative structures tend to create greater liking among the group members and better solutions to problems. The size of the group and the combination of personalities brought together may also have a significant effect. Generally, groups of small size that are composed of people who are similar in the degree of their need for affiliation but are balanced in terms of how many members possess dominant and submissive traits and are mixed in sex composition will have the best interpersonal relations, although task requirements concerning the abilities of the various group members must also be considered. Those people who determine the setting for discussion must evaluate the social implications of alternative locations, including whose territory is chosen, the cues existing in the environment about what kinds of activities are supposed to occur there, and the appropriate spatial relations for the particular group purpose. An attractive and comfortable setting will usually contribute to a positive emotional atmosphere, although it is possible for people to be distracted by arrangements which are "too comfortable."

Some elements of the group situation can be manipulated in advance; some can be altered after the group is together; and others must simply be enjoyed or endured. Recognition of the potential effects of social context should help discussion participants to make intelligent choices about the conditions under which they interact.

STUDY SUGGESTIONS

1. Identify some setting variables other than those presented in this chapter which might have a significant impact on the morale of a discussion group.
2. How would you evaluate the grading system that is used in most colleges and universities as an "input variable" in affecting classroom interaction and morale? What about the age differential between students and teacher?

Chapter 5
The Development of Group Cohesiveness

The term "cohesiveness" is metaphorically suggestive. In everyday parlance, it means "sticking together," as when one substance is glued to another. In physics, it indicates the state which exists when some force holds molecules together. And in group theory, it refers to a significant aspect of group functioning: the attraction that group members have for one another.

This feature of groups has been operationalized in research studies in two ways: (1) the investigators sum the ratings on attraction which individuals give for each other group member; or (2) they sum the ratings on attraction which individuals give for the group as a whole. *Each* of these kinds of attraction tends to affect the other, and so, recognizing that they are closely related but not identical, we include both meanings in our definition of cohesiveness. Whichever method of measurement is employed, the "cohesiveness score" of a group reflects a matter of degree, and not of kind. There are not "cohesive" and "uncohesive" groups but, rather, more and less cohesive groups. Although it is possible for a group to have "negative cohesiveness"—for the members to actually be repelled by one another or by the group as a whole—in practice this seldom occurs because under such circumstances the group would be unlikely to stay together.

Why should members of groups be concerned about cohesiveness? After all, couldn't they work together without liking each other or enjoying the interaction if they were motivated strongly enough to accomplish the task? Perhaps the answer is "yes," that it would be possible for them to function more or less as though they were thinking machines, but this would be an uphill struggle.

In the first place, highly cohesive groups are more likely to stay together. Partly this is because attraction to others in itself keeps people coming to meetings, but it also happens that members of highly cohesive groups tend to more satisfied with their work than others (Van Zelst, 1952). Of course, there are other factors which tend to hold people in groups. They may have a strong belief in the purposes of the group even though interaction is unpleasant, or they may be fearful of the disapproval of people who want them to retain membership. Cohesiveness is only *one* force which promotes group survival. However, there are also other reasons why cohesiveness is important.

Attraction among members helps groups to achieve their goals (Shaw, 1976, pp. 205–208). However, this is not quite the same as saying that cohesiveness always contributes to group productivity. If the goals are imposed from the outside and the members are not motivated to achieve them—if the purposes are not the *group's* purposes—then cohesiveness can be detrimental to productivity (Stogdill, 1972). The group can become a "social club" where the members share their complaints about the task and working conditions.

People who are attracted to each other and who are also interested in what the group is trying to accomplish perform more effectively for a variety of reasons. To begin with, they are ordinarily more loyal, so motivation is further enhanced. But, in addition, increasing cohesiveness has certain positive effects on communication, which in turn influences productivity. Feelings of attraction open channels of communication since people interact more with those they like (Moran, 1966). Also, once a group has established a state of high cohesiveness, uncertainty about emotional relations with others declines, and more energy can be devoted to the task. For example, a study by Larsen and Gratz (1970) showed that college students enrolled in courses where sensitivity training methods were employed performed more effectively together on problem-solving tasks than did those who had received training only in the logical aspects of discussion. Presumably, the students who had explored their relationships were more ready to work together even though the other students had received more instruction specifically related to problem solving.

Even if high cohesiveness does not always lead to enhanced productivity, there is another reason for considering this topic: Feelings of liking others and of being liked are intrinsically rewarding. It is simply more enjoyable to participate in a group where there are strong bonds among the members. As a result, people learn more about themselves when new behaviors can be tried out in a secure environment. It is therefore easy to see why cohesiveness is so important to therapy and encounter groups, although the principle applies to all other kinds of groups as well.

In the previous chapter, the authors discussed some aspects of the social context of groups which affect the way people feel about one another. A group that starts with the advantage of compatible personalities and favorable working conditions must still make an effort to realize its full potential for cohesiveness. Cohesiveness is not automatic; it arises out of the way people communicate with one another. On the other hand, even initially incompatible people can grow to like one another through conscientious attention to their interpersonal relationships. The development of attraction usually occurs gradually, and it begins the moment the group members come face to face.

FIRST IMPRESSIONS

When people arrive for the first meeting of a group, the personalities of the other members are mostly unknown, as is the question of how these people will respond to one another as a group. Thus, the individual member is likely to begin to assess these people, either consciously or unconsciously, as a means of reducing uncertainty in the situation. And each member may make some attempts to control how he or she is perceived by others. The formation of "first impressions" of individuals and of the group as a whole is certain to have an effect on attraction in the initial meeting and may have an enduring impact on group cohesiveness.

We remind you that communication is a transactional process, that meaning is the product of both the perceiver and the perceived. Culture leads to certain common ways of interpreting aspects of appearance and behavior, but it is doubtful if any two people form *exactly* the same impression of the same individuals on any occasion. Therefore, each statement made below about how people read such messages is a generalization subject to individual variation.

Impressions of Individuals

One of the most widely investigated topics relating to interpersonal behavior is that of "person perception"—the process by which people make interpretations about other individuals. Mostly, these studies concern assessments of personality traits, although people also make guesses about occupations and other facts concerning the lives of those about whom they form impressions. Although some theorists have suggested that the very first reaction tends to be an enduring one (Thibaut and Kelley, 1959), it should be noted that impressions will also change over time as more information is received about the individuals being judged.

Impressions may be based on physical appearance and dress alone. Judging from the fact that people are often consciously concerned with producing an "image" by means of the clothing they select, it is not surprising that research has shown dress to be a factor which is capable of influencing impressions. In one study, for example, people gave more favorable personality ratings to strangers who were "dressed up" than to those who were "dressed down" (Hoult, 1954).

Perhaps more surprising is the fact that people also tend to assign personality traits to others with faces having certain physical characteristics. For example, in one study, an older face with thin lips and wrinkles at the eye corners was considered by observers to be distinguished-looking and intelligent and to have an "air of responsibility" (Secord, Dukes, and Bevan, 1954). In addition, a number of studies have shown that people tend to associate certain body types identified by Sheldon (1954) with configurations of personality traits. Fat people, whom Sheldon calls "endomorphs," are frequently seen as relaxed, cooperative, affable, and softhearted; thin people, or "ectomorphs," are often perceived as detached, shy, introspective, and cautious; muscular, athletic-looking people, or "mesomorphs," are often seen as dominant, energetic, determined, and outgoing (Wells and Siegel, 1968; Strongman and Hart, 1968; Walker, 1963).

Voice quality can also lead to inferences about personality. For example, Addington (1968) found a "breathy" quality in a male voice to connote youth and artistic qualities; in a female voice, it suggested femininity and shallowness. In both male and female voices, "nasality" was perceived as being associated with a number of undesirable traits.

When we come face to face with another person, we naturally have more information on which to base a judgment than we would simply by looking at a photograph or by listening to a recording of the person's voice. We can see the other person assuming certain postures, moving in certain ways, revealing his or her reactions to ongoing happenings. People who hold their arms in close to the body and hang their heads may be seen as "shy" and "self-conscious," while those who take up space with their arms and legs and hold their heads erect may be seen as "self-satisfied" and "casual."

The performance of such behaviors which create impressions in others may not necessarily be spontaneous and unrehearsed. As Goffman (1959) has pointed out, people are often aware of holding their bodies and controlling their movements in such a way as to appear as they would like others to see them. For example, a person who wishes to give the impression that he or she is open to contact from others will maintain a friendly, alert tonus in the face and an active, responsive quality of movement. This "performance" may be dishonest in that it creates a false impression, or it may be quite honest in the sense that it reflects the genuine desires and motivations of the performer.

Although we consider nonverbal behavior to be especially important in impression formation, we do not mean to exclude verbal acts. Obviously, what a person says or how much he or she talks during a first meeting of a group will also lead to inferences on the part of others. It is likely, for example, that a talkative person will be seen as a potential "leader" of the group. If the group is seen as one where there are appointed or authorized leaders, the "high talker" will be evaluated as "overly aggressive" if he or she does not occupy an official leadership position, whereas the same person will be evaluated as "helpful" if he or she is the sanctioned leader (Damusis, 1972).

In light of what we have said about the kinds of messages people use to form first impressions of individuals, the practitioner of discussion should keep certain points in mind:

1. As a *sender* of messages about the self, the participant should be aware that others do tend to form first impressions, many of which are based on widely held stereotypes. For example, the research on facial stereotypes shows that people generally agree on what photographs of faces should go with what occupations or personality traits (Secord, Bevan, and Dukes, 1953), and they are often rather confident of their judgments (Secord, Dukes, and Bevan, 1954). We do not mean to suggest that people ought to invest in plastic surgery, body-building courses, voice training, expensive clothes, and acting lessons, but simply that they ought to know some of the bases on which others develop first impressions. At times, when they consider it important to make a good impression, they may want to give some thought to their selection of clothing, their grooming, and the attitudes with which they approach the situation.

2. As a *receiver* of messages, group members should be aware that first impressions are *frequently inaccurate* from the point of view of self-descriptions by those who are judged. This is rather clearly true of judgments based on facial characteristics (Secord and Dukes, 1953) and voice quality (see Knapp, 1978), where studies have consistently failed to show a correspondence between perceptions of personality and actual scores on personality tests. The most notable exception appears to be body type, since there is some evidence that stereotypes about fat, thin, and muscular people match to some degree the self-descriptions of individuals with these physical characteristics (Cortes and Gatti, 1965). Even if these stereotypes do apply in a general way, however, there is considerable possibility for error when this concept is applied to a particular individual. On the whole, researchers have not been very successful in uncovering characteristics of posture, facial structure, or voice quality which would serve as reliable indicators of personality or other stable individual qualities. It may be, of course, that while most people are not very accurate, there are some very perceptive individuals who make fewer mistakes in their first

impressions (see Argyle, 1969, pp. 160–164). However, if reliable signs which could be taught to others do exist, we do not know what they are. At the same time, you should keep in mind the transactional nature of communication. In a certain sense, there is no such thing as an "accurate" interpretation since even a person's self-description involves a transaction between the individual and his or her own behavior.

3. Nothing we have said here should be taken to mean that people cannot recognize expressions of emotion in others. Rather, we have argued that it is the more enduring personal qualities which may be mistakenly identified at a first meeting. The group discussant should be aware, however, that people often confuse emotional responses with personality traits when they form first impressions. In the studies of personality judgments based on photographs of faces, for example, people often inferred traits from such factors as whether the person being photographed looked toward or away from the camera or was smiling. It is possible, therefore, that the mood a person is experiencing on a given day might be taken by others to indicate a more lasting trait.

4. We should also qualify our conclusions to point out that the dangers of stereotypic impression formation may not be quite as great as the research would seem to indicate. It is probably true that there are certain kinds of people who do not very often form strong first impressions, and the tendency to resist such responses may exist in everyone to some extent. Also, it seems likely that when people meet others they do not make evaluations based on one cue only—such as physical appearance or voice quality—but rather they probably assess many cues simultaneously. If the cues are not consistent with one another, they may cancel out in their effects on judgments. However, if the cues are consistent, it is possible that a rather firm impression will be developed. It seems likely that judgments of multiple cues will be more accurate than those based on one or two indicators.

We believe that first impressions of individuals, regardless of their inaccuracies, probably exert a rather strong influence on group interactions. The larger the group, the more we would expect this to be true. Our reasoning is that stereotypic responses should dissolve somewhat as the perceiver gathers more information about the person being judged. In a two-person group, each person gets to talk a good deal, and each can devote considerable attention to the other. With increasing group size, there is less data on which to base an evaluation and less time to form an impression of each person. As a result, in large groups people may fall back on standard and habitual ways of perceiving others.

Impressions of the Group as a Whole

When people first enter a group, they begin to develop impressions not only of other individuals, but also of the group as a whole. In fact, this impression might be the strongest one that is taken away from the initial encounter, since a person ordinarily has little opportunity to get to know others on a one-to-one basis in the first meeting. As the participants gather and then begin the discussion, people may be thinking about a number of questions: (1) *What feelings do I get about the emotional tone of this group?* Is it tense, jovial, or relaxed? Do people seem involved or detached? (2) *Will these people be able to work well together?* Is there competition for the floor? When someone talks, do others seem to listen attentively? Or do they simply wait for their turn? (3) *How will I fit in with this group?* Will I be bored? Will I be able to get into the conversation? Do I feel comfortable with these people?

To some extent, of course, the answers to questions such as these come from the impressions one develops of the individuals who make up the group. But there is something else added: People do more than just respond to individuals; they also calculate how this *combination* of personalities (or, rather, the combination of what *appear* to be the personalities of the group members) will work out. In addition, it is possible for people to have somewhat different impressions of the group as a whole and of some of the individuals who comprise it. It is not uncommon for a person to say, "I met a couple of nice people, but on the whole, it seems like a pretty stiff group." Or, conversely, "There were a couple of rather obnoxious people there, but on the whole it looks like a good group."

Although there has been much research on the perception of individuals, it is surprising that the perception of groups has received very little attention. However, in the investigations which have been conducted, the results suggest that people do develop impressions of the group as a whole. Usually, studies of this type involve having people hear a discussion on an audio tape and then asking them to evaluate or characterize the group in some way. Research has revealed several factors which influence impressions.

1. What is said in the discussion, of course, will have an effect. For example, in one study, the more the group members made agreeing statements, the more they were seen as "cohesive" by observers (Damusis, 1972).

2. The attitudes of the perceiver toward the topic being discussed may also influence what is "heard." In the same study referred to above, "pro" listeners thought that the group members were likely to vote "pro," while "con" listeners thought the opposite, despite the fact that both heard the same discussion. Thus, there is a tendency for people to hear what they want to hear. This can create problems in the development of cohesiveness later, when participants discover differences among themselves in ideas and emotional style which they did not perceive when the group first met.

3. In addition, if the person anticipates belonging to the group, the

conditions under which he or she is brought into membership may affect perceptions. In one study, for example, some young women were given a "severe" initiation while others received a "mild" initiation.[1] They then heard a tape recording of a particularly *dull* discussion and were told that this was the group they were going to join. The women found the discussion more "interesting" when they had gone through the severe initiation. It would appear that having experienced an unpleasant procedure to get into the group, they wanted to see the group in a positive light in order to justify what they had gone through, thus distorting their perceptions of the discussion (Aronson and Mills, 1959).

First impressions of both individuals and the group have two especially important effects on group process. In the first place, group members begin to establish feelings of attraction or dislike for other participants and for the group as a whole and, thus, influence the likelihood of high or low cohesiveness. In the second place, members also begin to develop expectations about the way others will behave in the group. These expectations may become self-fulfilling prophecies, thus establishing actual patterns of interaction.

THE EVOLUTION OF IMPRESSIONS

First impressions are rather important because they set a tone for what follows. However, despite the initial impact of this process, people gain more information about one another as they interact over time, and their impressions undergo some changes. Certain factors tend to influence the outcome.

Changes in Interpersonal Attraction

Generally, people tend to like others whom they find to be *similar* to themselves in attitudes and/or personality. This conclusion is so widely supported by research that we will not cite all of the studies here but rather suggest that the reader consult a summary of this research by Shaw (1976, pp. 86–91). Most investigations have been concerned with attraction in dyads, although apparently similar results are produced in larger groups (Good and Nelson, 1973). Obviously, this process requires some amount of time for mutual exploration among individuals since these bases of similarity will not often be apparent in the first meeting (Newcomb, 1961). People seem to find it rewarding to discover that

[1]Subjects were told that the topic of the discussion group they were going to join concerned "sex." The authors of the study describe the conditions of the study as follows: "In the severe condition, subjects were required to read some embarrassing material before joining the group; in the mild condition, the material they read was not very embarrassing" (Aronson and Mills, 1959, in Cartwright and Zander, 1968, p. 120).

others share their feelings about certain issues and about themselves, and they also gain confidence that they will be understood and appreciated by such people in future encounters. In addition, there is some evidence that people prefer to work with those of similar abilities (Senn, 1971; Shaw and Gilchrist, 1955), presumably because such situations reassure individuals that they will neither lag behind nor be let down by other group members.

There may be some rare cases, however, in which dissimilarity contributes to attraction because of a certain combination of personalities. Earlier, we noted that highly dominant people do not get along very well with one another in groups and that a mix of ascendant and submissive individuals is optimal. Of course, dominance may not overshadow all other traits, so that feelings which dominant persons ultimately come to hold for one another may be partially dependent on the degree to which they discover that they have other traits in common.

Changes in Attraction to the Group as a Whole

Just as first impressions of individuals evolve, perceptions of the group as a whole may also undergo change over time. It seems likely that attraction to the goals, activities, or prestige of a certain group initially creates a positive bias toward liking that collection of people. Then, as the discussion progresses, participants have an opportunity to test whether the motivations of others match, complement, or conflict with their own. As they reassess their ideas about the attractiveness of membership, they may correspondingly increase or decrease their commitment to the people in the group as well.

Later, group members have an opportunity to assess the group's performance of its task. Another aspect of cohesiveness which has not been studied, to our knowledge, is the effect of successful goal achievement on interpersonal liking. Investigators have tended to assume that the correlation between cohesiveness and productivity observed in field studies of groups means only that attraction leads to effective task performance, and not the converse—that productivity also increases cohesiveness. In our experience, however, goal achievement does tend to facilitate attraction to the group as a whole, although it is seldom sufficient to create high cohesiveness by itself.

Finally, over and above the feelings that group participants have about emerging group goals and task performance, attraction toward the group as a whole may increase simply as a function of the amount of time that the group members spend together. The existence of this relationship between interaction and positive sentiment was originally suggested by George Homans (1950). Since then, others have apparently found the idea intuitively attractive since it is often cited by other authors. Some studies support this conclusion, although most of them deal with attractions formed among people in housing units rather than those involved in continuous group interaction. For example, a classic study of friendship development in a housing project showed that people who lived close to one another or who were otherwise likely to come into contact at their mailboxes or other places were also more likely to form interpersonal relationships (Festinger, Schachter, and Back, 1950). Duetsch and Collins (1951) found that more intimate relationships among blacks and whites developed in an integrated than in a segregated housing project. In a study specifically concerned with group discussion, Snortum and Myers (1969) observed that members of a sensitivity training group increased steadily in feelings of closeness over a series of meetings. However, not all research has obtained the same result, and Newcomb (1953) has suggested the proposition that the more people interact with one another, the *stronger* their feelings become, whether positive or negative. Thus, although there is probably a general tendency for members to become more attracted to the group as time goes by, this effect is not inevitable.

The Development of Differential Attraction

At times, certain group members develop strong attractions to one another and form subgroups within the larger group. These relationships may come about rather naturally as the result of prior friendships or the discovery of similarities in personalities, attitudes, or abilities. As such, they do not necessarily create a problem as long as the subgroup members are attracted to the group as a whole and maintain lines of communication with others. However, attraction within subgroups is sometimes accompanied by neutral or negative reaction to others. These "mutual support coalitions" may have a divisive effect on the cohesiveness of the entire group.

COHESION-BUILDING BEHAVIORS

Thus far, we have assumed that the bases of interpersonal attraction are more or less *discovered* by the participants as they get to know one another. We have given little help to those who wish to *promote* greater cohesiveness. It is time to rectify this omission. The development of cohesiveness is not simply a matter of people gathering information about one another, but rather it is something which can be worked on gradually through dozens, hundreds, and even thousands of "little acts" of courtesy and consideration. In this section, we will describe the normal processes without which it would be very difficult for a group to achieve a high degree of mutual attraction. Although these acts occur again and again in the life of the average group, we will describe them in the order they might take place within the course of one group meeting. It should also be noted that these behaviors are skills which can be acquired by individuals through awareness and practice.

1. Greeting Behaviors. Obviously, people do not just sit down and begin a discussion of the designated topic. Each time the group comes together, individuals go through a process of acknowledging one another. Whether everyone exchanges greetings with everyone else depends on the size of the group; a large group makes a complete round of salutations difficult. In any case, this behavior serves an important bonding function. If the customary rules of greeting behavior are not followed, some people may feel slighted. For example, as Goffman (1971, pp. 80–91) points out, the length and elaborateness of greetings depend partly on how long people have been separated, a long separation calling for a more extensive greeting.

Salutations will typically involve direct eye-contact, a verbal request for information about the other's welfare, and oftentimes some form of touching (a handshake, a touch on the arm, or a hug). Where people greet each other from a distance across a room, eye-contact may be supplemented by smiles, waves, or possibly a raising of the eyebrows. As more and more people enter the room, there will be various acts of inclusion— making room, pulling up chairs for others, and adjusting body position so that at least part of the body is oriented toward the newcomer (see Scheflen, 1974, pp. 61–65). The meeting may be called together by a verbal announcement (e.g., "I think we should get started") or by several people "pulling up to the table." Even after this point, late arrivals are likely to be acknowledged with a glance and a smile.

2. Choices in Spatial Arrangements. There is a certain latitude of choice in a group about who sits close to whom, although this is reduced somewhat as available seating places are filled. Generally, people sit closest to those they like and those they want to engage in social conversation (Russo, 1967; Campbell, Kruskal, and Wallace, 1966). Thus, it is often easy to recognize "mutual support coalitions" when the same people sit together at each meeting. People also tend to sit across from those they expect to challenge (Steinzor, 1950). In a very cohesive group, these positions will change frequently, suggesting that there are a number of lines of attraction among the members and that people do not habitually challenge the same individuals. Likewise, people who wish to establish ties with a variety of others will tend to select different seats on each occasion.

3. Turn-Giving and Turn-Requesting. As a meeting progresses, there must be some way of organizing who speaks when; otherwise mass confusion results. To some degree, interruptions are used for this purpose, but if this behavior is practiced habitually by some group members, it suggests an attempt to dominate others (Rogers and Jones, 1975) and is unlikely to lead to mutual attraction. Individuals show regard for others by sending *turn-giving signals*, verbal and nonverbal messages which say, "It's someone else's turn to speak." Such signals include the dropping of a hand gesture, a lowering of pitch or volume at the end of a sentence, and establishing eye-contact with others after a period of verbalization (Duncan, 1973; Kendon, 1965). Sometimes turn-giving signals can be used as a means of showing differential attraction when a person consistently focuses remarks and eye-contact toward a limited number of people as a means of handing over the conversation only to close associates. But in a highly cohesive group, individuals will often look to the entire group or to a variety of potential respondents for the next statement. The other side of the coin consists of *turn-requesting signals*. Rather than interrupt, people who use these messages show respect for others by signaling that they would like to speak next. These behaviors include sitting foward, nodding vigorously, and beginning gestures preparatory to speaking (see Wiemann and Knapp, 1975).

Note that while the turn allocation techniques we have described here generally contribute to attraction within the group, the absence of simultaneous talking does not in itself guarantee good feelings. In fact, an overly polite discussion sometimes reflects the suppression of negative feelings and not the existence of positive regard. Also, an apathetic group seldom has a problem with turn allocation because it is easy for group members to talk when there are numerous periods of silence, but this does not suggest high cohesiveness. On the other hand, spontaneous interaction among people who are highly involved in the discussion oftentimes will be accompanied by lapses in orderly exchange, especially when the group is large and there is much competition for the floor. Under these conditions, the occasional emergence of confusion about who is supposed to speak can be a healthy sign. Attempts by the group members to solve problems of turn allocation are more important to the development of group atmosphere than is the strict adherence to rules.

4. Listening Behaviors and Gatekeeping. In addition to turn-giving and turn-requesting behaviors, there is another set of messages which contribute to the growth of group cohesion. These consist of verbal and nonverbal signals that encourage others as they speak or that aid others in getting into the conversation. Listening behaviors, or "back-channel signals" as Duncan terms them, are emitted by individuals simultaneously with the talk of others. They say, in effect, "I'm listening—keep going—I'm listening," and include such responses as repeated head nods, vocal expressions such as "uh-huh," and various appropriate responses of the face and head which show that the listener understands—raised eyebrows, head tilts, looks of sympathy, and so forth (Scheflen, 1974, pp. 67–69). Similarly, verbal statements which show that the listener acknowledges what has been said by others, including paraphrasings of ideas, have a positive effect. One particular technique, called "gatekeeping," is very effective in encouraging people to talk by drawing out those who are having trouble getting into the conversation, perhaps by asking silent members for their opinions or simply by asking if they have something to add. The effect of these various behaviors on group cohesiveness is obvious: People tend to like others who seem to want to hear what they have to say.

5. Behaviors Showing Sensitivity to the Feelings of Others. People do not always express their feelings clearly and explicitly in a group. There may be a number of reasons for this, including shyness and a desire not to interfere with the progress of the discussion. But it is important for group members to know how others feel about proposals and about their roles in the group if consensus and mutual support are to be achieved. Effective group participation is attuned to the emotional responses of others, and there are various ways in which feelings can be communicated and detected.

Frequently, the expression of feelings that people do not want to show in an obvious way takes nonverbal forms, especially in facial and postural behavior. Facial expression is the best single indicator of emotion. While it takes a fairly high degree of perceptiveness (which can be enhanced by training) for people to consistently recognize expressions of basic emotions and subtle blends of emotion in the face, it is fairly easy to distinguish positive from negative facial reactions.[2] In most cases, the face must be observed for the detection of specific emotions, but the rest of the body gives clues to the intensity of feelings (Ekman and Friesen, 1965). In addition, posture is a rather reliable indicator of involvement (e.g., leaning in) and withdrawal (e.g., leaning out). Sensitive group members pick up these signals and respond to them, either verbally or nonverbally. For example, he or she may comment, "I notice that you were bothered by that comment." Or, they may simply direct eye-contact toward the person who shows a feeling nonverbally, suggesting their willingness to hear anything the person may have to say.

6. Signals of Identification and Empathy. Besides picking up on the emotional messages of others, group members can also show that they identify with others and with their feelings. The effect is to cause people to feel that they have much in common, thus increasing their feelings of mutual liking. This can be accomplished with verbal expressions, such as "I know

[2] Readers interested in more information on the subject of facial expression are referred to Paul Ekman and Wallace Friesen, *Unmasking the Face* (Englewood Cliffs, N.J.: Prentice-Hall, 1975).

just how you feel." More often, however, it is done nonverbally by means of various kinds of mirroring expressions (see Scheflen, 1974, pp. 57–60) which can take the form of congruent body postures—two or more people adopting similar postural behavior, much as though they were mirror reflections of one another. A subgroup of individuals who consistently mirror one another in opposition to the postures assumed by other members of the group are indicating differential attraction. In contrast, members of a highly cohesive group will often adopt similar body positions all around the circle.

Mirroring can also involve facial expression, vocal intonation, volume, gestures, and various aspects of movement. In fact, Condon and Ogston (1966) have been able to show that people in conversations frequently "vibrate together" in such minute and precise ways that the pattern of mirroring can be detected in its entirety only by means of slow motion photography! If it is true that imitation is the sincerest form of flattery, as seen when a child copies the nonverbal behaviors of a parent or an admired adult, it is also true that reflection of the postures, movements, and various manners of expression among members of a group is a rather clear way of communicating attraction.

7. Departure Behavior. Just as greeting behavior serves a bonding function by reestablishing relationships among people who have been apart, departure behavior provides people with the opportunity to take leave without being abrupt and with reassurances to others that it is not the relationship which is being terminated but rather just the immediate encounter; that is, in most situations people do not simply get up and leave the room when they perceive that it is time for them to go. People who expect that they will have to leave before the meeting is concluded will often announce this fact early in the discussion, perhaps offering an explanation. When the time does come for them to depart, they will often make some kind of verbal and/or nonverbal "statement" that they "must" go, and this will often be acknowledged by others in some way. The other group members who stay until the end usually will coordinate their behaviors in such a way that everyone recognizes when the meeting is coming to a close, and someone will ordinarily make this "official" by saying something such as "I think that about does it," or, "I believe that's all the business we have for today." In some groups this procedure is formalized by a hasty vote on adjournment.

Knapp and his associates (1973) have suggested that "good-byes" have two primary communication functions. First, they "signal inaccessibility" by showing others that departure is imminent. Second, they communicate "supportiveness" by letting others know that the departure is a reluctant act which in no way suggests that something is wrong with the relationship. Knapp and his colleagues have confined themselves to the study of leave-taking in two-person settings, but some of their findings seem applicable to multiperson groups. For example, forewarning of inaccessibility can be shown by an increase in various body movements such as shuffling the feet, moving the upper part of the body, and changing body orientation away from a direct, head-on position. In groups, it often happens that people who are about to depart will also gather their materials together and push themselves back slightly from the circle or table. Supportiveness can be communicated by various behaviors such as a forward lean or an increase in head nodding. In groups, it often happens that after a person has signaled inaccessibility, he or she will perform the "leaning in" and "nodding" behaviors as a final act of participation before taking an early departure, perhaps followed with a look around the group and a wave directed to everyone, performed while getting up. If it is appropriate to interject verbal comments, individuals may make superlative statements ("Good meeting"), express appreciation ("Thanks for coming"), show welfare concern ("Take it easy"), and provide an internal legitimizer ("That's all I have to add") or an external legitimizer ("Sorry, I have another meeting"). The exact nature of the leave-taking behaviors employed will vary according to the context. If the individual will not be returning to the group for a while or if the entire group will not be meeting for some time, departures more elaborate and protracted than those in situations where everyone will be seeing one another again soon are customary.

The kinds of cohesion-building acts that we have described in this section are ones which occur rather naturally in the flow of interaction among people who are highly skilled in interpersonal relations. Where it seems appropriate, it is also possible for groups to engage in certain planned activities or exercises which promote similar ends. In the beginning of the group, for example, it is sometimes effective for participants to pair up, carrying on a conversation by themselves for a period of time with the objective of "getting to know each other," and then introduce their partner to the rest of the group. Since people tend to look for positive qualities in others and to stress those characteristics when introducing others in first meetings, this activity serves to increase the chances for the development of cohesiveness by creating positive first impressions and recognizing each participant as an integral part of the group. Later on, the group may choose to interrupt the normal course of business to engage in other kinds of cohesion-building activities. One exercise, called "strength bombardment," which is often used by human relations facilitators, involves having members of the group focus on one person at a time with each individual pointing out the positive and strong qualities they see in this person.

The appropriateness of such activities depends on the group's pur-

pose and on norms which have been established about how the participants are supposed to interact with one another; their practice would not
be recommended for every circumstance. However, even where formalized "getting together" experiences are not appropriate, there is much
that individuals can do to promote cohesion-building behavior within the
group. For example, they can "model" various behaviors such as active
listening and showing concern for the feelings of others which we have
described, perhaps calling attention to these acts by the degree of courtesy
and consideration shown. Likewise, they can reinforce cohesion-building
acts on the part of others by commenting on them (e.g., "I really appreciate the way you've been helping others to get into the conversation,
Jeanne") or by simply acknowledging acts of others with an approving
look.[3] Since cohesion-building acts are supposed to occur "naturally" in
most groups (despite the fact that few people are probably highly skilled
in all of the communication behaviors we have described), there is a certain amount of risk involved for people who take it upon themselves to
encourage these kinds of behaviors in others. For this reason, the individuals who are designated as leaders or who have special positions of status
in the group may find it easier to enter into this kind of teaching role than
others. In any case, the facilitation of cohesion-building should ordinarily
be done in a rather subtle fashion, unless it is explicitly recognized that
such training is one of the purposes of the group.

THE EMERGENCE OF HIGH COHESIVENESS

So far, we have been suggesting that the development of positive bonds of
feeling is a rather gradual process. At times, however, groups seem to take
dramatic "jumps" in cohesiveness. Although cohesiveness is always a matter of degree, group members often see this as an "all or nothing" condition, referring to "the day we really became a group" as a turning point
in their feelings of group closeness.

Certain kinds of acts seem to precipitate strong increases in cohesiveness. One such event involves an act of "sacrifice" by one or more group
members, such as giving up a long-held position or showing a willingness
to compromise. Another is an act of self-disclosure by someone in the
group which far surpasses the level of intimacy which has been shown
previously and which makes the person more vulnerable, thus encouraging trust on the part of others. Still another, perhaps less dramatic, event
occurs when someone introduces process discussion which leads the group

[3] Readers who are interested in more information on these kinds of facilitative skills should
refer to John Krumboltz and Beverly Potter, "Behavioral Techniques for Developing Trust,
Cohesiveness, and Goal Accomplishment," *Educational Technology*, 13 (1), 1973: 26–30.

members to examine their interpersonal relations.

A change in group attraction may also be precipitated by external events which are not within the group's control. Often, this takes the form of a threat to the group's existence or to the view that members have of themselves as a group. For example, a university administration could suggest that there is no longer a need for a certain academic department, or executives in a business organization could call upon a certain work unit to justify its continuance. In rare circumstances, the threat might even be a physical one, and it might happen that there was literally no group until the time of crisis, as when a group of commuters find themselves stranded underground in a stalled subway. Or, a group might suddenly find itself in competition with other groups to see which can perform more effectively. The presence of a threat tends to mobilize energies and to strengthen bonds because it forces group members to recognize their common interests and to view sources of dissension within the group in a new perspective. In addition, positive information about the group coming from the outside can have a similar effect. For example, public acknowledgement of a group for outstanding achievement can cause the group members to value their relationships with one another more highly.

The effects which we have described as stemming from acts of sacrifice, disclosure, or process intervention, and from external threats or rewards are not inevitable. When confronted by a crisis, group members also may withdraw from individual acts of commitment and fall into blaming one another. Fear of involvement and lingering bitterness over past relations can hold people back from meeting challenges to the group potential for cohesiveness. Ordinarily, however, there is a tendency for such conditions to enhance mutual attraction simply because most people would prefer to like those with whom they interact. To gauge the impact of emergent events as well as the more gradual influence of impression formation and cohesion-building acts, one needs to look for certain indicators of cohesion.

SIGNS OF HIGH COHESIVENESS

How can one tell when strong bonds of mutual attraction have been developed in a group? If we were conducting a research project on this subject, we could ask the members to fill out attitude scales at various points in the discussion process, registering their reactions to the other individuals in the group and to the group as a whole. For ordinary circumstances, however, we must be satisfied with looking for certain signs of cohesiveness and using intuition in order to make judgments. Our experiences with groups suggest that increases in certain behaviors provide rather reliable indices to levels of attraction.

1. Language. An increase in the use of certain kinds of verbal expressions often provides a good indicator. This is especially true when members begin to use the pronoun "we" in referring to the group, rather than saying "I" exclusively. In addition, participants will make statements of solidarity when feelings of satisfaction and attraction are being developed. Someone may say, "We're really getting somewhere," or "I feel good about this session." The repetition of such ideas by others, nods of agreement, and looks of approval in response to these statements strengthen the impression that the feeling is widely shared among the members.

2. Joking and Laughter. When people are enjoying their time together, they will often kid one another, using facial expression and vocal intonation to show that their remarks are not to be taken seriously, and this will often be accompanied by whole-hearted laughter. Of course, the absence of these behaviors is not necessarily an indication of low cohesiveness when the group is working on a difficult problem. As Bales (1950) has noted, this kind of spontaneous response of good humor should be distinguished from the nervous laughter which reflects tension.

3. Spatial Configurations. As we noted in the section on cohesion-building behaviors, physical closeness is a rather reliable sign of liking. In highly cohesive groups, there is a tendency for people to change their seating positions from meeting to meeting, thus expressing their liking for a variety of the participants. In addition, where it is physically possible, participants may pull their chairs together, decreasing the size of the circle as they grow to like one another more.

4. Bodily Expressions of Liking and Affection. There are other nonverbal means by which people can show attraction to others besides spatial relations. Where it is appropriate to the cultural and group setting, they may touch one another from time to time, especially during greetings and departures, but also occasionally within the course of the group discussion. Likewise, a relatively large amount of smiling (Reese and Whitman, 1962) and directness of eye-contact (Mehrabian, 1969; Exline, 1972) suggest attraction.

5. The "Early Arrival" and "Late Departure" Phenomenon. People who like one another are likely to want to spend time together beyond the confines of the official meeting times of the group. One way they can do this is to come to meetings early and remain after business has been conducted. If such behaviors are indicative of attraction, there will ordinarily be a good deal of animated social conversation at these times. Regular attendance at meetings is a related behavior; it suggests that people do not want to miss the opportunity to be with one another.

6. Sharing Behavior. Members may also show the desire to coalesce by offering help and assistance beyond the task requirements. For example, they may give one another rides home or even bring food and pass it around.

7. Withstanding Conflict. One final indicator of cohesiveness may seem paradoxical. It might appear that people who always agree must like one another, but, in fact, the avoidance of conflict may be a sign that they feel on tenuous ground in their relations. By contrast, those who are secure in their associations can argue more freely. This is a topic which we will develop in more detail in Chapter 8, "Conflict Management in Groups." For the time being, we will simply suggest that the ability to withstand conflict without withdrawal or rejection is likely to be found where there are healthy and positive mutual orientations.

We should qualify the above statements to some extent. The signs we have listed are certainly not infallible indicators of high cohesiveness. This is especially true if only one or two of these behaviors occur without others being present or if such events are uncommon in the life of the group. It is also true that the opposites of these signs tend to suggest low cohesiveness. For example, we could just as well speak of the "late arrival" and "early departure" phenomenon as an indicator of the lack of attraction, although, again, the significance of such occurrences would depend on confirmation from other behaviors which create a similar impression. Also, we want to point out that the validity of most of these signs of cohesiveness has not been tested in systematic investigations of multiperson groups. However, we believe that the ideas we have suggested have a certain degree of "face validity:" that is, these indicators may be immediately recognizable and intuitively sensible to you, and you can test these assertions by comparison with your own personal experience.

SUMMARY AND CONCLUSIONS

In this chapter, we have suggested that the enhancement of positive feelings of attraction generally contributes to group effectiveness, although we have acknowledged that it is possible for a group to spend so much time socializing that the task is neglected. We have suggested various ways in which cohesiveness may be increased. The development of favorable first impressions, the discovery of similarities among group members, the continuous performance of certain cohesion-building acts, and the enactment of individual commitment and responses to external forces of threat or reward all contribute to the total group atmosphere. We have also suggested that there are certain "shorthand" methods of detecting how group members feel about one another and the group as a whole.

However, since every group is a system, it is not entirely possible to distinguish between those events which contribute to and those which reflect mutual attraction. Every relevant act is both a potential cause and a potential effect in the ongoing development of group cohesiveness. Group members must be both sensitive to the signs and active in the process of bringing about an optimal level of attraction.

STUDY SUGGESTIONS

1. Try to recall the most attractive small group and the least attractive small group of which you have ever been a member. What factors caused you to feel so attracted to the first group and so repulsed by the second? With the other members of a group, develop a list of such factors and try to determine the most common sources of attraction and repulsion.
2. Are there certain kinds of groups (e.g., a sports team or an orchestra) in which interpersonal attraction among the members is less important to the effective accomplishment of the group's goals than in other kinds of groups (e.g., the cast of a play or a college seminar)? What are the reasons for your opinion?
3. Have you ever been in a group in which the level of cohesiveness decreased, rather than increased, over time? If so, why do you think that happened?
4. Prepare a table of "indicators of group cohesiveness" (as suggested in this chapter) in rows so that you can check off the frequency of their appearance. Then select two groups you know (as much alike in task and size as possible) and check the frequency of appearance of these indicators. You might want to estimate the general cohesiveness of the two groups before you record the acts and see if your overall subjective judgment matches the actual occurrence of these behaviors. Or you might want to choose groups you already believe to be high and low on cohesiveness.
5. Interview the members of a group noted for its high morale and commitment, and the members of a group with lower cohesiveness. In your interviews see if you can identify the personal sources and the group sources of high or low cohesiveness. To what extent is commitment to the group a product of individual personality and to what extent is it caused by actual group practices?

Chapter 6
Group Culture

A person who travels to an unfamiliar culture will find much that he or she does not understand. In a similar way, a newcomer to an established group will find that, despite superficial likenesses to other group situations, it takes a while to understand how to behave in this new group. We refer to this elusive quality as "group culture."

PARALLELS BETWEEN CULTURES AND SMALL GROUPS

When the term "culture" is employed in its usual sense, it refers to a certain way of looking at an entire society or a minority group within a society. Simply put, a culture consists of the "total lifeway of a people" or a "design for living" of an entire people. Theorists frequently break down the idea of culture into two subconcepts, *values* and *customs*

Values are conceptions of what is desirable, and as such they provide very broad guidelines for behavior which individuals must interpret in order to function in many different contexts. Lists of American values typically include such items as "individualism," "social and occupational mobility," "independence," "rationality," "planning for the future," and "change and learning" (see Condon and Yousef, 1975; Barnlund, 1975). As we have pointed out in Chapter 2, values tend to vary greatly from culture to culture.

Customs are traditional ways of doing things within the culture. They may be rather formalized, as are the dates for certain holidays and the ways that people are supposed to celebrate them. Or, they may consist of informal practices, such as the distances that individuals prefer to maintain between themselves in everyday conversation. Like values, customs differ widely according to the culture.

Customs and values are closely related, but they are not the same. Values are more abstract; they are the ideals toward which most people in a culture strive. Customs are more descriptive of how people actually behave. Values and customs are often consistent with one another, but not always. Sometimes customs lag behind a change in values. For example, the new emphasis on equality for women in the American culture is not reflected in the hiring practices of most organizations. Sometimes external pressures cause people to follow customs which at first glance appear to be at variance with their values. In the book *Tally's Corner* (1967), urban anthropologist Elliot Liebow provides an example of this principle as it applies to an American minority group. Like many other Americans, lower-income blacks hold the value that "the man should be a good breadwinner." Partly as a result of unemployment and crowded living conditions the custom has emerged in many inner-city neighborhoods for black men to stand around on the street during the day. The explanation is not that blacks value being out of work, but rather that jobs are scarce for minority group members. In fact, besides being a place for socializing, the street is also one place where information about employment can be obtained, but, as Liebow points out, middle-class whites traveling through a black neighborhood may misinterpret what they see.

If "culture" in its broadest and most accurate sense refers to the "total lifeway of a people," then the term "group culture" refers to the "total lifeway of a group." We use this term to stress the parallel between culture on the societal and group levels. The sense would be the same if we were to use the term "group personality," drawing an analogy to individual systems. As with the concept of societal cultures, we can break down the notion of group culture into two parts—group norms and group patterns.

Group norms operate in a manner similar to that of cultural values. They are group standards of appropriate behavior which are enforced by social pressure. In their simplest form, they can be described as a set of "do's" and "don'ts." Typical examples are as follows: "Do participate in the discussion"; "don't miss meetings except in unusual circumstances"; "do encourage others to talk"; "don't dominate the conversation or otherwise behave in a rude manner." Some group norms specify the roles that individual members are supposed to perform and may be described by statements about what each person is expected to do: "Sally will challenge ideas which are not well thought out." "Bill will open the meetings and keep us on the track." Obviously, a group norm is a type of rule, but it is not precisely the same, since an authority figure can bring about a grudging compliance to a rule. However, only a standard which is accepted as rightful by all or by a majority of the group members is a group norm, whether it is imposed from the outside or generated by the group itself.

Group norms are often derived from values, but they grow out of interaction and are specific to each group. For example, American values which favor "informality" and "deemphasis of status differences" may be translated and transformed in a particular group to a norm which says that "members should be friendly to everyone in the group." At the same time, norms cannot always be traced to cultural origins, and they may even be in opposition to societal values, as demonstrated by countercultural groups such as communes.

Group behavior patterns are analogous to cultural customs. They are the behaviors which characterize the way members of a group relate to one another. They are the ways the group usually functions. Patterns are often similar to customs, but they differ in that they are specific to a given group situation. For example, in the American culture, people customarily greet one another briefly when they arrive at a meeting, often with a smile and a nod or wave. In a particular group, these practices are likely to be followed, but they may be constricted or elaborated on in certain ways. In some decision-making groups, greetings will be minimal, and the members will get down to the business at hand almost immediately; in others, members will engage in social conversation before beginning the meeting. In some experiential groups, members not only acknowledge but also hug one another when they enter the room.

Group behavior patterns and norms are closely related, although they are not identical. Conceptually, they represent different levels of abstraction, as do values and customs. Patterns tell how people usually behave, while norms tell how they *ought* to behave in a more general way.

Behavior patterns and group norms usually develop together. If a group norm is established early in the life of a group which says, in effect, "we should maximize agreement at any cost," it would not be surprising to find later on that when disagreement is expressed someone will change the topic. Also, a pattern of behavior established early in the life of a group will often come to be accepted as a standard later. Repeated actions tend to contribute to a sentiment in favor of those actions; sentiments for certain actions tend to bring behavioral conformity; and so on.

The distinction between behavior patterns and norms would not be very important if it were not for the fact that they do not always correspond directly with one another. A lack of fit can come about in several ways:

1. A pattern of behavior can be imposed by an external source without acceptance by the group members. For example, in a study of boy's clubs (White and Lippitt, 1960), an autocratic adult leader was able to organize the activities of the children in a very strict manner. When the leader was absent, however, this regimented behavior fell apart almost completely. Even when the autocratic leader was present, group members expressed their dislike for the imposed rules by covert acts of rebellion, suggesting the existence of a group norm which was at variance with much of the members' outward behavior.

2. A group may adopt a way of doing things to which no one is attached. The pattern is simply comfortable and familiar but unrelated to norms. For example, the group may customarily meet in one place, but a change in location would bother no one.

3. Occasionally a group will fall into a pattern of behavior which no one really likes. For example, early in a discussion one person may perceive that others are not well qualified for the task, so he or she may take over and do most of the talking. This situation might persist for a while despite widespread dissatisfaction. Such a condition is often temporary. It suggests that the group has not yet worked out its norms to the degree that this situation can be dealt with effectively. Contradictory standards may be operating: "Don't create dissension." "Conflict is necessary to explore any problem." If someone were to protest this pattern of unequal participation, nearly everyone in the group might enthusiastically agree, with the possible exception of the person doing the dominating.

What is deceptive about the relationship between patterns and norms is that although most patterns are supported by norms, it is not always apparent whether or not this is the case, especially in the short run. One way of finding out whether a pattern represents a norm is to poll the group members about what they regard as appropriate and inappropriate behavior. Assuming that they can readily verbalize standards, this approach might work. Ultimately, however, the best test occurs when someone's behavior deviates from expectations. If there are no negative reactions, either subtle or direct, we may assume that no norm has been violated. On the other hand, if some kind of observable social pressure is exerted, we may assume that the pattern is supported by a group norm.

Violations seldom occur simply because a norm *is* a standard for behavior. How, then, can a person tell whether a pattern which goes unchallenged is supported by a norm? In this situation, the duration of the behavior pattern is indicative. The longer it persists, the more likely it is that an underlying norm is operating. Since norms and patterns are so closely related, in the remainder of this chapter we will often refer to them collectively as "group culture" or "group norms and patterns." At other times, however, we will want to retain the distinction, employing the term "behavior pattern" to refer to the routine ways that group members behave in relation to one another, and reserving the term "norm" to refer to accepted standards.

Group culture is one of the broadest concepts in this book. It touches on virtually every other idea we will discuss. In fact, although this concept is treated within the general topic of "interpersonal relations," we could speak of the "task culture" or of the "socioemotional culture" of a group. *Task culture* would refer to those behavior patterns and standards which regulate the way a group strives toward its goals; *socioemotional culture* would refer to those ways the group maintains relations among its members. However, we discuss group culture within the framework of interpersonal relations because of the moral imperative implied whenever a group behavior pattern is supported by a standard; that is, participants prove themselves worthy of acceptance as members of the group by their general adherence to norms. And acceptability is closely related to the degree of attraction that people feel for one another.

UNDERLYING CAUSES OF GROUP CULTURE

Every system must have some customary and accepted ways of doing things in order to function effectively. We referred to this principle as "homeostasis" in Chapter 2; it is the tendency of the system to return to a stable state. Individuals need personal values in order to be able to make choices, and they rely on certain habitual acts to carry them through the day. Societies require values and customs to coordinate the activities of their citizens, and, similarly, small groups need patterns and norms.

Group culture enables people to function efficiently in a smooth team operation. Respective responsibilities may be defined—like the positions on a football team—and each member is counted on to carry his or her particular share of the load. A group of friends who have bull sessions with some regularity will usually develop a customary gathering place so that time and energy are not expended trying to find one another. If students can carry into class certain established ways of relating to particular teachers or if a couple can make some automatic assumptions about how they should behave each time they attend a dinner party with a certain group of friends, this will save them the trouble of working out an entirely new arrangement on each occasion. To be sure, no two class periods or dinner parties will be exactly alike, and some adaptations will have to be made, but at least previous experience will provide a base from which to work.

To the extent that a group has not established clearly defined role relationships and accepted procedures, there will be considerable clanking and grinding of gears as it goes about its work. The members will have to expend a larger share of their energy figuring out and establishing a satisfactory pattern of interpersonal relationships. We sometimes wonder if, at the first meeting of any discussion group, anything more is accomplished than getting to know each other—the so-called discussion of the topic being simply a thin veil over the feeling-out of what is going on at a deeper level.

In addition to the need to conserve time and energy, there seems also to be a psychological cause for the development of group culture. People have a need to "know their place," to know "where they stand," to know "what is expected of them." Without any guideposts they become anxious, insecure, and sometimes even paralyzed. It is like going into a restaurant and being given a menu which is so long and has so many choices that one does not know where to begin the process of elimination. Complete freedom can sometimes be as immobilizing as total restriction. And so we search for some behavior patterns and norms which will help to orient us.

DANGERS OF GROUP CULTURE

As we have explored the reasons for the development of group culture, we hope that you have been somewhat frightened as well as enlightened. As we come to appreciate the need for patterns and standards, we must also recognize the dangers inherent in them.

Certainly people cannot function without habit. They would go crazy if they had to think anew about every move they were going to make. On the other hand, patterns and norms can become so ingrained, so automatic, so unconscious, that they are regarded as unalterable. Then the individual or group is encumbered with routines and relationships which are not only meaningless but downright dangerous.

To make this danger clear, let us examine a few illustrations. Most groups meeting for the first time assume that it is desirable for members to introduce themselves to one another, not only giving their names but perhaps also providing other labels of identification (such as groups, institutions, departments, or geographical areas they may represent as well as their jobs or professions). We may now see the purpose behind this: By identifying one another group members are aided in the process of establishing patterns of relationship. They are provided with clues as to what might be expected of each group member and what kinds of norms ought to be established so that no one is offended. If they discover that one of their number is a member of the clergy, they may be more cautious about the use of profanity. If they find that one of the participants has 20 years of professional experience with the problem to be discussed, they may be more careful about expressing their opinions.

All of this can enable them to function smoothly and efficiently. But there are also rather obvious negative results. Too much may be assumed on the basis of labels of identification. People who belong to the clergy are not necessarily intolerant of profanity; people who are trained in a certain field may not necessarily be informed on every issue related to their profession. False stereotypes may cause the participants to avoid statements which do not need to be avoided and to rely on others for judgments when they ought to express their own interpretations. In an experimental study of problem solving in three-man Air Force discussion groups, Torrance (1955) was able to demonstrate the disadvantages of rigid group norms and patterns. Each group consisted of a pilot, a navigator, and a gunner (the first two being officers and the last an enlisted man). The results showed that groups rarely failed to solve a problem when it was the pilot who had the right answer, but that frequently the group decided on the wrong answer when the gunner knew the right one.

Let us assume that a discussion group has developed as one of its operating norms that members are not supposed to interrupt each other but are to be patient and courteous at all times. (A norm, incidentally, can be implicit without ever being verbally expressed.) Such a standard might ordinarily be quite helpful in maintaining a maximum of mutual respect and a minimum of frustration with the group. On the other hand, there may be a time when one of the members is quite stirred up about a particular issue and feels that the rest of the group is dangerously complacent. This one individual may also feel, with considerable justification, that action has to be taken rapidly and that there is not sufficient time to sit around and hear everyone expound at length on the matter. So he or she may become a bit aggressive, interrupting others and pressing urgent pleas for action on them. If the group is so committed to its norm of courtesy and non-interruption that it resents this member's behavior and refuses to listen to what he or she has to say, the members may later discover to their dismay, if not their downfall, that they should have tossed their precious norm overboard.

In sum, a group or society cannot operate without traditions and rules. But when expectations become so binding that they are not open to reevaluation, that group or society loses the flexibility required to meet new challenges and may be on the road to extinction.

TYPES OF GROUP BEHAVIOR PATTERNS

What kinds of behavior patterns do groups establish? We remind the reader that "group behavior patterns" refers to the ways the group members coordinate their actions with one another. Each individual plays a part in group patterns by taking a certain role which is either essentially the same as or complementary to the roles played by others. Most enduring group patterns are eventually supported by norms—standards which describe, in a general way, how people are supposed to play their roles. In order to make it more clear what we mean by "group patterns," in this section we will provide examples of common patterns. So many can be illustrated, that the list could be inexhaustible. We have chosen to focus on two broad and rather inclusive aspects of group functioning: (1) "network" relationships or behavior patterns that determine who will speak to whom with what frequency, and (2) "emotional climate" or the feeling or tone that pervades the messages exchanged by group members. In the process of discussing these, we will examine the desirability of each alternative pattern.

Communication Networks

As people begin to talk together they not only develop specialized roles for themselves, but they may, as does a river, form well-defined channels for sharing their feelings with one another. Some of these networks are desirable and effective. They are desirable when they enable the group to make maximum use of the talents of its members, and they are effective when they contribute to speedy decision making. Others may exclude certain members or cliques and thus contribute to division, disruption, or disintegration. We shall describe four of the more common patterns, why they evolve, and how each of them may influence a group's effectiveness.

RECITATIVE PATTERN

The first communication network is called the "recitative pattern" because it is reminiscent of the sort of interaction one finds in so many classrooms. The teacher initiates all the questions to which, in turn, students are expected to give the right answers. Approval is given for the correct reply, disapproval for any other. In a discussion this means that most of the communication originates from, or is directed toward, one member of the group. Figure 3 illustrates this pattern.[1]

In spite of the absence of formal restrictions on communication during discussion there is a tendency for talk to center on certain individuals. Participants will almost inevitably direct their remarks toward high-status figures because they have a greater influence on decisions. Those who happen to be unusually aggressive or dominant will also tend to be at the hub of communications because they are likely to seize control of the group. Members with extensive knowledge of the problem normally will find themselves in focal positions. The locus of leadership in a group will almost certainly influence who talks to whom. If leaders see themselves as

[1] In Figures 3 to 6 the lines connecting people indicate an interaction between two members of the group. The short intersecting bars represent the number of times this channel was used.

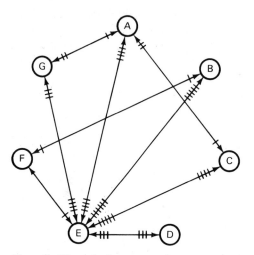

Figure 3   The recitative pattern of communication.

personally responsible for directing and controlling participation, then most of the talk will be aimed in their direction, since their permission must be obtained in order to "get the floor." If, on the other hand, there is no leader or if the leader plays a nondirective role, there is not as likely to be a consistent or inflexible pattern of communication. The focusing of communication on E in Figure 3 could indicate the presence of an undemocratic leader who has assumed the responsibility for herding the group along, or it may have resulted from someone monopolizing the conversation, thereby forcing others to speak to him or her.

Before taking any corrective action, it would be wise to make sure that the recitative pattern is not a result of legitimate, temporary factors. The presence of conflict in a group, for example, will often cause a momentary focusing of communication on a single member. Disagreement is immediately reflected in both the substance and direction of interaction. Leon Festinger (1950), who has directed some of the most successful studies of social influence, notes that: "The existence of a discrepancy in the group with respect to opinions and abilities will lead to action on the part of members of that group to reduce the discrepancy" (p. 171). In both laboratory and field studies, Festinger and his colleagues have found that the pressures to communicate are greater the more cohesive the group is and the wider the difference of opinion among the members. This is to say that whenever someone takes a position contrary to that of the group, communication will increase between the group and the deviant to reduce the margin of disagreement and facilitate unified action.

As we saw earlier, however, communication with deviants is likely to decrease after a time. Parties to the dispute may change their minds or, as a result of discussion, conflicting points of view may be integrated. In

some cases the group discovers that the deviant is unalterably and abso-
lutely committed to a position. People may then stop talking to that individual, not because of disagreement, but because he or she is seen as being
unreceptive and unyielding to argument. This raises an ethical problem:
If the individual refuses to change because the members of the group
have employed unfair tactics of social pressure or because the issue has
not been thoroughly explored, then the group will only be harming itself
by cutting off communication. The deviant may turn out to be right. If,
on the other hand, the members of the group have explored the controversy intelligently, we see no alternative but for the group to go on in
spite of his or her opposition. Otherwise the entire deliberative process
will break down.

Therefore, any decision to break out of the recitative pattern, requires some analysis of its causes. If it results from temporary or healthy
disturbance, nothing should be done to change the pattern. But if it reflects the presence of a dominating personality, a monopolizer, or someone who needs to be in the center of attention, some corrective action is
indicated.

SUBGROUPING

In subgrouping we find private conversations taking place within the
framework of the larger discussion. These conversations have the effect of
taking certain members out of the discussion and of splitting off attention
from the main job of the group. Subgrouping is illustrated in Figure 4.

Curiously enough, subgrouping can occur because of either too much
or too little interest in the topic. Participants can become so emotionally
upset over an issue that they must express themselves to someone, with the

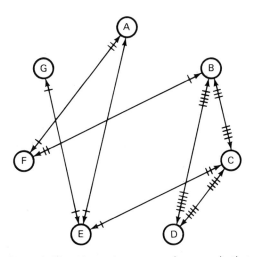

Figure 4 The subgrouping pattern of communication.

result that they split up into smaller groups to increase the number of available communication pathways. Whispering between neighbors is sometimes interpreted as a sign of apathy. Actually it often means that those engaged in side conversations are so interested that their enthusiasm spills over into private comments for which they do not wish to take the time of the group. Sometimes, however, if the discussion becomes tiresome, members seated beside each other will start a conversation about other matters. Their conversation may deal with more exciting aspects of the topic or with entirely irrelevant matters of personal interest (family problems, dating, vacation plans).

There is no reason to prohibit such occasional conversations, but when they become common and persistent they may indicate that something is seriously wrong. If subgrouping occurs because it is impossible to break into the larger discussion, then new openings must be made for those forced into private conversations.

DIALOGUE

A special case of subgrouping is found in the dialogue. In this case, a few people carry on their conversation, not privately, but in front of the entire group. One person offers an opinion. Someone else objects. As the two disputants begin to argue, they set up a private communication circuit in which each is forced to reply to the other. The remaining group members are forced into the role of helpless spectators, for the two people engaging in argument are oblivious to anyone else who tries to enter the conversation. Figure 5 illustrates a group in which two such dialogues have taken place.

This sort of public dialogue is usually a product of a healthy dispute

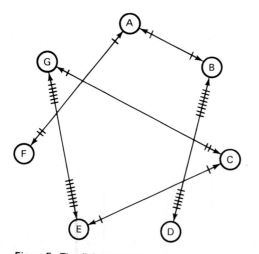

Figure 5 The dialogue pattern of communication.

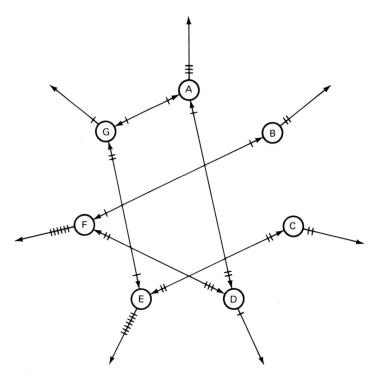

Figure 6 The multilateral pattern of communication.

between members of a committee. If this is the case, nothing needs to be done about it immediately, but if the dialogue continues very long, it may lead to apathy or interpersonal friction in the group. It can be overcome if other members are more aggressive in entering such an exclusive conversation by shifting to another issue or, if necessary, by appointing someone to control participation. Often, however, nothing more than pointing out the problem to the parties involved is needed.

MULTILATERAL PATTERN

What most discussion groups are striving for in the way of a communication pattern is diagrammed in Figure 6. In this instance, communication flows freely from person to person according to whoever is moved to speak or whoever has relevant information to contribute. Attention shifts randomly around the group, and departures from this pattern are a result of special issues that arouse conflict or of some other kind of temporary crisis.

In this diagram you will notice the addition of a number of lines which, instead of connecting people inside the circle, point away from the group itself. These lines are used to indicate what we shall call "group-centered" remarks, comments that are directed at the group as a whole rather than at a single committee member. One of the characteristics of a mature group seems to be the predominance of group-directed over person-directed contributions. Group-directed comments profoundly improve communication because they tend to open up the communication channels, encourage everyone to offer information and opinions, provide maximum feedback for the correcting of error, and facilitate better interpersonal relations. For example, Robert Bales (1950), in his studies of group interaction, found that on the whole, those exercising leadership in groups tend to make a larger proportion of group-centered contributions than do those who are not regarded as leaders. Expressing ideas in a way that invites comment from everyone is a way of "drawing out" those who may have something worthwhile to add by way of amendment, qualification, or objection to what has been said.

Emotional Climates

In a group situation, emotions are "catching." Sometimes the feeling that one person is experiencing will spread among the other participants, especially if he or she communicates that emotion in an emphatic manner by verbal or nonverbal means. Such a "charged" atmosphere may be rather transitory, so that a group may be characterized by apathy at one meeting, hostility at another, and friendliness at still another. This is especially common in encounter groups where people are encouraged to express and fully experience their here-and-now. feelings, but other groups meeting for social engagements, instruction, or decision making may evidence similar spontaneous changes. Where emotional climates are fleeting and unpredictable, they do not constitute patterns. But in many cases, phases of emotional change in a group will be repeated and, therefore, become predictable; in others, the group will fluctuate for a time and then arrive at a dominant feeling state. These regularized ways of relating constitute group patterns.

Emotional climates have been described with different sets of adjectives by various authors. British psychoanalyst W. R. Bion, who has worked extensively with therapy groups, has proposed a threefold classification (Bion, 1974): (1) pairing, (2) dependency, and (3) fight-flight. In a "pairing" group, the climate is one in which each member seeks out a close relationship with one other person in the group. A "dependency" group is one in which the predominant emotional problem being worked on is the relationship between the leader and the group members. Such groups frequently fluctuate between relying on the leader for direction and battling with the leader for control (counterdependence). In "fight-flight" the members are primarily in a state of mutual antagonism with one another. In this situation, the group tends to alternate between direct verbal warfare and behaviors of evasion and withdrawal.

Another popular set of categories are those which were used by White and Lippitt (1960) in their experimentation with various styles of leadership in small groups. Although designated primarily to describe different modes of leadership—autocratic, democratic, and laissez-faire—these adjectives are also widely used as labels for the emotional climate resulting from each of the three styles. An autocratic atmosphere is characterized among other things by competition among group members, scapegoating, buck-passing, and hostility (usually repressed) toward the leader. A democratic atmosphere is one of interdependency; that is, the members relate to one another in a spirit of equality and mutual aid. A laissez-faire situation is typified by an absence of impelling group goals, low motivation, and considerable withdrawal.

In *The Lonely Crowd*, a well-known book of the '50s, David Riesman characterizes societies as being predominantly tradition-directed, inner-directed, or other-directed. Although he is talking about societies at large, we might apply these categories to discussion groups as well. The tradition-directed group would be one in which the behavior of members is guided heavily by rituals and customs which have been handed down from previous generations or previous meetings. Relationships are highly formalized, virtually prescribed by formula. The Japanese culture might exemplify this kind of climate. The inner-directed group would be rather fiercely competitive, for each member is guided, according to Riesman's figure of speech, by a gyroscope which has been set in motion within the person by his or her parents. Such an individual has rather rigidly defined individual goals and notions of right and wrong and, thus, finds it difficult to work adaptably with others. Other-directedness is symbolized by Riesman as a constantly scanning radar set, which is to say that group members are constantly on the lookout for cues from others to guide their beliefs and actions. The urge to conform to the views of other people is their primary goal. Such a group would be compulsively cooperative and highly uncritical.

Virtually any set of categories which we might use to describe something as complex as group emotional climate would have some shortcomings. The purpose of presenting such classification schemes here is not to imply that reality can be captured by means of a convenient label, but rather to stimulate students to think about patterns of emotional reaction in groups to which they belong. Therefore, we present the following set of categories which we have found useful in training people to diagnose emotional climates, recognizing that a certain degree of oversimplification is involved and that a particular group may resemble one type only to a certain degree.

THE OVERLY COOPERATIVE GROUP

The prevailing norm in the overly cooperative group is one of suppression of conflict and of negative feeling. An artificial atmosphere of "sweetness and light" predominates, which is usually the case among people who have repressed or inhibited their feelings of antagonism toward one another or among those who are extremely fearful of causing offense to others. The pervading feeling is apparently one of friendliness and courtesy, but the way that people communicate suggests that some deception is going on: Nods of agreement or understanding may have an exaggerated quality; smiles may seem "pasted on"; and laughter may be too loud or have a nervous, tense quality. The underlying tone is one of anxiety or strained comradery, and the members are probably engaged in Bion's "flight" pattern.

THE OVERLY COMPETITIVE GROUP

This is the opposite end of the pole from the overly cooperative situation. A "dog-eat-dog" atmosphere prevails. Conflict is openly expressed but without the good humor and mutual respect that can accompany a difference of views. The dominant emotion of hostility is expressed openly by means of angry facial expressions and shouting, but it is more likely to be shown in less direct behaviors such as cold stares, frequent interruptions, and ego-deflating comments masked as jokes. This atmosphere is similar to Bion's "fight" situation, and the predominant leadership style is likely to be autocratic.

THE ANARCHIC GROUP

The anarchic group can best be characterized as rugged individualism run amuck. There is not enough cooperation to describe this situation as competitive, since each member is intent on his or her own goals or needs. The feeling tone is one of apathy or mild antagonism. Members may engage in behaviors which range from speaking without acknowledgment of previous comments and engaging in long monologues to sitting in inattentive silence and openly displaying boredom. Members may attempt to pair with others in private dialogues, or they may keep to themselves. This kind of climate generally develops under laissez-faire leadership and, like the overly cooperative group, represents another mode of flight from genuine interpersonal relationships.

THE RITUALISTIC GROUP

The prevailing norm in the ritualistic group is strict adherence to traditions and rules. Such groups often operate on the principle of "all business and no pleasure." Meetings are conducted very formally, completely dominated by procedural restrictions. The emotional quality is flat but polite, and there are few expressions of warmth and friendliness. Such a group represents one form of Bion's dependency, since it is likely to have a leader who is the keeper and enforcer of the rules.

THE INTERDEPENDENT GROUP

We would regard interdependency as the most mature of the five kinds of emotional climates we are describing. Differences are frankly stated and vigorously argued while common goals and sympathies are recognized. Verbal and nonverbal expressions of support and friendliness are common, but the deception signals characteristic of the overly cooperative group are absent. At the same time, the group does not expend all of its energy on maintaining relationships. As members work hard on some problem, tension builds and is then released in casual banter and relaxation.

THE DEVELOPMENT OF NORMS AND PATTERNS

We have discussed the fact that all groups have a need for a certain amount of stability and predictability in their interpersonal relationships. This explains *why* group culture is established. We have also given some examples of group standards and have described some of the behaviors which come to characterize group communication. What we have not examined are the means by which patterns come into being and the ways that groups arrive at understandings about the norms which guide their behavior. This is an extremely complex process which communication scholars and other social scientists have only started to unravel.

One thing we do know is that behavior patterns begin to develop as soon as the group members commence their interaction. Let us suppose, for example, that the first individual to speak in a discussion carefully avoids revealing any strong feelings toward the topic being considered. If the next two or three contributors follow suit, a climate has already begun to develop in which strong feelings are unlikely to be expressed. The fourth participant, sensing the atmosphere, avoids making a forceful commitment by employing ambiguous language. The fifth contributor will be even more likely than the fourth to respect this rapidly developing mood. Like the proverbial snowball rolling downhill, the pattern gains momentum.

While patterns may come about with each person playing a nearly equal role, as in the example described above, it frequently happens that one person emerges as the most forceful and influential group member in establishing a pattern of behavior. Dr. Fritz Redl, a psychiatrist with wide experience in working with children's groups, suggests that the predominant emotional tone of a group is set by what he calls the "central person." Redl identifies ten different types of such people and describes the kind of emotional effect they have on others (Redl 1955). For example, Redl describes type 9, "The Bad Influence," as a person with few inner conflicts. Such an individual expresses feelings which the other group members have been suppressing. The behavior of this person is infectious because it relieves the guilt feelings and anxieties of others and allows them to act out what they had secretly wished to do. For example, a student might serve as a "bad influence" if he or she created a disruption in class by talking loudly to another student across the room and others then commenced to do the same.

A person who is appointed the official leader of a group or who possesses some other form of status which is recognized by the participants at the beginning will be in an especially strong position to exert influence. Since the other group members are uncertain exactly how to behave, this person will often be used as a model for imitation. It is little wonder, therefore, that the members of sensitivity training groups are often frustrated and confused when the leader withdraws after making an opening statement, leaving them to their own devices.

It takes a certain amount of training and perceptiveness to tell when a pattern has emerged, but it is even more difficult to say at exactly what point a standard for behavior has been established. Occasionally it will become obvious because someone verbalizes a norm and others readily agree. For example, in a group where numerous side conversations are going on, one person may say, "I think it would be better if we spoke one at a time," and others may respond by changing their body positions toward the center of the group and nodding approval. Perhaps more often, however, the standard is not verbalized, and it thus becomes difficult to tell whether sentiment has crystallized into a rule for group behavior. In this case, the longer the behavior persists, the absence of signs of dissension or unrest in itself becomes evidence for the existence of an underlying standard. Ultimately, however, the strength of the presumed rule is not tested until someone deviates from a pattern in an overt and obvious manner. At this time, if the unexpected behavior is in conflict with norms, the group will exert social pressure in an effort to bring the deviant into line.

THE MAINTENANCE OF GROUP NORMS

There has been a large amount of research concerned with the process and effects of group social pressure. In one classic study, Stanley Schachter (1951) was able to show what factors motivate majority members to exert influence on a deviant and also how they may use communication to bring about compliance. Schachter accomplished this by "planting" people in the groups who were instructed to disagree with majority opinion just as a decision was about to be reached. For one thing, his results showed that the more cohesive the group (the greater the attraction the group holds for its members), the more likely it is that the members will bring pressure to bear on the deviant to conform and that they will reject the deviant if he or she fails to conform.

Also, the extent to which social pressure occurs and rejection takes place is directly proportional to the relevance of the issue to group functioning. This finding can be applied to other situations by implication. For example, taking a drink at a gathering of ladies of the Women's Christian Temperance Union would bring greater pressure than would wearing an out-of-style dress. Schachter also found that when a participant challenges group opinion, communication will tend to flow in the deviant's direction in an effort by the majority to achieve consensus. This concentration of attention on the dissenter will continue either until he or she has modified the discrepant view or until certain group members decide the deviant is "impossible" and thereafter stop talking to that person altogether. Questionnaires administered after the experiment showed that majority members who cut off communication in this way also strongly rejected the dissenter. Finally, there was one other particularly interesting feature of the Schachter study. Some participants were instructed by the experimenter to disagree with the majority at first and then to "slide" toward agreement. The results showed that there were no attempts to isolate these individuals from further communication, nor were such individuals rejected; that is, the "prodigal son" was welcomed back into the family.

Note that opposing majority opinion would not constitute a violation of a norm in every group. In the Schachter study, there must have been a norm in each of the groups that "members should not challenge an emerging group consensus." Since the participants were new entrants to the group, this norm must have been established rather quickly, and perhaps it was derived from an American value which they shared: "The majority should rule." Despite this cultural tendency toward conformity in opinions, it is possible for a group to adopt a different norm which says, in effect, that "members should challenge the majority position until all are satisfied with the conclusion." If this had been the case in the Schachter experiment, there would have been no attempt to isolate the deviant, and rejection of the deviant would have been less likely.

Social pressure need not involve the kinds of extensive verbal interaction found in the Schachter study. A passing comment repeated over a period of time by various members of the majority may serve the same function. For example, one observation study in a factory setting (Roethlisberger and Dickson, 1939) showed that members of work groups established certain informal standards for the amount each person was supposed to produce. Deviants were exposed to teasing and ridicule, those who exceeded the norm being referred to as "ratebusters," and those who produced under the norm being called "chiselers." Nonverbal behavior may also be used as a group sanction. For example, a particular college class developed a strong norm that class members should attend all meetings. One person was absent several periods in a row and did not provide an excuse to the group when he returned. Later, when this group norm was discussed in the class, he reported that the day he came back to class he noticed others avoiding eye-contact with him. (He did not miss class after that day.)

Social pressure can exert considerable influence over group members. In the first of many studies of this phenomenon, Asch (1951) placed unsuspecting subjects in groups where all the other members were secretly cooperating with the experimenter. The participants were asked to judge the relative length of a number of pairs of lines which were shown to them, the unsuspecting subject being asked for a judgment after all the fixed contributors had stated theirs. In some cases, the fixed participants all gave the wrong answer, and in others, they were instructed to be divided in their judgments. It was then possible to determine the extent to which these judgments influenced the naive subjects to contradict what their eyes told them and to give wrong answers. It was found that approximately one-third of these subjects yielded to group pressure and distorted their answers in the direction of majority opinion. Of further significance was the finding that majority pressure was more effective when it was unanimous than when the majority was divided. When the unsuspecting subjects were given just one "true partner" (a participant who gave a right answer when all the other contributors gave the wrong one), they were able to withstand social pressure to a far greater extent than when they stood alone.

The Asch study and many other related investigations suggest that people tend to succumb to the views of a united majority, especially when they are not supported by anyone else in the group. This effect is accentuated when people anticipate staying in the group for a long time (Lewis, Langan, and Hollander, 1972). Nevertheless, there are some people who can resist group pressure better than others. In Chapter 4, "The Social Context of Discussion," we alluded to the findings of studies which show that men tend to conform less than women. Other studies show that personality differences can also play a part. Generally, people who are high in self-confidence are less swayed by majorities; for example, people who rate themselves positively on leadership abilities are less conforming than others (Frye and Bass, 1963). Also, young children and adults are less subject to majority influence than are adolescents (Costanzo and Shaw, 1966). Despite these qualifications, however, it is clear that groups frequently attempt to change and often succeed in changing the behavior of individuals who violate norms.

CHANGES IN NORMS

There is one other possibility that we have not yet discussed: The deviant may succeed in modifying the attitudes of the majority. This brings us to the matter of change in group norms, for in spite of the needs which they fulfill and their general resistance to alteration, norms are sometimes overturned or become transformed. The process by which this occurs is now apparent. Some individual who does not believe a particular standard to be valid either speaks out against it or violates it in action. If there is sufficient latent sympathy within the group for this new point of view or if a majority can be persuaded to accept the new mode, the old norm is overthrown and a new one established.

Actually this sounds easier than it is. In the first place, it requires that individuals who formerly accepted the norm must suddenly become assertive enough to challenge it. This means not only contesting the norm itself but often displacing from their position of leadership those people who formerly dominated the scene. They are not likely to withdraw easily. Another common difficulty is that, although unexpressed dissatisfaction with present norms may have grown within the group, the entrenched leader may have done such an effective job of dividing and conquering that the other members either are unaware that their desire for change is shared by many others or are unable to unite their forces sufficiently to overcome firmly established patterns. After all, theirs is the uphill battle.

On the other hand, there are a number of forces which may serve to aid the proponents of change and make it possible for them to overcome the obstacles they confront. A shift in personnel may automatically bring about modifications. Old leaders may gradually and imperceptibly lose their influence until they no longer shape the goals of the group. Dissatisfied members, discovering they have support, may simply begin to behave differently and gain acceptance without talking about it with the entire group, or the group may slowly adapt itself to changing environmental conditions without the stresses and strains of a major upheaval.

If these changes do not occur naturally, there is another way to bring them about—through a process of conscious and deliberate "feedback." *Feedback* is a term which has been borrowed by social scientists from the physical sciences and refers to that process which is illustrated in the operation of a thermostat. Very simply, the thermometer in the dining room records the temperature of the house and feeds it back to the furnace controls, "telling the furnace" whether it is giving off enough heat or needs to change its "behavior" in order to adapt to the changing climatic conditions.

Similarly, the members of a discussion group can occasionally interrupt their regular business and ask, "How are we doing?" "Is our pattern of interpersonal relationships satisfactory?" "What are our norms in regard to emotional climate, for example, and do they serve our purpose?" In other words, the group engages in a conscious, critical examination of its own interpersonal patterns with a view to determining what, if any, changes are desirable. In this way the hidden agendum, if there is one, may be brought to the surface, and a clearing of the air can take place. Often, merely facing these questions openly will improve the climate. Just as in individual psychoanalysis, the process of making the unconscious conscious, or analyzing the taken-for-granted, can bring about considerable change. It might be that overtalkative participants were not aware of how much they were dominating the conversation or of the effects of their monopoly on other individuals. Having this brought to their attention might alleviate the situation.

As in psychoanalysis, however, simply bringing a problem into the open and talking about it may not be enough. New habits have to be formed to replace the old ones, and this can be accomplished only through action and experience, not merely talk. Once group members are aware of norms which underlie their unsatisfactory patterns, they must do more than verbalize new standards. They must actualize altered norms by instigating new patterns of behavior.

Finally, there is a point at which our analogy between group feedback and individual psychoanalysis breaks down. Unlike individual therapy, there are certain kinds of norms or hidden agenda in a group which do not lend themselves to open discussion or which are not worth the time and effort to probe. It might be that discussion of such matters would create new problems for the group that are worse than the old ones. Some organizations, particularly social clubs in high schools and colleges, regularly hold what they call "truth sessions" (or some similar terms). The purpose of these meetings is for each member to tell the others exactly what he or she thinks of them. Although presumably such an affair should serve the values we have been discussing above, it is obvious why it might not. Unless skillfully handled, such a meeting might do no more than create hard feelings and compound the tensions that up to that time had been fairly manageable. For someone to accuse another member, in front of the whole group, of overdominating the meetings because of a neurotic need for attention would not usually serve any constructive purpose.

On the other hand, we do not wish to create the impression that a group should avoid discussing touchy interpersonal matters. A guiding principle is that the issue should involve the functioning of the group as a whole and not be an isolated private dispute between two members. (An exception may be found in experiential groups where individual goals are given more emphasis.) Of course, some discussion may be required before it is clear whether or not this principle is being followed. If the feeling is widely shared that meetings are a waste of time because the leader is not interested in the group's goals but is simply using the group as a means for building personal prestige on the outside, it might well be that an open confrontation of this issue could be the best thing that might happen to that group. It is unlikely that after such an airing of feelings interpersonal relations will remain unchanged. Whether the change is for the better will depend on how well the process of feedback and evaluation has been handled.

SUMMARY AND CONCLUSIONS

Just as societal cultures may be analyzed in terms of their values and customs, "group cultures" may be described in terms of "norms" (standards of behavior accepted by the group members) and "behavior patterns" (habitual ways of behaving in the group). The best way of telling whether a pattern represents a norm is to observe whether the violation of an expected pattern by an individual results in negative sanctions from others. Group culture is needed in order to provide a sense of order, but its danger is that the group may have trouble changing to meet a new challenge.

Communication networks and emotional climates provide two examples of behavior patterns. Desirable patterns may be illustrated by the multilateral network, where group members tend to interact rather freely with one another, and by the interdependent climate, where both challenging and supportive behaviors are common.

Patterns are often instigated by acts of prominent group members; when the behaviors become accepted, implicitly or explicitly, by all or a majority of the membership, a norm has been established. Thereafter, social pressure is exerted in both subtle and direct ways to enforce norms, although these standards for behavior can be changed if deviant acts gain support or if the group engages in self-analysis.

Each of the aspects of group culture which we have examined in this chapter plays a role in the survival of the group as a social system. Behavior patterns provide for an efficient mode of operation in the group and a comfortable routine for its members. Norms and social pressure promote homeostasis, a stable state to which the system can return when an accepted pattern has been broken. And when established routines no longer serve the group's purposes, changes in norms permit the group to evolve.

STUDY SUGGESTIONS

1. Try to identify the norms of a group to which you belong. List 10 or 12 norms. Then conduct interviews with at least two other members to see what they would describe as the norms of the group. What might be the effect of discussion of those norms on which there is agreement? What might result from disagreement on other standards?
2. Observe a group to which you do not belong, preferably one in which you know none of the members personally. Try to identify the behavior patterns of this group. When you think you have identified the principal ones, report your observations to the group and ask them to tell you which patterns are supported by norms and which are not.
3. Families, like problem-solving groups, develop norms of their own. What are some of the norms in your own family which you feel are healthy and satisfying; what are some of the norms which you feel are unhealthy or frustrating? Healthy or unhealthy for whom? Why?

4. Try to trace the failures or frustrations you experienced in an unproductive group to which you have belonged to the patterns of behavior or the norms that evolved within them.
5. Lead a discussion in a group to which you belong on the topic of "Which of our norms in this group fit and do not fit the task or the goals we see for the group?"
6. Can you think of any groups in which you have participated where a prevailing norm differed significantly from the norms of the larger society of which the group was a part? How do you account for that phenomenon?
7. Have you ever been in a group when one of its norms or values underwent a noticeable change? How and why did that occur?
8. Are there particular kinds of groups in our society that tend to exhibit more often than others (a) overly cooperative behavior; (b) overly competitive behavior? Why do you think this is so?

Chapter 7
Involvement and the
Problem of Apathy

One of the most persistent and difficult of all the problems that beset groups is that of apathy. To be sure, discussions often suffer from lack of organization, inadequate information, improper leadership, and interpersonal friction, but few of these seem as difficult to diagnose or remedy as that of lack of interest on the part of group members. A committee plagued with apathy is about as efficient in discharging its responsibilities as an automobile engine without spark plugs.

Here, again, it is clear that the small, face-to-face group tends to be a society in microcosm, in that the motives found in groups often duplicate those we find in society at large. The apathetic committee member is the counterpart of the apathetic citizen. Periods of apathy tend to go in cycles. In the 1950s, the "silent generation" earned its nickname from its passivity toward public issues. McCarthyism would never have gained a foothold in a nation of alert and responsible citizens. However, even in those times there were stirrings of involvement, not the least of which was the black movement for social equality. The '60s were years of much greater involvement in which general dissatisfaction with the Viet Nam War galvanized many people into a reexamination of a wide variety of

American institutions, including not only militarism but also racism and sexism. The '70s may have represented a return to earlier periods of apathy. Despite a continuing fight for the rights of women and minorities and despite evidence of a growing concern for ecology, this decade was a time characterized by withdrawal. If past experience is a guide, there should be a new emergence of involvement, but the timing and complexion of that change are not clear.

Erich Fromm (1941), in exploring the case of prewar Germany, reminds us that apathy has national significance:

> We have been compelled to recognize that millions in Germany were as eager to surrender their freedom as their fathers were to fight for it; that instead of wanting freedom, they sought for ways to escape from it; that other millions were indifferent and did not believe the defense of freedom to be worth fighting and dying for (p. 5).

Perhaps by studying the phenomenon of apathy in the small, face-to-face group we can learn something about its sources within individuals and how it helps them adjust to their environment.

There are a number of theories we could borrow and use as a basis for studying this aspect of interpersonal behavior. The ideas of W. R. Bion, which we discussed in the previous chapter, seem especially helpful. As you will remember, one of the patterns which he identified was that of "fight-flight." In this climate, members express their motives through personal attacks on each other or through withdrawal from participation in the group.

In general, people seem to regard the attitude of fight as the more serious one. Teachers label as "problem children" those who are disobedient, demanding, talkative, or nonconforming to classroom rules. Few parents look upon a quiet son or daughter with anything but fondness. They worry instead over the child who demands attention, who fights back, or who is difficult to live with. However, are these really the "problem children"? Or are they more likely to be the docile and submissive children who make no attempt at all at self-expression?

Psychiatrists, for example, find that treating violent or hostile patients is extremely trying. But they will readily admit that there is no case more serious than that of catatonics—people who have withdrawn so completely from participation in life and relations with other human beings that they cannot even communicate their problems to others. Violence can be redirected into healthier and socially more acceptable channels, but therapy cannot reach the mentally withdrawn patient. While we do not mean to suggest that the nonparticipating members of groups are "psychological cases," some light is thrown on their motives and patterns of behavior through study of more serious types of withdrawal.

Our experience with small groups—in classrooms, industrial plants, churches, and civic organizations—forces us to join the psychiatrist in regarding apathy as a more serious problem than hostility. Overly aggressive, dominating members of a group undoubtedly cause trouble and discomfort for other members, but they are at least striving, even if unsuccessfully, for some sort of self-realization. There is always the potential for transforming hostility into creative aggressiveness, a possibility which we will examine in Chapter 8, "Conflict Management in Groups." The cynical, the passive, the unenthusiastic, on the other hand, may be trying to avoid becoming anything at all. We do not mean to underestimate the "fight" side of this question, but for the time being we will address ourselves to the problem of "flight."

THE SOURCES OF APATHY

How can the pattern of flight be explained? Why do people who are physically members of a group withdraw from it psychologically? Why do committee members prefer to remain silent in a meeting when their help is needed? What has paralyzed their creativity?

Sources Outside the Group

The way in which one acquires membership in a group can have a great deal to do with the enthusiasm one feels for participating. Membership is often forced on people. They are pressured into attending meetings on one pretext or another. Perhaps they are members of a department or organization that needs to be represented in negotiations; or they are accidently present when the committee is being set up; or it is simply their turn to shoulder some of the responsibility for decision making. Either their stake in the outcome of the meeting has never been made clear to them or they do not really have cause to be involved.

There is an amazing number of irrelevant criteria used to select the members of deliberative bodies. It is not surprising that people appointed on the basis of artificial reasons see little point in investing much energy in the work of the group. Students who are forced to attend college by overzealous and ambitious parents can hardly be expected to attract notice by their enthusiasm in the classroom. Members of a department who are mechanically assigned to committees, regardless of interest, qualification, or personal experience, cannot be expected to enter eagerly into deliberations.

Apathy is a condition under which many discussion groups begin their investigation of a problem. The "chosen" few feel little or no concern over the issue; they are indifferent to its solution; and they will be unaffected by the decisions that are made. Like the proverbial horse, people may be forced to join a committee, but you cannot make them talk.

Sources Within the Group

Apathy is sometimes generated by the group itself. Members of the committee are eager to get started and are full of optimism at the outset, but their ardor soon cools. Perhaps the leadership is repressive, the norms of the group restrictive, or the interpersonal relationships strained. Disillusionment is followed by indifference.

To begin with, there simply may not be an opportunity for everyone to participate. A committee of 30 people, for purely physical reasons, may make it difficult to get into the conversation. The presence of a few monopolizers—those who talk too frequently and too long—may inhibit others who are less aggressive and unwilling to interrupt. Often the temperamentally excitable, or the exceedingly well-informed, or the effusively enthusiastic, take over a discussion. The more they talk, the less time remains for others. The effect is to "short out" all the less aggressive members. As one wag put it, "Those who hold a conversation ought to let go of it once in awhile." When the overly talkative do "let go" of an issue, it is usually after it has been thoroughly exhausted and nothing more remains to be said.

Perhaps the most important of the internal conditions that lead to withdrawal is found in the group's "culture." Patterns may be established that are inconsistent with the goals of the group. The meetings may be too highly organized (so that spontaneous contributions are stifled) or too disorganized (so that people have no idea of where they are on the topic and, hence, of what to say). The group atmosphere may be too formal or too informal for productive work. The discussion may move forward too rapidly, allowing the slower and, sometimes, the more thoughtful members no chance to enter, or too slowly, boring the more alert.

Also, failure to participate in the opening moments of a discussion or in the first of several meetings of a committee can make it doubly difficult for people to take a more active part later on. In remaining silent for a time, members create a group norm according to which they see themselves as "nonparticipants" and are regarded as such by other members of the group who expect them to continue in that role. Getting into the conversation at that point takes an extra effort to break through the previously established tradition and create a new, and more active, role for one's self. Unless the group is relatively flexible, this may be difficult to do.

The attitudes of high-status members of a group also have something to do with participants' eagerness to enter the discussion. Teachers who punish students, via grades, for original or heretical opinions are hardly in a position to complain about student apathy, yet they sometimes do. Businesspeople who create boards of totally acquiescent representatives or who monopolize their own meetings are themselves accountable for the irresponsibility they condemn. A survey of communicative practices in factory and office units by Thomas Nilsen supports this analysis. Nilsen found that members of management were disillusioned by the fact that after inviting employees and supervisors to consult with them, they encountered almost total indifference toward the affairs of the company:

> Long-standing habits of communication are difficult to overcome. This would seem at first to be too obvious to mention, but the surveys revealed that management personnel . . . were at a loss to understand why supervisory personnel would not talk when given the opportunity although they had not had such an opportunity before. . . . There were many factors entering into this lack of discussion, but it seems clear that one important factor was that . . . supervisors had never talked frankly to or discussed problems with management in the long history of the company, and habits of nondiscussion were firmly established (Nilsen, 1953, pp. 398–399).

On the societal level, there is a counterpart for this phenomenon in relations among the races. As Andrea Rich (1974) points out, in this country whites have long expected blacks to play only certain roles. While many blacks have learned to speak out against conditions forced on them, those who have worked their way into the establishment sometimes feel that the risk to their individual positions is not justified by the chances for change. People who have learned to play an expected role keep their jobs by telling whites what they want to hear. Therefore, it is not surprising that when a white authority figure asks for an opinion, blacks are sometimes cautious and suspicious because they do not believe that the request is sincere. After months or years of abuse, involvement is not brought about by a few well-chosen words.

Sources Within the Individual

Much of what we call apathy, then, is a result of the psychological climate that prevails in a group. But, in addition, each person brings to the group a specific personality whose architecture is very largely completed. This personality, with unique needs and patterns of expression, is partially created out of earlier contacts with parents, friends, and associates. Every human relationship leaves its trace. While one group may bring out a different facet of an individual's personality or will permit greater or lesser flexibility in roles, there is a strong tendency for personal habits of expression to change very slowly. Freud used the term "transference" to refer to our inclination to behave toward other people and to communicate with them as if they were our parents. People who tended as children to be submissive or dominant in their relations with their parents may repeat these same reactions in a wide variety of human situations.

Broadening the meaning of the term somewhat, we might say that in any group there is a tendency for people to act out patterns of behavior which they acquired through long experience. In some cases, this results in a strong aversion to groups in general. Psychiatrists speak of "twofers," individuals who feel comfortable in two-person relationships, but who become increasingly anxious and alienated as the number of people in a social situation becomes larger. For them, nonparticipation may be the preferred mode of coping with a threatening or unpleasant environment. This condition is not pathological unless such people have a phobic reaction so extreme that it does not permit them to tolerate being in groups at all. Those people who wish to change can do so by means of a professionally guided program of systematic desensitization (see McCrosky, 1972).

More commonly, individuals feel an aversion to groups because they do not know how to handle the requirements of certain social circumstances, and not because of deep-seated personality tendencies. Their reaction is not a general one, but one that applies only to special contexts in which they have not had experience or training. Decision-making groups provide an example of such a context. The failure to practice democracy in our schools, factories, and homes is hardly calculated to prepare people for effective participation when the opportunity occurs. One is not born with talent for democratic action any more than one is born with the ability to play a Beethoven sonata.

Each failure to submit a problem to discussion deprives people of the chance to develop the confidence and skills which make participation attractive. During World War II, for example, an experiment was conducted at Fort Eustis, Virginia, to test various methods of reeducating German prisoners of war. Former German soldiers were given this training, on a voluntary basis, just before being repatriated. The program consisted of a series of 12 lectures followed by one or two hours of discussion, with opportunities for attending additional lectures and films on American institutions. While the POWs showed considerable interest in the programs, they had great difficulty in discussions. Questionnaires completed by nearly all the 20,000 soldiers who took part reveal that they were most dissatisfied with their own inability to think together, to express themselves, to argue rationally, and to conduct orderly meetings. To participate in a group, then, requires more than a favorable climate of opinion; it requires certain technical skills as well. Nonparticipants in discussion may not be uninterested; they may simply be unsure of how to make use of their intelligence in this type of social situation.

Even when their opinion has a solid basis in fact, group members may not believe they are up to the job of defending their judgments. Individuals who are mature in many ways may withdraw from a conversation when they are the only liberal in a group of conservatives, the only believer in racial equality among segregationists, the only independent among fraternity members. Fear of ideas can also take another form. Committee members in a group of well-prepared and well-informed people may doubt that they could have any ideas worthy of consideration. A mental paralysis, growing out of a feeling of intellectual inferiority, may keep them from contributing. Silence seems the best defense against having our intellectual inferiority—whether real or imagined—displayed publicly.

Another reason for the withdrawal of the members of a group is lack of confidence in their ability to interact successfully with others on an equal basis. Members of a discussion group may not be threatened intellectually, but socially, by the demand for spontaneous and informal human relationships. The possibility of getting into arguments, of risking interpersonal frictions, and perhaps of alienating people may prompt some members to remain silent. Those who are normally indirect in their relations with others may balk at having to express themselves so frankly and directly and on such an intimate basis.

Then there are apathetic group members whose withdrawal from discussion springs from cynicism. Having been members of unsuccessful committees—where decisions were never reached or were never put into operation—they have become thoroughly disillusioned with democratic processes. Convinced that nothing will come of it all, they remain silent and thereby do everything in their power to make the prediction come true. Past failure to work effectively in group settings is projected onto the new situation and provides a motive for withdrawal. Often these nonparticipants demoralize a group because they communicate nonverbally—through posture, facial expression, and gesture—how hopeless they regard the whole situation to be.

THE GROUP AND THE INDIVIDUAL

In explaining the causes of psychological withdrawal, we have implied that it is undesirable. But is this really so? Do the privileges of citizenship not include the right to stay away from the polls altogether? Does freedom of speech mean that all must publicly announce their private thoughts? Does one have the right *not* to contribute to a group? The issue is far too complicated to permit an easy "yes" or "no" answer to these questions. Before we proceed to a discussion of how to overcome nonparticipation, first we should clarify our goals. What is the responsibility of the individual member to the group? And, in turn, what responsibility toward its individual members must the group assume?

If we are going to place individual values above all others, then we must say that a person has the right to develop whatever means of personal expression—even nonexpression—he or she chooses. Privacy, in some respects, is the greatest of all democratic privileges, but at some point, a group member or a citizen who fails to accept *some* responsibility for maintaining democratic processes may be said to have failed to live up to his or her responsibilities. The examples of such exploitation are legion: the non-union worker who benefits from all the advances gained by dues-paying members of the local; the student who learns from her classmates but refuses to contribute her own ideas; the apathetic member of a committee who gets as much credit as anyone else for making a wise decision. The member of a crew who does not pull his or her own oar gets there just as certainly as the others, but at their expense. Any collaborative effort involves us in the sticky question of where the line should be drawn between the obligations of member to group and group to member.

Individual Responsibility

We turn first to the individual. Under what circumstances do all participants have a responsibility to contribute to a group's deliberations? We would suggest the following:

1. They should contribute whenever they have *information* that is needed by the group. This does not mean bringing in unnecessary or irrelevant factual material, nor does it mean talking just to impress others.
2. They should present their *point of view* on the problem whenever that view has not been presented by someone else. They should contribute a promising hypothesis or solution even if they do not support it personally.
3. They should participate, even when they have nothing new to add, in the *evaluation* of the opinions and information presented by other group members. It is up to each person to examine, criticize, and explore the views of others.
4. When all the previous items have been taken care of, an individual has some responsibility for assisting in the *process* of discussion. He or she may be useful to the group in encouraging the participation of other members, in clarifying misunderstandings, in resolving conflicts, in formulating decisions, or in keeping records.
5. Finally—even if the group is functioning intelligently and efficiently—individual members are obligated to express their *understanding and approval* of the action being taken, even when this requires no more than a nod of the head, a smile of agreement, or the saying of "aye" or "nay."

If individual members are reasonably sure that these needs are being met by others in the group, then they are justified in remaining silent. Perhaps at a later time or at subsequent meetings their skills or knowledge will be required. If not, then they have failed to prepare adequately or their appointment to the committee is without purpose, since they duplicate the qualifications of other members of the group.

Group Responsibilities

Since the source of many of the causes of apathy is the group, rather than the individual, some of the responsibility for nonparticipation must be shared by the group as a whole. In order to avoid blame for forcing withdrawal of some of its members from a discussion, a group must, in our opinion, maintain two conditions.

First, there must be an equal opportunity for all members to enter the discussion. To attach the stigma of "nonparticipant" to someone who has tried repeatedly to obtain a hearing is totally unwarranted. Free competition in the marketplace of ideas is as important as in the marketplace of goods and services. And just as antitrust laws are necessary to protect the relations between corporate entities, so, too, a discussion group must limit those who might abuse the privilege of talking and so prevent others from entering the conversation. This is not to say that everyone must participate equally in the mathematical sense, but that everyone, regardless of status, must have equal access to the floor. There is a great difference between "equality of opportunity" and "equality of participation." Discussion—or, for that matter, democracy itself—would not last long if everyone, fool and genius alike, exercised the same influence on public decisions. But all must be given a chance to contribute their ideas, so that we can discover which are the wise and which the foolish.

Second, equality of opportunity is not very meaningful unless the group establishes a climate favorable to participation. The right to speak is an empty privilege if social pressures are brought to bear against those who use their time to express unpopular views. Therefore, a group needs to create a permissive psychological climate as well. This means that people must not only listen, but also *show* that they are listening by their nonverbal behavior. It also means that, regardless of who is expressing an opinion or what the opinion may be, the remark will be discussed openly, honestly, and without prejudice. This is not as easy to bring about as it sounds since there is a tendency in groups to ignore the ideas of infrequent contributors and other low-status members.

On occasion, it may be necessary to go one step beyond these minimum provisions to secure participation from all members of a group. Shy, reticent people may temporarily need encouragement before they feel accepted enough to voice their opinions. All people are not equally aggressive, equally articulate, equally confident of their convictions. The group should take into account that its members may differ in reaction time, general spontaneity, and willingness to engage in an intellectually vigorous argument. A special effort to aid the less experienced or less self-confident may sometimes be necessary.

This delineation of responsibility between individual and group, however, is not as sharp as our treatment suggests. Just how often should a group depart from its assigned task in order to increase the interest and skill of an individual member who is bored or inactive? When should a group give "aid and comfort" to its ineffective members? Some of the critics of discussion may be justified in complaining about groups in which therapy and training are continually given precedence over productivity and efficiency. It takes time away from the group's main purpose to help people to express themselves. An atmosphere conducive to personal growth may be bought at the expense of speed and efficiency in decision making. On the other hand, a group which disregards the personal needs of its members may fail to cultivate people who might contribute valuable information, original ideas, or interpersonal talents that may be needed at other times.

The specific point at which training should be given priority over task performance is one to be decided in the particular social context. Participants should bear in mind this principle: The group must perform well not only in the short run, which might excuse the group's neglect of some member's needs, but also in the long run, where the survival value of the group will reflect its ability to marshal the combined capacities of its members.

Thus far in our discussion of individual and group responsibilities we have treated apathy as though it were only a problem of nonparticipation by a minority of the members of a group. However, it is also possible for an entire group to become apathetic. This seldom means that everyone withdraws completely and that the group sits in silence. Someone will carry the ball, since the very basic rule of interaction is that group members must fill the time with some kind of verbalization (Goffman, 1967, pp. 33–35). Rather, this kind of emotional climate is likely to be characterized by aimless wandering, irrelevant comments, complaints about outside authorities, and a general lack of nonverbal responsiveness. It may also be accompanied by frequent absenteeism which operates in such a way that the composition of the group shifts from meeting to meeting. Obviously, this pattern constitutes a serious problem for the group, and the situation becomes even more acute if such behavior persists for some time and is supported by a norm that "group members should not express enthusiasm or involvement." In this case, responsibility for change must be shouldered by the entire group; something is wrong with the way the group system is functioning, and it cannot be blamed on isolated individuals.

HANDLING THE PROBLEM OF APATHY

The potential for involvement can often be enhanced by careful planning. In the first place, it should be evident that appointment to a committee should be made, as far as possible, on a voluntary basis. Trying to coerce people into behaving democratically and spontaneously is to engender not only apathy but a host of other motivational problems as well. People can hardly be blamed for indifference or for dodging their share of the work when a problem does not touch their lives in any recognizable way. Whenever possible, persons who already have some experience with the problem or who are deeply affected by current policies concerning it should be named to a committee. Committee members will often work surprisingly hard when given a chance to correct problems which they themselves have had to face.

However, even groups which have been composed in a judicious manner may run into problems later. Once the group is in motion, a number of techniques for dealing with the problems of apathy recommend themselves, and, as has been our habit throughout this book, we will describe them as objectively as we can, leaving to our readers the issue of selecting the preferred approach.

The Directive Approach

There are two quite different schools of thought concerning the proper way to deal with noncontributing members. The first and most familiar of these can be broadly characterized as directive in method. It is based on the belief that inarticulate people need to be encouraged to express themselves more freely and more fully. Through a little prodding here, a few well-placed suggestions there, or some persuasion at another point, nonparticipants will be temporarily pressured into joining the discussion. Before long, these artificial techniques of motivation will be unnecessary, for participation will become its own reward; group members who were formerly withdrawn will begin to feel some of the satisfaction that comes from exchanging ideas in a spirited discussion.

Perhaps the committee never gets off the ground because few of the participants are deeply concerned with the topic. In this case, some members might take it upon themselves to deepen the level of emotional involvement. Through viewing a controversial film on the subject or through participation in a dramatic reenactment of some aspect of the problem, the group might obtain a fresh perspective on its topic. A field trip may translate a seemingly abstract issue into more tangible form. There are many students who have taken a fresh interest in mental illness, juvenile delinquency, or drug addiction after visiting a mental hospital, accompanying a social worker on his or her rounds in the slums, or spending a day in court. A bored discussant may become much more excited about a topic after reading provocative or controversial articles on the subject.

The chairperson, or any member of the group for that matter, may use stronger medicine. He or she may take the role of the "devil's advocate" by assuming, for the sake of argument, a point of view that is unpopular or that is being disregarded by the group. The spokesperson for the devil may improve decisions by forcing groups that are too homogeneous in their outlook to consider ideas that are unusual, unfamiliar, or original. In addition, even if the ideas proposed by the devil's advocate are rejected, the group members must mobilize their efforts to meet this challenge, and the process of exerting social pressure on the deviant is likely to create greater involvement.

When the problem of apathy seems to stem from disproportionate participation caused by large group size, coacting groups can be employed. The meeting is broken up into several smaller groups which work on the entire problem being considered or each on a specific issue related to the overall topic. When all of these smaller groups have reached decisions, the larger group can meet again to hear reports from each unit, or representatives of the subgroups can meet in the center of the entire group for a discussion to which the other members on the outside listen. This allows more individual participation while still permitting the group to function as a whole.

Another suggestion is to give inactive members a specific assignment within the group and make them responsible for carrying it out. Students in elementary and secondary schools who are shy and withdrawn are often brought out of their "shells" by being given a position of authority in school activities. Why not do the same for adult members of discussion groups? One person might be made responsible for reporting on this phase of the subject, another on that phase. Or, perhaps, nonparticipants could be put in charge of summarizing the discussion, keeping records of the meeting, or even leading the group from time to time. This may put some pressure on them to become better informed so they will be prepared to take part. Giving them responsibility for the conduct of a meeting may supply the motive for developing the skills they lack.

In some cases, active members of a group might call on nonparticipants by name and ask them for their opinion. While this may be justified if the nonparticipants are simply shirking their share of the work, it is not always effective in bringing them out. To be put on the spot for an opinion may be exceedingly embarrassing—as students well know—if one does not happen to have anything worthwhile to say at that moment. This technique usually works best when the person calling on another member happens to know, perhaps from conversations outside the group, that the individual has something to say on the specific issue being discussed. Sometimes calling on others will be effective when a sensitive group member picks up a subtle nonverbal cue that an inactive participant would like to make a comment but doesn't know how to get into the discussion.

As we noted earlier, the problem of apathy can become so serious that only one or two members of the group carry the discussion, and even they may lose most of their enthusiasm. When apathy has become the accepted mode for most of the group members, the methods of changing norms discussed in the previous chapter will apply. At the very least, some rather extensive group self-evaluation is needed. Sometimes this can be done effectively by directive means. One person who wants to change things may be able to prod the group into self-examination. But in the specific case of widespread apathy, where momentum has been lost almost completely, the exertion of energy by one or two group members may not be enough. A more risky method known as "nondirectivity" may be required.

The Nondirective Approach

The nondirective approach to problems of personal and social adjustment is usually associated with the name of Carl Rogers.[1] The fundamental premise underlying the nondirective approach is that human beings have within themselves constructive impulses which can lead to creative and mature behavior. Much as the body restores itself to health, so the psyche, if permitted, can shrug off its inhibitions. What causes withdrawal from satisfying human relationships is the subversion of natural impulses through past failure to relate successfully to one's family and culture. As a result, a person loses the desire for risking interdependent relationships with other people. Directive and manipulative techniques, according to Thomas Gordon, one of Rogers' students, only intensify reactive and defensive behavior:

> We have seen, too, how authority produces reactive rather than constructive and creative behavior. We have evidence of the reluctance of people to "show their ignorance" in the presence of the expert, or the well-informed person. People apparently must feel secure and free from threat in order to be themselves, in order to participate freely, in order to expose their ideas or feelings to others. Traditional leadership, it seems, rarely gives people such security and freedom (Gordon, 1955, p. 334).

The job of the nondirective psychotherapist, according to Rogers, is not to manipulate the client—by stimulating, diagnosing, or prescribing—but to create an accepting situation in which the client may cure himself or herself. The ideal is to make the client more autonomous, more self-energizing, not less, and, therefore, the therapist avoids responding to appeals for help.

In a group of apathetic committee members, what would this mean specifically? Someone who has been active in the past or who has an official position of leadership would call the attention of the group to the pre-

[1] Readers who are interested in studying in detail the applications of nondirective methods in the field of teaching, counseling, and leadership should read Carl Rogers, *Client-Centered Therapy* (Boston: Houghton Mifflin, 1951).

vailing mood of apathy. But there would be no overt gestures on this person's part to salvage the meeting or save the committee members from their predicament. This creates a leadership vacuum and invites others to respond. Probably at this point the nondirective leader would simply sit quietly until someone takes the initiative, or, if necessary, until the group adjourns. This is tantamount to saying: "I believe we have a problem here. It is not my problem any more than it is yours. We may wish to do something about it, but, on the other hand, we may not. I am prepared to listen to whatever anyone has to say."

This is a difficult kind of approach to take, for it puts a strain on the person doing it and on the rest of the group as well, especially if they are not accustomed to facing up to their interpersonal problems in this way. Unless those who initiate such action are reasonably secure, they may be tempted, in the silence that follows their calling attention to group apathy, to propose solutions to the problem. However, it is also a strain on the other members of the group who must finally face up to their own impulses and motives. It is quite true that this method may lead in many directions—and one who adopts it had better be prepared to accept any outcome. The group may disintegrate, either because the members finally see that there is no real reason for its continued existence, or because they are not up to the self-analysis that such an approach provokes. Or the group may reassess its old goals and formulate new ones that are more realistic. But the group that does survive this kind of self-analysis, or group-analysis, is likely to emerge from it with stronger and more genuine reasons for acting.

Briefly, the result of the directive approach is to revitalize a group through temporary expedients that will keep it going. By artificial stimulation a group can be kept functioning in the same way that the temperature of a person with a high fever can be forced down by administering drugs. Simple palliatives may do the job. But apathy or fever may be a symptom of a more serious malady within the organism. If it is, then a different cure may be in order. The group may be pursuing the wrong goals, it may have already achieved its goals, or its members may need to face squarely the motives for withdrawal within themselves. If so, less directive methods may be of value.

SUMMARY AND CONCLUSIONS

Apathy is one of the more persistent and serious illnesses from which discussion groups suffer. Committee members who are physically present may not actually take part for a variety of reasons. For one thing, they may have been appointed to the group but have no interest in the problems being investigated. Many people regard committee work as something inescapable and not to be looked forward to with happy anticipation. Yet, sometimes, committees are composed of deeply concerned people whose original interest was snuffed out after a brief time. In these cases, withdrawal has its source within the group itself. The overly talkative and dominant members may discourage some people. Others may find the pace too fast or too slow, too formal or too anarchic. Social pressure is sometimes manipulated so as to threaten anyone who does not conform in thought, dress, or manner. But nonparticipation may also reflect the individual's motives and fears programmed through past experience. To engage in discussion may be regarded as dangerous or difficult—dangerous in the sense that earlier family and group relationships were personally painful, and difficult in the sense that a person may feel incapable of articulating his or her ideas successfully. Cynicism, too, can play a part when people have participated in one group after another without feeling any sense of accomplishment.

The group and the individual member share in the responsibility for failure to make maximum use of the talents of group members. The individual is obligated to contribute whenever he or she has information or ideas to offer, when the opinions of others are not being adequately tested, or when the group needs help in some area of its own process. The group, as a whole, should be held responsible for forcing people out of discussion when it fails to provide equal opportunities for all to participate or when it does not maintain a climate conducive to thought and open communication.

Involvement can be encouraged in the group through directive or nondirective methods. A greater degree of involvement may be produced through reading provocative materials, field trips, or role-playing scenes. Some members, by playing the devil's advocate, may "smoke out" some of the less aggressive members. Nonparticipants may be assigned specific duties, or the group may be divided temporarily to allow people to establish new roles and new channels of communication. If the nondirective approach is adopted, members will simply bring the problem of apathy to the attention of the group, encourage members to analyze their own goals and motives, and be prepared to accept changes in either the aims of the group or the attitudes of individual members.

STUDY SUGGESTIONS

1. Do you believe that group apathy is most frequently due to sources outside the group, sources within the group, or sources within the individual? On what do you base this belief?
2. Construct postmeeting reaction sheets, permitting group members to indicate the extent of their satisfaction with the leadership, agenda, norms, and accomplishments of their groups. Have these sheets filled out anonymously by members of four groups to which you belong. Then tabulate the answers and identify: (a) the group which reflects the greatest extent of apathy; (b) the major

sources of that apathy within the group. Pretend you are the group leader and design a plan to solve the problem.

3. Reflect on the groups to which you now belong (or have recently belonged). Select the group toward which you feel the most apathy (prefer not to attend meetings, fail to pay dues or hold office, fail to take responsibility, etc.). Do an in-depth analysis of the sources of your apathy within: (1) the *group*—its atmosphere, norms, leadership, membership, and (2) your *self*—past experience, communicative style, interpersonal skills, knowledge and involvement with the task, and so on.

Part III
PROBLEM SOLVING IN GROUPS

CHAPTER 8
Conflict Management in Groups

When modern social scientists first began to study the phenomenon of conflict, many of them assumed that conflict was undesirable, although perhaps necessary, as a temporary state. The objective was to find ways to *resolve* it, to bring the conflict to an end. It is not surprising, therefore, that the first scholarly publication in this area was called *The Journal of Conflict Resolution*. Commenting on this choice of title in a special issue of the journal, Kenneth Boulding made the following observations:

> I am not sure now . . . that "resolution" was the right word. Perhaps "management" would have been better, for the distinction between constructive and destructive conflicts is not necessarily the same as the distinction between those which are resolved and those which are not. Conflicts are sometimes resolved in ways which are highly undesirable for one party if not for both. Sometimes there is a need for protracting conflict and for keeping it unresolved, perhaps by diminishing its intensity and increasing its duration. Thus the more neutral word "management" may better describe the objectives of our enterprise . . . (Boulding, 1968, p. 410).

We are entirely in agreement with Boulding's statement. "Conflict management" is a more neutral term than "conflict resolution" because it does not imply that conflict must always be dealt with in such a way as to bring it to a speedy conclusion. For example, it seems obvious that the struggle for civil rights in this country cannot be concluded with any easy solution or an uneasy compromise. Even the landmark Civil Rights Law of 1964 was only a stage in the process of this conflict. In the same way, it is not always necessary or desirable for small groups to resolve all their conflicts. Sometimes it is more important to find ways in which the group can sustain a dialogue among conflicting factions. At the same time, the word "management" does not exclude attempts to resolve conflict, and we will have much to say about how this can be done. But first, we must define the nature of conflict itself.

THE NATURE OF CONFLICT

In the broadest sense, "conflict" refers to any circumstance in which "disagreement" or "antagonism" is expressed. These terms are not synonymous. There can be disagreement with no appreciable amount of anger or annoyance; and people can be hostile toward one another without actually disagreeing on ideas, although this is probably not common in learning or decision-making groups. However, it is not uncommon to find that disagreement—especially prolonged disagreement—is associated with personal antagonism. We may refer to a brief episode during which disagreement is expressed and then resolved as "momentary conflict." For the most part, in this chapter our concern will be with what we may call "sustained conflict"—situations in which disagreement is extended or where hostility is a frequent and recurring event in a group. We often speak of groups as being "in a state of conflict" when disagreement and/ or antagonism are a major feature of their interactions.

In *The Functions of Social Conflict*, Lewis Coser offers a definition of conflict which is *within* the meaning we have described above but which is more specific, in that it stresses the elements of *competition* and *power manipulations* in conflict situations:

> For the purpose of this study, [social conflict] will be provisionally taken to mean a struggle over values and claims to scarce status, power and resources in which the aims of the opponents are to neutralize, injure or eliminate their rivals (p. 8).

At first, it may appear that Coser's definition does not apply at all to what happens in most small group discussions. The "life and death" struggle which he appears to suggest may seem more characteristic of international conflicts over boundary lines or of labor disputes where the stakes are high and management and workers are polarized and hostile. But with some qualifications, it can be seen that the circumstances covered by Coser's definition are not unusual in small group settings. "Neutralizing" an opponent might simply mean getting him or her to stop objecting to your proposal. "Injury" might be nothing permanent—a cutting remark which reduces the other's status temporarily, for example. And even "eliminating" a rival might simply involve getting someone to withdraw from the argument. We would add, however, that in conflict there are other aims pursued which are less drastic and which may open up lines of communication rather than destroy them. For example, one may engage in conflict not with the hope of "winning" completely but rather that of gaining some concessions. In fact, a useful strategy sometimes involves demanding more than you hope to gain in the end. In addition, people sometimes engage in conflict simply for the purpose of securing an open discussion of the issues, especially if they are part of a suppressed minority in the society or in a small group.

In one respect, Coser's definition is useful because it calls attention to parallels between small group disputes and conflicts involving larger units, including global confrontations. But it also makes an important point about the nature of conflict in groups: there is potential for the expression of conflict in nearly any group because the benefits available to the members are often in limited supply. This is most obvious in situations that are analogous to games like poker or monopoly, where the gains of some must be losses for others. For example, a group of salespeople may be called on to decide on a system for evaluating their job proficiency. The weighting of various criteria may favor some individuals over others. If the total monetary value of sales is taken as the only significant factor in rating the salespersons, individuals who perform other services for the company, such as maintaining good customer relations after the sale, may be slighted. Each potential group solution may give advantages to some and handicaps to others. Competition may also occur among members who share a common interest in the quality of the solution but who cannot be equally influential, thus creating conflict over status.

However, Coser's emphasis on competition may obscure an important fact: *Group conflict situations always involve both cooperative and competitive orientations.* Consider a basketball game as an example. Essentially, this appears to be a competitive situation; one team must win, and one must lose. But the teams must also cooperate in order to stage a game. They will have common goals, such as getting some exercise, sharpening their skills, respecting the rules, or attracting a crowd to an arena. The point may become even clearer if we examine the relationships among the players of one team. Essentially, this appears to be a cooperative situation; the entire team wins or loses. If an individual player shoots when he or she should pass off to others, the team effort suffers. But it is also true that the more shots an individual player takes, the better are his or her chances of being the leading scorer. So there are also competitive motivations within the team.

Most group situations involve *mixed motives;* each participant must make choices between stressing individual gains and sacrificing for the good of the entire team. It is important to note that group members may *choose* to see a particular set of circumstances as necessitating primarily cooperative or primarily competitive behavior. Although we believe that from the perspective of the entire group it is often advantageous for members to strive for cooperation, this can be overdone. Since there are always cooperative goals involved in conflict, often it is better to allow competition to reign for a period of time in order to assure that all points of view are expressed.[1]

THE FUNCTIONS OF GROUP CONFLICT

Everything that we have said thus far implies strongly that conflict is a "good thing." In fact, we could go even further to say that a group which experiences little or no conflict may well be in danger of failing as a viable and creative entity.[2] But why? What are the positive outcomes of group conflict?

Values of Conflict

First, one of the most obvious effects of group conflict is emotional arousal. Although some of the feelings created may be negative, they *are* evidence of involvment, and, thus, conflict often can be an effective antidote to apathy. Conflict may serve an *involvement function* in groups.

Second, and perhaps less obvious, is the fact that a group which permits—and encourages—conflict has a better chance of avoiding sudden and inappropriate "explosions" of emotion than does one which has suppressed disagreement and antagonism. When people do not feel free to express disagreement and hold back negative feelings for a long period of time, the hostility which flows out with the "straw that breaks the camel's back" may be altogether out of proportion to the issue involved at the time. The release of such feelings before they build up serves the *safety valve* function.

Third, and even less obvious, perhaps, is that in a group which has a

[1] The value of encouraging conflict can be seen in a study by Maier and Solem (1952). They instructed leaders in some groups to encourage participation, to urge members to explore a wide variety of solutions, and to protect the rights of minorities to disagree. Those groups were more effective in decision making than were others whose leaders were told simply to record the group decisions.

[2] In one study, Barnlund (1959) found that a major reason for decision failure in groups was the absence of conflict. However, he also found that the "presence of unresolvable conflict" was another important characteristic of unsuccessful decision making, suggesting that groups need conflict but also must know how to handle it. Methods of dealing with conflict are taken up later in this chapter.

history of successfully sustaining and sometimes resolving conflict to the satisfaction of all without breaking up, the bonds among the group members can actually be strengthened. In their book *The Intimate Enemy* (1968), Bach and Wyden describe how this happens in marriages when the partners learn to "fight fair." Couples may actually become closer by learning to deal with their differences. In the same way, groups in which everyone experiences the freedom to express their feelings and opinions tend to become more cohesive. This is the *inclusion function* of conflict.

Thus far, we have mentioned only the socioemotional outcomes of conflict. But there are distinct advantages in terms of the task dimension of groups as well. Conflict also serves an *idea testing* function. Only through disagreement can ideas be examined thoroughly. In this way, the group can avoid superficial decisions. Even if people who initially disagree with a proposal eventually change their minds, the group can have more confidence in those decisions reached after potential weaknesses in thinking have been explored.

In addition, conflict can serve an *innovative function*. This is especially important when the members of a group have long held an assumption which may no longer be functional. Suppose, for example, that a manufacturing company has produced a certain product for many years and that now sales are declining. Board members may propose various ways of increasing sales, but it may be that the company needs to produce a new product and move into a more viable, growing market. This innovative idea may be met with staunch opposition, especially among those members of the group who were instrumental in developing the old product. Conflict will be necessary to insure that the new idea gets a fair hearing. On the societal level, the phenomenon of the women's movement provides an example of conflict brought about by the challenging of basic and long-held assumptions.

Risks of Conflict

It is probably much more common to hear group members express pride in their group by saying "we always get along" than to hear them express positive feelings about productive episodes of disagreement. Why is it that groups so often resist and avoid conflict? Some of these responses undoubtedly stem from the personality traits of group members. Individuals who have feelings of inadequacy about dealing with antagonism and disagreement or who have a strong need for structure and certainty in relating to others may avoid conflict because they cannot cope with the unpleasant feelings they may experience. But surely everyone has had some negative and unproductive experiences with conflict, and not all of these can be traced to personality failings. What is the case for avoiding conflict?

There are some inherent dangers whenever a group engages in a prolonged state of conflict: (1) Conflict is time-consuming. Where efficiency and speedy solutions are considered all-important, taking time to disagree or to express negative feelings may seem to sidetrack the group from its mission. The criticism is especially salient when the group becomes bogged down in minor disagreements and fails to move on to important matters. (2) Negativism can *spiral*, so that group members become more and more hostile toward one another. If carried far enough, this often results in people withdrawing and avoiding communication with one another. (3) Eventually, the group can dissolve altogether.

Although we recognize that these dangers exist, we would argue that the risks of avoiding conflict are even greater and that often insightful handling of conflict can overcome the potential problems. Our answers to each of the specific objections to conflict are as follows:

1. In general, groups are "inefficient" if they function as they should. Most of the time, individuals can reach decisions more quickly by themselves, perhaps consulting with others before reaching the decision alone. But when the advantages of real group deliberation are sought, the risk of losing time must be accepted. In fact, it depends on how one defines "losing time." Efforts in the direction of an improved group product are not a "waste" of time unless one assumes the prime objective to be the reaching of *some* decision immediately, regardless of the quality of the solution.

2. The danger of spiraling negativism can usually be skirted if group members express disagreement and even anger in a *supportive* way; that is, the manner in which a negative reaction is presented can be positive if a person shows involvement and interest, rather than rejection, toward those being thus challenged. And if spiraling hostility does occur, group members can often change the direction of events by pausing to examine as a group how they are communicating with one another.

3. Ultimately, of course, when all attempts to sustain and resolve conflict fail, the group can break up. We would argue that this is not necessarily bad. When there has been open and direct communication in a group and when the individuals discover that their interests are so divergent that they cannot work together on a common goal without making unacceptable compromises, separation may be the most logical course. Where such a solution seems unthinkable, the group can sometimes cease deliberations temporarily and then return to work on the conflict. Both approaches—dissolving and taking a "breather"—seem preferable to avoiding conflict altogether.

THE SOURCES OF CONFLICT

When a state of conflict does emerge, it is often helpful for the group members to identify the causes. Sometimes this can occur on the individual level; other times, the entire group may want to step back from the conflict to analyze it for a while. When the sources of the conflict have been recognized, the group members can decide what, if anything, to do about it. To aid you in this analytical process, we offer a typology of the sources of conflict.

Goals and Means

As Coser points out, conflict over "goals"—the main objectives of a group—is usually more disruptive than disagreement about "means"— conclusions about how to accomplish goals that everyone accepts. Closely related to goals are basic procedures about how the group will make decisions. If, for example, some members of the group believe that it is the responsibility of the chairperson to make the ultimate decisions and that the purpose of the group is simply to advise, while others feel that the entire group must make the decision, the conflict may be as basic and disruptive as if the group could not arrive at an agreement about the purpose of the group. Clearly, when the conflict stems from goals or basic procedures, the group should deal with these issues before moving on to consider specific solutions. Otherwise, a puzzling situation may result in which some group members submit one proposal after another, and other members reject each one. The underlying problem may not be the character of the solutions themselves, but rather the goals to which the solutions are directed or the conception of the roles that various group members will play in the decision-making process.

Personality, Status, and Ideational Conflicts

Disagreement or antagonism may be focused on one or a combination of three kinds of issues, regardless of the degree of disruption which occurs. When people come to dislike one another because of personal qualities that each possesses, the situation is ordinarily called a "personality clash." Two individuals with dominant personality styles, for example, are likely to come into such conflict. In many cases, however, it is not so much that people differ or fail to complement one another in basic personality traits as it is that some aspects of their communication behavior create a problem. For example, if one person has a boisterous and joking manner, while another is soft-spoken and serious, they may have trouble in arriving at a way of dealing with one another.

Closely related to conflicts stemming from personality factors are clashes over status. Two dominant individuals may conflict not only in styles of behavior (both cannot talk at the same time), but also in the desire of each to be the most influential person in the group. This need not have anything to do with personality, however. Two people who are otherwise quite compatible may each have a genuine wish to be elected chairperson of a committee or, where the structure of the group is less formal, to be seen by others as "the leader."

Finally, a conflict may have little or nothing to do with how people feel toward one another as individuals or with how they feel about their relative position in the influence hierarchy of the group. Rather, the disagreement focuses on *ideas*.

It is not always possible to separate the three kinds of conflict. As we have pointed out, personality conflicts may evolve into a leadership struggle. In addition, people may disagree with one another primarily because of mutual dislike. And status may be intimately related to an issue involving ideas; if two people each champion opposing ideas, the one who prevails also gains status over the other. On the whole, however, if the group can separate these issues or if they diagnose how the issues are related, they can deal more effectively with the specific nature of the conflict.

Hidden Agenda

Sometimes the issue around which conflict appears to revolve is not the actual cause of disagreement or antagonism. In Chapter 3, "Individual Motives and Group Goals," we referred to the phenomenon of "hidden agenda" where individuals have underlying motivations which they do not reveal for fear that these motives will be regarded as socially unacceptable by others. We now turn to an examination of the ways in which hidden agenda may play a role in conflict.

Conflict involving hidden agenda usually takes one of two forms: (1) It may be a status conflict masquerading as an ideational dispute. Perhaps a person wants to be the most influential member of the group. Or maybe he or she just wants to be listened to and agreed with more often. But to say this may be risky; others may reply, "What do you mean? We're supposed to be equals here." What is more, this person may be somewhat unaware of his or her underlying motivations. So, instead, this individual disagrees with the ideas of the other person contending for the top status position or with the ideas of those who are more influential. (2) Although the issue may be purely a socioemotional one at heart, it surfaces as ideational conflict. Perhaps the individual finds the behavior of another person particularly annoying for some reason or feels that certain others shun and dislike him or her. To reveal this reaction, however, might be to expose some degree of insecurity or to show what others might regard as temperamental behavior. So, once again, the individual resorts to challenging the logic or evidence presented by others.

Sometimes it is possible to recognize these hidden agenda conflicts by observing the manner in which certain individuals express their disagreement with others over time. Both kinds often surface in the form of cutting remarks and negative nonverbal reactions. When individuals consistently direct these responses toward those with whom they usually disagree, there is evidence that a hidden agenda involving status or socioemotional causes is present. When the attacks are directed by one or both of two frequent talkers against each other or by less frequent talkers against the more influential group members, it suggests a status conflict. When two individuals or factions are vying for influence, often they will align themselves against one another physically, sitting directly across from those they expect to challenge. The signs of underlying socioemotional conflict are often more subtle. An individual who is usually an attentive listener may become inattentive when certain members of the group speak, denying eye-contact and the usual nodding behavior which says "I'm listening, I'm listening." If this behavior is accompanied by ideational conflict with the same people, the presence of hidden agenda involving personality differences seems likely. Or, occasionally, volatile outbursts may occur among disagreeing group members, seemingly without warning or apparent justification, again suggesting the presence of a personality clash.

There is another kind of hidden agenda conflict which is perhaps less common than status or socioemotional differences disguised as ideational dispute, but which is even more disruptive. In this case, the conflict has little or nothing to do with the immediate group situation. The causes are hostility or frustration brought in from outside the group. This kind of persistent negativism is very difficult to identify, but its hallmark is that it seems to have little to do with the behavior of others. It may take the form of attacks on nearly everyone; the antagonist picks no favorites. Or, where it is directed at specific others, the recipients of hostility are attacked more for what they represent than for how they act in the group. If, for example, the hostile group member has negative feelings toward authority figures in general, whoever fits this category best may become the target. In this case, it could be the chairperson, the oldest group member, or the person whose occupation outside the group (e.g., policeman, teacher) is acknowledged as an authority role.

Dealing with hidden agenda conflict is often difficult. Even if someone has the insight to recognize the actual cause of the problem and the courage to bring it up before the rest of the group, those who agree may remain silent, and the "accused" may become defensive. Those with disguised motives may be unwilling to admit their real motivations. Especially in the case of generalized hostility, individuals may be unable to face up to the causes of their feelings, and groups may not be willing or able to administer psychotherapy. Such conflicts do not always create a serious problem for the group. It may not be necessary to have all motivations out in the open in every case. In fact, conflict stemming partially from hidden agenda sometimes has positive results: Ideas get tested as a side effect. However, when group members become frustrated and confused or when apathy results despite a shared and genuine interest among the group members in reaching a collaborative decision, it may be time for someone to initiate group self-analysis.

Group members who are involved in a conflict situation will find it helpful to keep in mind the types of conflict which we have described in this section. If the source of the difficulty can be clearly identified, the group can direct its energies toward handling the problem. When goals or basic procedures for decision making are involved, the group should deal with these issues before considering specific solutions to the problem under discussion. While an emphasis on ideational conflict is often desirable in moving the group toward its goals, it should be recognized that conflict also arises from matters of status and interpersonal relations, and these are also a legitimate concern of the group. Group members should also be aware that conflicts may stem from hidden agenda. Whether attention should be directed to underlying causes depends on the importance of the conflict to group functioning and on the apparent possibilities for clarifying the situation.

Group members should keep in mind, however, that it is not always possible to separate the causes of conflict from one another. This is especially true when there is a mixture of status and ideational conflict, since the status positions of individuals may be closely linked to how their ideas fare in the group. We have already made some suggestions for dealing with socioemotional problems in the section of this book on interpersonal relations. We will now turn to problems of dealing with conflicts where status or ideational issues, or a combination of both, are involved.

STRATEGIES OF CONFLICT MANAGEMENT

In any group that has been together for some time, issues of power are likely to involve conflict. We define power as "a person's potential to influence the behavior or fate of others in a consistent way." Whenever this is brought into force, we say that the person "exerts power." In "pure" ideational conflict, one's power stems from his or her ability to influence others with ideas. But instances where pure reason prevails may be rather rare. Status considerations—matters of prestige—often enter the picture and affect how people react to the ideas presented, so that people derive their power from sources other than their rational persuasive abilities. In some cases, an individual or individuals may be sanctioned to make certain decisions regardless of what a group decides. The "boss" who asks his employees to discuss an aspect of their working conditions but who then ignores the group consensus and acts on his own is exercising this kind of status power. In other situations, the group may have the ultimate authority to make a decision, but certain individuals, because of their credibility or their past history of influence in the group, may have the majority "in their pocket." Also, some individuals gain prestige by being reliable members of a solid majority.

We believe that discussion is at its best in those situations where status is relatively equally divided or at least where it has little to do with judgments of the merits of ideas. Besides the fact that we favor the fullest sort of democracy as a matter of principle, we would also point out that only when the ideas of everyone can be heard and carefully considered on their intrinsic merits rather than on the prestige of their authors can the advantages of conflict be most fully realized. However, we do recognize that even where lip service is given to the idea that everyone has an equal say, there are often strains in groups toward the avoidance and suppression of conflict. Frequently, those high in status employ various tactics to achieve this end, but sometimes, in groups where everyone is very fearful of disagreement, both those high and low in status may cooperate in avoiding conflict. It is important that group members be able to recognize these diversionary strategies and also that they be familiar with more constructive ways of dealing with conflict. So we will first discuss the "strategies of the powerful": avoidance and suppression. Then we will examine those tactics which can be employed by the "less powerful" or by all members of the group who wish to base decisions on ideational rather than status considerations: strategies of prolongation and collaboration. Our list of strategies will only be suggestive and not exhaustive.[3]

Strategies of Avoidance

The simplest and most efficient way of eradicating conflict is to head it off before it happens. Group members who wish to avoid conflict send a clear message: "If you're not in agreement, don't bring it up." One way of doing this is to set an agenda which excludes controversial items. Issues of potential conflict are simply not offered for consideration. Another approach is to make a verbal appeal for unanimity at the outset of the discussion. Sometimes arguments are presented as to why the group must "stick together" in this "time of crisis." However, where avoidance has become a norm for the group, this appeal may be presented briefly only as a reminder of the way group members are expected to act. When an issue is first introduced, people who wish to avoid controversy may also attempt to categorize the problem or the participants in such a way that others will be reluctant to disagree. This may take the form of moralizing about what position will be taken by "every good American," "every responsible faculty member," or "every loyal employee." Group members might also be complimented or patronized with such statements as "I'm

---

[3] Another list of strategies, similar to this one in some ways but having to do specifically with *interpersonal* conflict, may be found in Frost and Wilmot (1978), pp. 114–143.

sure you will want to do the right thing," implying that the "right thing" is what the speaker advocates.

Another type of avoidance tactic depends on timing for its effectiveness. Pleas for a speedy solution may be made. Frequently, if the entire group is not aware of an impending decision where a deadline must be met, knowledgeable members of the group may introduce the issue for consideration at the last minute while also offering a prepared solution. Perhaps the most extreme measure of this type is to call a "surprise" meeting at a time when it is known that certain group members who are likely to oppose a recommendation will be absent.

Strategies of Suppression

Once an issue has been raised and the group is in a state of conflict, some group members may continue to use tactics of avoidance, but they may also employ new, more drastic techniques in an attempt to shut off the debate. Some of these approaches may be rather direct. Members of the group may refer to threatening outside forces: "If we pass this resolution, we're all likely to receive salary cuts." A member may attempt to "pull rank": "As chairperson of this group, I urge you to consider what a risky step this proposal entails." Closely related to the strategy of bringing up threatening outside forces is the technique of pulling rank in the name of an absent authority figure: "The boss won't like this."

The most direct method of suppressing conflict is to bring parliamentary rules to bear in order to end discussion. The group may take a vote on whether to permit further debate. We do not mean to say that this tactic always stems from pernicious motives. At times, when the discussion has gone on at great length and a few group members are filibustering, this action may be necessary, but a premature closure on arguments may also be used as a method of silencing a dissident minority.

Other approaches to suppressing discussion may be rather indirect, but they may be nevertheless quite effective. Cutting remarks may be used against opponents, or high-status members may persistently interrupt others, preventing them from fully expressing their ideas.

Strategies of Prolongation

In the face of attempts at avoidance and suppression, often led by the more powerful members of a group, the less powerful, or others who wish to avoid a premature conclusion, will need an antidote. And even if differential power is not an important element, groups may need to work at tolerating—and sometimes enjoying—the strain of disagreement or antagonism. For these purposes, group members need strategies for sustaining conflict.

At times, the less powerful may be able to turn the tables by using the strategies of the powerful against them. Some of these include monopolizing, countermoralizing, interrupting, and employing cutting remarks. In some cases, even thinly veiled personal threats or references to outside threats (other than those which give the powerful their power) may be used. The minority can also threaten to leave the group altogether.

But effective use of such table-turning strategies is limited. Monopolizing is difficult for those who are in a minority. Calls for unanimity will not usually work because the majority has the votes, although occasionally urging a compromise might succeed. The less powerful cannot pull rank if the power structure is against them. And others may be only too happy to see them leave.

In some cases, this approach of "fighting fire with fire" can accomplish some temporary or short-range purposes. Action by the powerful may be delayed by a stalemate. The minority or the less powerful may be able to make themselves so troublesome that the powerful will give in on some points, and, sometimes, only by creating a disruption can the minority receive a hearing. But for the most part, what disruptive strategies fail to accomplish is a change from power tactics to more constructive processes of dealing with conflict in the group. For this purpose, it is necessary to influence those high in status to give up power for the good of the entire group.

Two techniques seem especially useful for sustaining conflict in a way that still keeps the group together. One approach is for members of the group to persuade others of the values of conflict. Even groups in which the members are convinced of the advantages of conflict will sometimes need reminders in the form of encouragement when they are suffering from "battle fatigue." Sometimes this can be done quite effectively and in a subtle manner. For example, a group member may simply interject a statement expressing solidarity in the face of conflict: "We're certainly getting all the issues out on the table!" Or, individuals may engage in gatekeeping, helping dissident group members to get into the conversation.

A second approach is for participants to make process comments about how the group as a whole or individual members are reacting to the conflict. This may take the form of comments about specific behaviors: "I notice that whenever Bill tries to explain his position, others interrupt him." Or, interventions may be more general, referring to the way the group as a whole is responding and calling for group discussion about this process: "People are getting very excited and hostile here. Is there anything we can do about this?"

Certain kinds of comments of this type may be especially successful in helping the group to sustain conflict. In particular, comments made at the time when the avoiding or suppressing is happening are likely to be effective because they pinpoint the behaviors at issue. At times, such observations can be presented as a problem of communication in the group rather than as a personal attack on certain individuals. And when it is necessary to direct remarks to specific individuals in the group, those making such comments can sometimes reduce the tendency of others to respond defensively by speaking in the first person, making it clear that they are aware that their observations are tentative and grow out of their own perceptions: "I'm bothered by the way you keep referring to what the boss will say when we're trying to discuss this issue." In addition, the manner in which such comments are made can have a significant effect on the reaction of the person who is confronted. The person voicing the criticism can make it clear that he or she is rejecting only a part of the behavior of the other, and not the whole person. For example, even an expression of strong anger, shown in the face and voice, has a different meaning when the speaker maintains direct eye-contact rather than looking and turning away from the person being confronted. With eye-contact, such an expression invites response; without eye-contact, it suggests rejection or an attempt to cut off response from the other person.

Strategies of Collaboration

Groups that are able to prolong conflict without disintegrating and without the more powerful members resorting to strategies of avoidance or suppression are well on the way toward collaborative action. However, something else is needed before conflicts can be resolved in a way which will be satisfactory for everyone: Status and power must be relatively equal among the group members. This means that each participant has more or less equal control over the fate of others, that who influences whom is fluid and changing rather than static and inflexible, and that the composition of majorities can shift from topic to topic. In addition, it will be helpful if socioemotional conflicts have been resolved to the point where people can listen to one another and argue rather freely. Under these conditions, it is possible for the group to focus on ideational conflict, the hope being that the group will arrive at a solution which is better than any one of the various positions taken by the conflicting parties in the beginning. The strategies which may be employed in this creative search for consensus may be described as a series of progressive levels of discussion.

LEVEL OF ASSERTION
Controversy usually begins with the assertion of conflicting statements of personal preference or belief. "Capital punishment should be abolished." "Strikes in energy industries should be outlawed." "Affirmative action discriminates against whites." "The schools should return to their primary function of teaching reading, writing, and arithmetic." "A teacher's sexual

preference should not be a criterion for hiring in the public schools." "Teaching should count more than publication in the evaluation of college professors." Opinions such as these, when germane to the problems under discussion, deserve to be analyzed and explored.

On examination, the difference of opinion may turn out to be nothing more than a semantic problem. If so, then once the opposing members clear up what they mean by their statements, the disagreement will dissolve. For example, what one person means by "socialized medicine" may turn out to be a government-supported private insurance program, which is what the opposition favors too. The members of a group who disagree over the purpose of a liberal education may discover they agree that some courses in the curriculum should have an occupational focus while most may have broader aims. If this is the case, group members need only to define their terms to resolve the difference.

However, the conflict may involve more than a matter of clarity. If so—and if the disagreement is genuine—group members are likely to continue at the same level of assertion, repeating their remarks over and over again in the hope of discouraging the opposition. The person who argued for a return to the three R's will state that "The schools must cut out the frills added to the curriculum in the last three decades," or "The schools must get back to subjects that discipline the mind, rather than entertain the student." Even when the conditions for collaborative discussion have been met, those who disagree, after running out of ways of repeating their views, may question the integrity or intelligence of those who oppose them. They may insinuate that other group members know very little about the subject or that they have not thought about it sufficiently. Someone may suggest, "You ought to visit the schools and see what's *really* going on!" or "Do you *honestly* believe that labor unions control our economy?" At this point the group faces not one, but two problems—how to settle the issue itself and how to reestablish healthy relations among the group members. If, on the other hand, a new dimension can be added before the conflict deteriorates into a clash of personalities, it may be possible to explore the disagreement further.

LEVEL OF REASONING

One way of moving beyond such a deadlock is to approach the argument from a more rational level. In observing two housewives screaming at each other over their back fences, Sydney Smith once commented that they could not agree because they were arguing from different premises. Someone in the group needs to ask those locked in argument to state the *reasons* for believing as they do. In answering this request, discussants will naturally be forced to expose the logic of their positions and thus enable other members of the group to understand their positions better. Group members who believe in capital punishment may argue, for example, that it is necessary "in order to protect society" or "to set an example for others who may be contemplating the same crime." Those who favor liberal education over job training may argue that colleges do a better job of teaching students to think than of providing them with occupational skills.

Forcing the conflict onto this new level has certain beneficial effects. First, it minimizes the chances of the argument becoming personal. When people begin to criticize each other, it is usually because they have run out of ammunition on the original issue. Also, by asking the disputing parties to be more precise about the bases for their opinions, the original generalizations will be given more specific meaning. Group members may, in reviewing the bases of their beliefs, begin to see some merit in each other's arguments. Some may back down from their position, or they may find that a compromise solution takes account of valid arguments from initially opposing points of view. Forcing the argument to the level of explanation, then, may ward off personal attacks, clarify the locus of the disagreement, encourage the testing of arguments, and lead to a settling of the dispute.

But it may turn out that consensus is still not achieved and that the group finds it has exhausted the usefulness of further talk at this level. Members may feel that no really valid objection or argument has been given or that the explanations are trivial and inconsequential. Before long, members of the group are hastening toward a premature vote on the issue or are charging each other with being ill-informed or incompetent.

LEVEL OF EVIDENCE
If the dispute has not been settled at the second level and if the lines of reasoning of the participants have been fully explored, then the conflict should be moved to still another level, the level of evidence. When people disagree over whether or not capital punishment works as a deterrent to crime, figures on the comparative crime rates in states which have and do not have the death sentence should be studied to ascertain which conclusion is supported by the evidence. Arguments over the discriminatory effects of affirmative action programs may possibly be settled by an examination of the relative qualifications of whites and minorities admitted to professional schools or hired as college faculty. If the facts do not resolve the entire matter, the group again faces the prospect of the dispute turning into a stalemate, forcing recourse to other methods of settlement.

LEVEL OF VALUES
Our conflicting beliefs about labor unions, capital punishment or race relations are not always a product of having been exposed to different facts. Nor do they always reflect a difference in our ability to draw logical inferences from the facts. If this were the case, all controversies, even the most serious, could be resolved in time. But our convictions often turn, in-

stead, on the assumptions we make about what is "good," "desirable," "proper," "just," and "virtuous." These, we say, are questions of value.

A conflict which involves a difference in values is the most difficult of all to resolve. Disputes over the costs of free public abortion programs or the effects of affirmative action programs on hiring practices can usually be settled by referring to the facts. But what sort of investigation will reveal whether abortion is "moral" or affirmative action is "just"? Some people believe such questions to be unresolvable. They see no possibility of settling differences between communist and noncommunist nations as long as their underlying political beliefs are so contradictory. They say it is useless to seek agreement between blacks and whites or between labor and management because their systems of values are so different. When members of groups take the position that their values are givens, beyond criticism and incapable of rational justification, there are several alternatives available: They may personally withdraw from the group; the entire issue can be shelved; a vote can be taken; a third party can be brought in to settle the dispute; or a group solution can be reached through undemocratic processes.

Another position, and one which we endorse, is that preferences and values—like any other ideas—can be subjected to critical analysis. This may be carried out in one of two ways: (1) by ferreting out and testing the theoretical assumptions on which the asserted value rests; (2) by examining the consequences of any belief empirically, through direct observation and experience.

The testing of underlying assumptions may be illustrated by the following example. Let us suppose the argument centers on whether American Nazis or other advocates of racist and totalitarian doctrines are entitled to freedom of speech under the First Amendment. While most Americans believe in freedom of speech as a general principle, there are many who think it does not extend to those who, if they had their way, would destroy that very freedom. To counter that kind of value judgment, it would not be sufficient simply to argue that freedom of speech is good because the First Amendment says so. One would have to explain *why* freedom of speech, even for racists and totalitarians, is valuable. In other words, even the *bases* of the principle would have to be examined.

In the writings of John Stuart Mill we will find such a rationale. Any limits placed on the exchange of opinions is fundamentally unsound, according to Mill, because it robs the human race of new ideas. He gives four distinct arguments in support of the value of free speech:

> First, if any opinion is compelled to silence, that opinion may, for aught we can certainly know, be true. To deny this is to assume our own infallibility.
>
> Secondly, though the silenced opinion be an error, it may, and very commonly does, contain a portion of truth; and since the general or prevailing opinion on any subject is rarely or never the whole truth, it is only by the col-

lision of adverse opinions that the remainder of the truth has any chance of being supplied.

Thirdly, even if the received opinion be not only true, but the whole truth; unless it is suffered to be, and actually is, vigourously and earnestly contested, it will, by most of those who receive it, be held in the manner of a prejudice, with little comprehension or feeling of its rational grounds. And not only this, but, fourthly, the meaning of the doctrine itself will be in danger of being lost, or enfeebled, and deprived of its vital effect on the character and conduct: the dogma becoming a mere formal profession . . . preventing the growth of any real and heartfelt conviction, from reason or personal experience (Mill, no date, pp. 65–66).

Now that free speech has been given a rationale, the members of a group can evaluate whether or not this value judgment deserves support.

In a similar way it is possible to explore critically the value structures of a liberal and a conservative in an argument over social welfare measures, of labor and management over the right to strike, of teacher and student in a dispute over course requirements.

In the last analysis, the supreme test of the validity of our values is to be found in experience. Suppose the members of PTA, in advising their school board, find themselves divided over the relative merits of traditional and progressive methods of teaching. It turns out that the disagreement rests on the relative weight they assign to the importance of order and discipline in teaching. If an examination of the arguments in favor of the two philosophies does not settle the question, committee members might wisely decide to visit classrooms and see for themselves what it is actually like to learn under each of these conditions.

By elaborating and critically examining the values which lie behind our judgments we may be able to reduce or clarify the area of disagreement beyond what has been accomplished at other levels. But it is not easy. It takes a great deal of time to isolate the assumptions on which our attitudes are based. And often the motivation is lacking. What is more, to undertake to change our values is to modify, in some cases, our whole personality. This requires considerable moral courage as well as an alert and critical mind.

The relationship among the strategies for the creative exploration of conflict can be summarized in the diagram below:

The Cone of Consensus-Seeking

Assertion..Assertion
Reasons..Reasons
Evidence...Evidence
Values.................................Values

Conflict, as we have pointed out, can begin on any level. No matter on what level the controversy begins, it often must be taken to other levels to be understood and/or resolved. When an argument persists on any one level for a long period of time, it is likely to go from bad to worse, from problem to people. Therefore, when the possibilities for agreement have been exhausted on one level, the group should move on to the next. Note however, that this process does not assure consensus, nor is it certain that the group members will narrow their areas of disagreement as they progress from one level to the next. It is not necessarily the gap of disagreement which narrows as a group goes down the cone, although this may well happen, but rather it is the gap of misunderstanding about the focal point of the conflict which is decreased. The procedure we have suggested here simply increases the *chances* for agreement.

COLLABORATIVE ALTERNATIVES TO CONSENSUS

As we have suggested above, it is not always necessary to resolve conflict in order to manage it. Where resolution is necessary, however, the seeking of consensus is an especially desirable approach. It is likely to produce in group members a willingness to expose and reexamine their own motives and their perceptions of the motives of others in order to find common purposes and to readjust conflicting purposes. Hence, the group's decision is likely to be a good one, and once it is reached, the chances of cooperation in its implementation are at their optimum. However, it is not the only collaborative method of conflict resolution available to groups. If a careful exploration of the conflicting points of view under discussion does not produce agreement and if it is imperative that the group take action, then there are two other alternatives which may be selected: majority vote or arbitration. Compared to consensus, each of these approaches has certain shortcomings, but they also have certain redeeming features in overcoming a stalemate or avoiding an uncomfortable compromise.

Majority vote is probably the most widely employed method of handling conflict. Although a vote is sometimes used simply to formalize or record a unanimous or a compromise agreement, it is more frequently employed as a means of actually settling a disagreement. Here the assumption is made either that further talk will not change anyone else's mind, or that the issue is not worth the time it might take for more prolonged discussion. Each member is expected to vote in behalf of his or her own best interests, and, therefore, "the greatest good for the greatest number" will result.

We note several questionable assumptions here. First, are the motives of the members really so much in conflict that, given more time for exploration, they might not be able to come to an agreement? Second, is time really at a premium? Third, will a majority vote truly produce the greatest good for the greatest number when the members of that majority have not had an opportunity to come to a full appreciation of the minority's feelings?

Granted, there are innumerable situations when the answer to these three questions is "Yes." If so, the method of majority vote would certainly be appropriate. In addition, in some circumstances, there are truly conflicting motives or interests which should not be glossed over with a coating of superficial harmony. The so-called "happy medium" is not always happy. Although compromising on a goal here and there may often be preferable to a total defeat, there are some compromises which are worse. (The old story of Solomon offering to cut a child in two in order to settle the dispute between conflicting "mothers" amply illustrates this truth.) Also, sometimes a minority does not care to explain or argue for its position beyond a certain point, but would rather simply record its dissenting votes and then go along with the majority.

The second collaborative alternative to consensus, arbitration, consists of airing the controversy before a neutral third party or parties whose decision the disputants have agreed in advance to accept. As with majority voting, the assumption is made that the conflict is irreconcilable and that positions will be won or lost. It is hoped that because of the presumed impartiality of the arbiters, justice will be done. Obviously this is not always what happens.Nor do individuals, having freely and voluntarily agreed to submit themselves to arbitration, always gracefully accept the settlements which are handed down to them. Still, if the participants are so embroiled in the conflict that they can no longer reason together and if majority voting does no more than to record the numbers who stand on each side of such a dispute, arbitration may be superior in the sense that it allows the question to be settled by those who can view it with some objectivity.

THE LIMITATIONS OF CONFLICT

Throughout this chapter we have stressed the positive values of conflict. If you have not been exposed to these ideas previously, this point of view may have been rather surprising since "conflict" is a term which has negative connotations for most people. Given that conflict can be viewed in a favorable light and that when properly handled it ordinarily brings positive benefits to group discussion, it is now time to qualify our position. Like nearly every process of discussion, an assessment of the advantages and disadvantages of conflict depends on the purposes and the values which one brings to a situation.

First, conflict serves some group purposes more readily than others. Summarizing the results of a number of studies, Hawes and Smith (1973) reach the following conclusion:

> Communicative behaviors expressing conflict are functional in facilitating search and evaluation of information but dysfunctional in generating information and selecting outcomes (p. 433).

This suggests that groups in which members become committed to points of view are likely to do well in examining the validity of facts and ideas which are presented. On the other hand, there are two situations where conflict may not be productive: (1) If the primary purpose of the discussion is to produce a wide variety of opinions and solutions but not to test them, disagreement may inhibit the creative potential of the group members. In fact, in one form of this kind of discussion, called "brainstorming," criticism of ideas is not permitted, while "hitchhiking"—adding to the ideas of others—is encouraged. (2) If it is especially important that the group reach consensus on some kind of solution, and the quality of the decision is less important than the necessity of arriving at a unified position, conflict may be counterproductive. Early conflict may make later agreement more difficult.

In many—and perhaps most—cases, decision-making groups will be called on to perform all three of the functions described above. They must search and test facts *and* discover solutions *and* arrive at a decision. As we will show in the next chapter, successful groups with these multiple purposes tend to solve this problem by concentrating much (but certainly not all) of their conflict activity in the middle of the discussion process, but end with substantial agreement. Of course, this flexibility is enhanced when group members have developed positive attitudes toward and skills in the management of conflict, and that is much of what this chapter has been about.

There is a second issue, beyond group purposes, which must be considered in an evaluation of the advantages and limitations of conflict. How people judge the role of conflict in discussion will depend on their feelings toward disagreement, antagonism, and harmony. This brings us back to the subject of group norms, which we discussed in Chapter 6. Some people believe that, in the long run, more will be accomplished when members of groups and societies stress their similarities and de-emphasize their differences. There are some cultures which downplay disagreement and hostility at all costs. This is true, for example, of many Asian societies. Also note, however, that these same cultures are likely to stress status differences as a means of decision making and as a way of maintaining unity. Within the American society, there are those who argue that minority groups will do the most for their cause not by confronting the power structure and stressing their separateness but by proving themselves as individuals and assimilating, thus gaining acceptance.

We do not take an ethnocentric view which would imply condemnation of cultures which value harmony over conflict. But it should be clear to our readers where we stand with regard to the values of conflict in the context of the American society.

SUMMARY AND CONCLUSIONS

Although people tend to think of conflict as something negative, it ordinarily contributes to group effectiveness by getting participants involved, providing a safety valve for frustrations, strengthening bonds after the expression of disagreement, testing ideas, and insuring a fair hearing for innovative points of view. The risk in conflict is that it is time-consuming and can lead to group disintegration, so it must be dealt with skillfully. It is easiest to handle when it concerns means rather than goals and when its source can be clearly identified. Especially difficult is the situation in which "hidden agenda" of personality or status conflicts emerge as ideational disputes.

Various strategies may be employed in conflict situations. Powerful group members sometimes try to *avoid* or *suppress* conflict, but where an equal role is sought for all participants, strategies of *prolongation*, in which conflict is sustained so that the group does not break up, and strategies of *collaboration* are especially important. Ultimately, if a conflict of ideas is to be resolved, group members must collaborate in seeking consensus. This can often be achieved by finding out whether the disagreement rests on the level of assertion, reasoning, evidence, or values. However, when consensus cannot be obtained by these methods, the collaborative strategies of majority voting or arbitration can be employed.

Finally, although conflict has many advantages which can ordinarily be realized by the intelligent use of strategies, it also has its limitations. Unless valued by the group members, conflict will be dysfunctional. On the other hand, although conflict is necessary for the testing of ideas, groups need periods of relative harmony when creative ideas are generated and group choices are supported. Ways in which both kinds of activities can be employed are explored in the next two chapters on "The Process of Decision Making."

STUDY SUGGESTIONS

1. Do you agree with the general attitude toward conflict that we have presented here? Have we underplayed its negative features? Or overemphasized its values? Why do you feel as you do about it?
2. What did we mean when we said that "groups are 'inefficient' if they function as they should"? Do you agree?
3. What are the advantages and disadvantages of treating a hidden agenda status conflict as though it were a disagreement over ideas?
4. Observe a decision-making group in which conflict is likely because the group is composed of "representatives of various interest groups." You may want to tape-record the session, if possible, to improve your later analysis. Afterwards identify one or two critical areas of conflict and try to analyze the following: (a) How did the group explore the conflict? (b) What difficulties complicated their reaching an agreement? (c) What are some alternative approaches that might have been productive?
5. Write up a case report of a conflict in which you have participated or design a simple situation for role playing which involves proponents of fundamentally

different positions. Select players in class and have one class member play "negotiator," "group leader," or "facilitator" in a scene he or she did not design. See how effectively members of the class are able to keep a conflict open, productive, and free of personal attacks and hidden forms of derailment. Have the class analyze the effectiveness of the group in handling the conflict.

Chapter 9
The Process of Decision Making: Descriptive Approaches

A great deal of criticism has been leveled at the operation of the typical committee. Meetings seem to consume endless hours of valuable time only to lead to questionable decisions or to no decisions at all. The criticism comes from many quarters—from social scientists, from people in business, even from committee members themselves. Dissatisfaction with the conduct of policy-making bodies has led one wag to satirize a committee as "a group of the incompetent, appointed by the unwilling, to do the unnecessary." A somewhat more serious analysis of the situation was offered by Leland Bradford, who described the problem in these terms:

> Against this background of desperate need for understanding and skill in group productivity is the really tragic picture of the almost universal inability of people to operate effectively in group situations. Anyone familiar with the average committee, with its difficulties in reaching decisions, its incomplete discussions and immature ideas, its personality clashes and emotional stress, and its inability to move from decision into actions, should have no difficulty accepting this statement (Bradford, 1948, p. 3).

Apparently group members are also aware of this problem in their own deliberations. In one study, for example, participants in discussions commonly acknowledged their inability to organize themselves as a major source of dissatisfaction with the group process (Herrold, et al., 1953).

How should discussants attempt to improve the organization of problem solving in groups? Advice on this subject varies. Some authors suggest that group members devise a careful plan—an agenda—to follow throughout their discussion. We will refer to this as the "prescriptive approach." Others simply describe the results of research studies which show how trained, experienced, or reasonably successful groups go about organizing themselves and then recommend that the group "let nature take its course." The implication of this "descriptive approach" is that through awareness of what has been discovered about other groups and through their own experience, discussants will arrive at a "natural process" which will maximize their effectiveness.

We believe that advising group participants to follow their natural inclinations can be overdone. Sometimes groups need help in organizing themselves, and prescribing an agenda is one way of doing this. However, there are some good reasons why it often makes sense for groups to "dive in" with little planning. First, group members often need to learn not to get discouraged when the process of discussion does not run smoothly. This is especially true when the group experiences a good deal of conflict. A lack of structure can be frustrating, but a process that seems disorganized and chaotic may "organize itself" as the group goes along. Second there are some potential dangers in using an agenda: (1) The plan for discussion may not match the problem, and the group may waste a lot of energy trying to make the topic fit some ritualistic pattern. (2) An agenda can stifle creativity so that the process of associative thinking—following an idea in new and unexpected directions—is restricted. (3) People may lose emotional involvement and spontaneity and come to feel that they are just "going through the motions." (4) And, finally, an agenda can sometimes be manipulated to avoid or suppress conflict, even though conflict may be desirable.

At this point, we believe it would make sense to describe how people ordinarily behave—or, at least, how experienced discussants behave—before offering any prescriptions. So, first we will describe those "natural processes" revealed by studies of problem solving in small groups.

MICROPROCESSES IN POLICY-MAKING GROUPS

A "process" is anything which shows continual change over time. As we have tried to show in Chapter 2, "Group Communication: Transactions Within Systems," communication in general, and group discussion specifically, is certainly a phenomenon which shows continual change over time. If we can make sense out of the extremely complex activity of discussion—show some regularities within the continual change—we can throw some light on how group members can better manage the process.

There are two levels of abstraction on which we can view group process—the "microscopic" level and the "macroscopic" level. Literally, "microscopic" means "too small to be seen without magnification," while "macroscopic" means "visible to the naked eye." In the sense we employ these terms here, they are a matter of degree and not of kind. A "microscopic process" or "microprocess" refers to the level of short sequences of discrete comments or nonverbal acts. A "macroscopic process" or "macroprocess" refers to grosser changes. For example, a group may go through certain identifiable "phases" while working on a task, and this we may call the "macroprocess." The many brief exchanges occurring within these phases are microprocesses.

Scheidel and Crowell's "Reach-Test Model"

Scheidel and Crowell conducted a study of five trained discussion groups. Each group engaged in a two-hour discussion in which the members evaluated a local newspaper. The investigators tape-recorded the discussions and scored each contribution according to type of comment.

One might expect the essence of critical, decision-making discussion to consist of the initiation of ideas, followed by responses which *test* each idea. For example, one would ordinarily expect to spend a good deal of time disagreeing with an idea or else correcting and "honing" the initiated contribution by expressing it in a new form, modifying it in some way, or relating it to another idea. In fact, Scheidel and Crowell had categories for each of these kinds of idea-testing and idea-changing comments but very seldom found behaviors which matched these descriptions. Surprisingly, most of the comments on the contributions of others were very positive. A fourth of the contributions simply agreed with the ideas. Another fourth were devoted to clarifying (rephrasing) and substantiating (providing supporting evidence). Very little time was spent on extending, modifying, and synthesizing.

The typical pattern of responses went as follows: Someone would suggest a new idea. Then others would agree, add examples to clarify the point, and suggest that their information confirmed the assertion. Only very rarely did someone disagree with an idea, and this almost never happened right after a new idea was presented. Scheidel and Crowell call this process the "reach-test motion" of group thought. An idea is suggested; others essentially agree and verify the idea; and then, if at all, someone may criticize the idea in a negative way.

Scheidel and Crowell suggest that this seeming overabundance of positive reactions in a group is "probably basic to the loyalty to the group solution so often observed in participants in group discussions" (1964, p. 143). In other words, everyone has a chance to express himself or herself on each succeeding idea, if only in agreement. With this "anchor" of agreement, the group can move forward to make decisions. If most group members simply sat by while one or two others presented ideas, they would not feel the same commitment to the final solution. Thus, the group must "reach" (make sure everyone understands the idea) before it can "test" (criticize the idea when necessary) in order to "anchor" decisions in group commitment.

In a follow-up study on "feedback" in group decision making, Scheidel and Crowell (1966) provide data which suggest an additional, psychological explanation for why there was such a large quantity of positive responses in the groups they studied. It may be that group members engage in positive comments not only to make sure they have their say but also to provide a substantial amount of agreement (and implicit approval) to each other so that people will be encouraged to go on contributing.

In this investigation, Scheidel and Crowell focused on the occurrence of "feedback loops," sequences of events in which one person (X) initiates a comment, another person (Y) responds, and the first person (X) speaks again. Fully 35 percent of the total interaction was devoted to these XYX events. By far the most common Y or feedback response was a simple statement of agreement (34 percent). The original speaker (X) then usually voiced agreement (with the agreement of the other person to his or her own idea!) or further clarified his or her point. In short, it appears that in those instances where one person speaks, another responds, and the initial speaker talks again, the intervening comment *reinforces* what the speaker has said. The positive response of another seems to encourage the original speaker to talk again.

Imagine a very different set of circumstances: Each time a person speaks, someone else *disagrees* with him or her, or else the second speaker *modifies* the first speaker's idea in a significant way. At first, the tendency may be for the initial speaker to defend himself or herself. Or he or she might be uncertain that the second speaker got the idea completely, in which case the first speaker might attempt further clarification. But it is also possible that the first speaker will be silenced for the time being. After a while, if this pattern continues, he or she may stop contributing. Eventually, the discussion may grind to a halt, or at least a good deal of frustration and perhaps avoidance of the task may result.

The cumulative effect of continued disagreement or negative modification of ideas can be seen in the following example. There is often one committee member who continually engages in this kind of challenging behavior. He does not voice his negative contributions in an angry or destructive way, but rather his penchant for the exact use of language leads him to continually qualify and modify the statements of others. The feelings of a number of group members seem to be summarized by the comment made by one fellow group member after a meeting: "Doesn't *anything* satisfy him?"

If it is true that the microprocess of group discussion can ordinarily be described accurately as "reaching" or "anchoring" and that new ideas are usually positively reinforced, what happens when an initiated idea does receive almost immediate disagreement? A study by Gouran and Baird (1972) suggests the answer. These investigators observed a tendency of group members to *change the subject* shortly after a disagreement was expressed. Somewhere between two and four comments after an expression of disagreement, the group would proceed to a new topic. In other words, when the group did not discover an "anchor" of agreement readily, the theme was dropped rather abruptly, and group members began to search for a new source of agreement.

Implications of the "Reach-Test Model"

If it is assumed (as we have done in the previous chapter on conflict management) that the quality of a decision is enhanced by conflict—by disagreement—the results of the studies cited above are rather discouraging. The picture which emerges—at least the one based on the groups studied by Scheidel and Crowell and by Gouran and Baird—is that groups tend to evade conflict in their pursuit of consensus. Certainly, this is a danger. The findings may not be quite as hopeless as they seem, however. You should know that the averages reported by these investigators are based on entire discussions from beginning to end. Research to be reported in the next section of this chapter on "macroprocess" suggests that groups often enter a *conflict phase* after a period of relatively high agreement, and afterwards may return to a period of greater agreement. The disagreement occurring during a conflict phase of interaction could be overshadowed in a report of results based on the total number of contributions.

Another implication of these findings is that although groups need conflict for maximum productivity, from the point of view of cohesiveness, groups thrive on an abundance of agreement. Hopefully, group members can learn to accommodate a fair degree of conflict, but too much negative response that is not preceded by some positive reinforcement may be frustrating and prevent the achievement of consensus. Experience with receiving comments on papers and oral class presentations has familiarized students with this principle. If all of the teacher's comments are negative, the effect is demoralizing.

A final implication of the findings is that the average group may well need to build up its "conflict tolerance" muscles since the "natural" tendency is to avoid conflict. This can be done in various ways, such as verbalizing the positive values of conflict and expressing disagreement so that it is clear that the idea is being challenged but that the person is not being rejected, as we suggested in Chapter 8. We should add, however, that we have seen groups in which conflict is prevalent but not really accepted. Strong disagreement exists as a *pattern of behavior*, but not as a *norm* (i.e., a standard for behavior). Under such circumstances, extended periods of disagreement tend to be followed by objections to the group's "negativity" or by long silences and other forms of withdrawal. While this may be a rather rare occurrence, it does happen. Such groups need to work on increasing their tolerance level for disagreement just as much as do groups which agree too readily. Perhaps a combination of more clarification and substantiation *and* reassurances that disagreement is acceptable and productive is the antidote to this particular problem.

MACROPROCESSES IN POLICY-MAKING GROUPS

If we look at microprocess only, we miss the real complexity of decision making. Groups not only repeat certain patterns (anchoring, reinforcement, etc.), but they also *evolve* as they move toward agreement on a solution—they pass through certain stages or phases, each of which is characterized by certain kinds of activities. This is the macroprocess of the group.

Bales' "Equilibrium" Model

Robert Bales (1950) was the first to conduct controlled scientific studies of the phases of group process. He developed a method of studying group interaction which has been widely imitated. First, he established a set of categories for the purpose of classifying comments by type. Then, he had observers watch or listen to a group discussion and assign each comment to one and only one category.

Drawing on the theories of the sociologist Emil Durkheim, Bales developed a theory which guided his choice of categories. He conceived of all groups (whether entire societies, organizations, or small groups) as having two basic functions, two problems to solve. One was the "task" function: The group had some difficulty which it was trying to solve by means of collaborative decision making. The other function involved the "socio-emotional" or "maintenance" problem: holding the group together, making everyone feel that he or she has a part in the process.

These two functions are both necessary, said Bales, but they are also essentially in conflict with one another. As a group begins to work on a task, leaders begin to emerge. This causes some dissatisfaction on the part of the less influential group members, thus creating a "maintenance" problem. In Bales' view, a successful group has to establish a "balance" or "equilibrium" between these opposing forces, that is, to pay attention to both the task and the maintenance problems. It cannot focus only on the

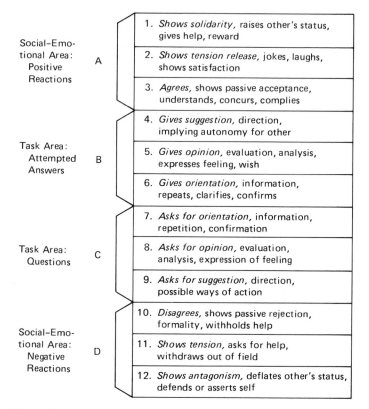

Social–Emotional Area: Positive Reactions   A

1. *Shows solidarity,* raises other's status, gives help, reward

2. *Shows tension release,* jokes, laughs, shows satisfaction

3. *Agrees,* shows passive acceptance, understands, concurs, complies

Task Area: Attempted Answers   B

4. *Gives suggestion,* direction, implying autonomy for other

5. *Gives opinion,* evaluation, analysis, expresses feeling, wish

6. *Gives orientation,* information, repeats, clarifies, confirms

Task Area: Questions   C

7. *Asks for orientation,* information, repetition, confirmation

8. *Asks for opinion,* evaluation, analysis, expression of feeling

9. *Asks for suggestion,* direction, possible ways of action

Social–Emotional Area: Negative Reactions   D

10. *Disagrees,* shows passive rejection, formality, withholds help

11. *Shows tension,* asks for help, withdraws out of field

12. *Shows antagonism,* deflates other's status, defends or asserts self

Figure 7 Interaction process categories defined and grouped by types. [From Robert F. Bales and Fred L. Strodbeck, "Phases in Group Problem Solving," *The Journal of Abnormal and Social Psychology* 46(1951): 486.]

task without creating socioemotional problems. On the other hand, it cannot work only on maintenance of interpersonal relations without abandoning the task.

The influence of Bales' theory on his category system can be seen in Figure 7. Six categories pertain to the task dimension—three for questions and three for answers. Six categories pertain to socioemotional contributions—three for positive responses and three for negative responses. By using the category system to score behavior in a large number of discussion groups, Bales (and his collaborators) found results which supported his theory. The findings of Bales and Strodtbeck are presented in Figure 8. You will notice certain features about the socioemotional responses: (1) Positive responses outnumber negative responses in every phase. Perhaps this trend is similar to the findings of Scheidel and Crowell in the sense that groups not only may need more agreeing than disagreeing responses, but they also may need more positive than negative emotional "strokes." (2) Negative responses increase from the first to the second phases and

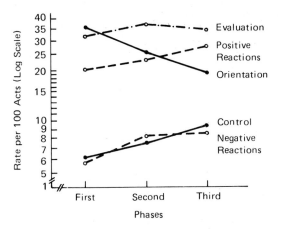

Figure 8 Relative frequency of acts by type and phase, based upon twenty-two sessions. [From Robert F. Bales and Fred L. Strodbeck, "Phases in Group Problem Solving," *The Journal of Abnormal and Social Psychology* 46(1951): 488.]

then level off toward the end of the decision-making process; that is, the "maintenance" problem sets in as group members of lesser influence begin to respond negatively.

In the meantime, certain changes are occurring phase-by-phase in the contributions which are directly related to the task (categories 4–9). Bales and Strodtbeck say that groups go through three stages in working on the task: orientation, evaluation, and control. This does not mean that groups *only* "orient" (ask for and give information) in the first phase, *only* evaluate (ask for and give opinions) in the second phase, and *only* control (make procedural suggestions, arrive at conclusions) in the third phase. Rather, it means that each of these activities reaches its *peak* in one of these phases. Orientation is at its maximum in the first phase, evaluation in the second phase, and control in the last.

Control increases steadily throughout the three phases; that is, group members make more and more procedural suggestions as they go along, offering comments like "Why don't we discuss this solution first?" And, as they get toward the end of the decision-making process, it is more and more likely that they will say "Can we drop this idea, then?" Or they will conclude, "We all seem to be in agreement on this solution."

From these results, one can see the interplay of the task and the socioemotional dimensions of the group process: (1) As the group begins, information-giving predominates. There is a need for positive emotional responses at this point, but not as much as will be needed later. (2) When more opinions are expressed and the group begins to arrive at some tentative decisions, some people will emerge as leaders, and, as a result, others will be less satisfied with their roles. Furthermore, the closer the group gets to making a decision, the more restricted members will begin to feel, causing them to experience greater tension. In this kind of emotional climate, the negative socioemotional responses occur more frequently, and these will be balanced by more positive socioemotional responses. In other words, the negative reactions of some group members will be expressed, thus "bleeding off" negative feelings to some degree. (3) This may be necessary before the group can proceed to the final stage where control reaches its peak and group members are finally able to agree on a decision.

What are the implications of Bales' model for the practice of discussion? Whether or not one accepts Bales and Strodtbeck's interpretations of their data in their entirety, this research does make a contribution to our understanding of the process of decision making by showing the importance of the socioemotional dimension of group interaction. One implication is that the way people feel about the group and one another can influence how they work together on a task. For example, it often happens that a person who has found himself or herself disagreed with consistently or who has had trouble getting into the conversation later disagrees with others or expresses a negative reaction by withdrawing or making an antagonistic remark. Another closely related implication is that the process of gaining the emotional commitment of group members takes time and should not be short-circuited. A group which ignores the way people feel about their roles and attempts to suppress emotional reactions does so at its peril.

Fisher's Model of Decision Emergence

While Bales stressed the interplay of the task and socioemotional dimensions of groups, some later investigators have focused more narrowly on task behavior. The work of Aubrey Fisher is especially interesting because he was able to describe in detail the intricacies of the idea-exchange aspects of group process. Fisher (1970a) used a method of exploring group phases which was similar to that of Bales in that he employed a system of categories to record the behaviors of group members as they worked their way to a final decision. However, his approach differed in two ways: First, he did not include categories for socioemotional responses; second, he did not record all task responses but simply studied what happened each time a solution was proposed, recording the responses which related to each proposal. Fisher came up with four phases which seemed to characterize the "decision emergence" process of the ten groups he studied. The phases are called orientation, conflict, emergence, and reinforcement.

1. *Orientation.* Fisher found that when group members first begin discussing, they spend a good deal of time agreeing with one another and giving information which clarifies the proposals made by others. In addition,

they very seldom disagree with one another in this phase, but rather express their ideas *ambiguously*. It is as though they do not want to offend others by stating a definite point of view, or they do not want to take a position which they might have to repudiate later. Rather, they "hedge" somewhat, leaving the door open for themselves to disagree with others later. In this phase, seldom is a favorable response to an idea followed by another favorable response. Rather, the group members tend to skip from one idea to another, voicing agreement briefly in a tentative form, and then moving on to a new idea.

2. Conflict. As the tentative expressions of the orientation phase begin to disappear, disputes arise in the second phase. Disagreeing responses become much more common while ambiguous statements subside. Group members tend to *polarize* on two sides of each proposal, with each person reinforcing the ideas proposed by his or her side and opposing those of the opposition.

3. Emergence. In the third phase, group members tend to soften their stands. Numerous ambiguous statements are made, much like the first phase, but the difference between this and the orientation phase is that the group members are no longer casting about for ideas, but rather are "mellowing" in their opposition. Their ambiguous statements in this phase are a prelude to agreement, and more agreeing statements are voiced. Polarization tends to dissipate.

4. Reinforcement. During the emergence phase, group members have more or less arrived at a decision. Yet, in the reinforcement phase, they go on talking about it, continuing to provide evidence in support of the emergent decision. Ambiguous statements also decline. It is as though the group feels the need to reassure themselves that they have made the right decision. They "reinforce" one another and coalesce in consensus.

The model described above sketches in broad outline form the phases that groups tend to go through as they work toward consensus. However, it leaves two important questions unanswered. How do group members work out the conflicts that occur among them? And while this is going on, what happens to specific decision proposals which are brought up?

THE PROCESS OF CONFLICT INTERACTION

Ellis and Fisher (1975) explored the first of these questions in a study where they examined brief episodes of "conflict," defined as instances where disagreement was expressed in a group. They traced what kinds of comments were most likely to *follow* statements which were unfavorable to a specific decision proposal. They found that, early in the discussion, group participants were likely to give information just after someone objected to an idea; the conflict was avoided by an excursion into more neutral data. Later, however, group members were more likely to follow up on an objection to a solution by further objecting; that is, more participants began to agree with the person disagreeing with a proposal as the discussion progressed. Still later, however, they tended not to follow objections with further objections; disagreement with proposals "died out." In other words, having avoided head-on conflict early in the discussion when various solutions were expressed, they then went on to a period of more intense conflict in order to test their proposals and finally began to accept a certain solution by no longer supporting objections to it. Thus, the ultimate solution "survives" conflict.

THE PROCESS OF DECISION MODIFICATION

The second issue concerns what happens to the specific proposals while a group is working out its disagreements. One possibility would be that group members might keep bringing up new solutions throughout the discussion. If this were the case, each solution would be eliminated as opposition developed, and finally someone would have to come up with an idea against which there was little objection, thereby achieving consensus. Obviously, if this were the way the process operated, it would be rather dangerous for participants to bring up a good idea early in the discussion. Also, the group might soon run out of fresh ideas, and the discussion would be stalemated.

Fortunately, this does not seem to be the way groups function, as Fisher (1970b) discovered in a study of "decision modification." The group does not have to continually come up with new ideas. Rather, old ideas are "reborn," often in modified form; that is, the first time a solution is suggested, it is likely to draw some opposition, or else the topic may be simply dropped. Later the idea may reappear, usually in altered form if there were objections to the idea the first time it was brought up. The same basic solution may go through a number of such transformations before it is accepted. Ideas which do not continue to reemerge in new form do not survive. This is what Fisher calls the "decision modification process."

IMPLICATIONS OF FISHER'S THEORY

If Fisher's model is an accurate representation of the phases through which successful groups progress in reaching a decision, what does this suggest about how groups ought to manage their macroprocess? First, as we have argued in Chapter 8, conflict is a natural, essential feature of group discussion. But group members must also get along with one another, and perhaps they can only tolerate extensive disagreement for a certain length of time. They might work out this problem by having a conflict phase during which disagreement is especially prevalent in their interaction. It should be noted that Fisher's conclusions do not suggest that disagreement occurs *only* in the conflict phase. Rather, a certain amount of disagreement occurs throughout group decision making. But there is more disagreement in the second phase, and at this time people stick to their positions more tenaciously than they do at other times.

Earlier in this chapter, when discussing the "microprocess" of groups, we said that an assertion was much more likely to be followed by a favorable than an unfavorable comment and that when disagreement did occur, the topic was soon dropped. This conclusion, which suggests that groups tend to avoid conflict, must now be qualified. It is not that groups evade conflict altogether. Rather, they *concentrate* on conflict in the second phase of their activity; then, they go on to phases when they are less certain about ideas and more likely to agree with others (emergence), and, finally, to a phase when they agree with and support one another strongly (reinforcement). In effect, they "get it over with," although certainly *not* completely, in the conflict phase, thus securing for themselves the productive advantages of conflict without having the communication break down altogether.

A second implication of Fisher's findings is that a successful group probably should go through all four stages. Consider the possible consequences of "skipping" phases:

1. If orientation is circumvented and the group plunges directly into conflict, members are in danger of creating a hostile atmosphere in which the positions which members take seem arbitrary and uncompromising.
2. If the conflict phase does not occur, a superficial solution may emerge. Possibly the group will have to undo this decision later.
3. If, on the other hand, the group never "emerges" from conflict, no conclusion can be reached.
4. The absence of the final reinforcement phase might not be as critical an error as the omission of an earlier phase from the point of view of the group's product, but the satisfaction which the participants feel toward the group consensus may be reduced.

PHASES IN EXPERIENTIAL GROUPS

The steps or phases that a group goes through will depend in part on the purpose of the group. Certain phases have been observed in psychotherapy and encounter groups whose processes are somewhat different from those found in policy-making groups. Such groups have certain distinctive features in common. Their primary purpose is for people to become more sensitive to emotions—to their own feelings as well as those of others. Unlike policy-making groups, *interpersonal relations* are the problem to be solved. The leader ordinarily gives less "help" than group members initially expect. Group members soon learn that they are supposed to help themselves, for the most part, rather than depend on the leader as the sole source of insight.

At first, it may seem to you that we have abandoned the topic of "decision-making processes" in discussing the stages of experiential groups. In fact, however, groups which are oriented primarily toward interpersonal relations and individual goals must make decisions, although these are of a different type than those of policy-making groups. Even in a casual group, where individual as opposed to group goals receive maximum emphasis, decisions may be made, although this may involve something as simple as a group conclusion to move from the dining room (after a meal) to the living room to continue a conversation. Cathartic groups make decisions about such matters as whether to demand that all group members take part or whether the discussion will be highly personal or more abstract. These decisions tend to be more procedural than substantive—more related to the internal functioning of the group itself than to external problems which the group confronts—that is, unlike policy-making groups, they seldom make recommendations to pass on to someone else, but rather make recommendations to themselves about how to proceed.

Tuckman (1965) and Tuckman and Jensen (1977) arrived at conclusions about the phases which are ordinarily followed in experiential groups by surveying a large number of studies by others concerned primarily with psychotherapy and human relations groups. Two kinds of activities were identified—those oriented toward interpersonal relations (group structure) and those involving decision making (task activity). These were seen as functioning together in each of several distinct phases (see Table 1).

We may draw certain implications from Tuckman's work for the practice of experiential group discussion. Just as in the case of the phases in policy-making groups, certain "pathologies" of group process may occur when the phases do not occur as they ordinarily do in successful groups.

1. Forming. The group may grasp at an easy and premature solution to the problem of dependence. For example, members may appoint a substitute leader, adopt a superficial topic, or lapse into apathy. It is fairly rare, however, for such groups to stagnate at this level.

2. Storming. Rather than entering this phase, the group members might engage in avoiding conflict at all cost. One way of doing this would be to plead with the leader to give them direction. Or, the group might become

Table 1   PHASES FOLLOWED IN EXPERIENTIAL GROUPS

	GROUP STRUCTURE	TASK ACTIVITY
PHASE 1: "FORMING"	Testing and dependence. [Here, the first reactions of the group members to the unexpected abdication of the leader may be seen. What ways of relating interpersonally will be accepted by the group are explored. Members are especially concerned with what the leader expects.]	Orientation to the task. [In the absence of strong leader direction, the group members try to decide on goals and "ground rules."]
PHASE 2: "STORMING"	Intragroup conflict. [Group members begin to respond with frustration to the lack of structure brought about by the nondirective stance of the leader. Resistance as various group members attempt to fill this perceived "vacuum" can be seen.]	Emotional response to task demands. [As goals and group rules begin to emerge, members resist not only the leadership of others, but also the emerging requirements for goal-directed behavior.]
PHASE 3: "NORMING"	Development of group cohesion. [Frustration and hostility can only be endured for so long. They give way to acceptance of the idiosyncrasies of other group members. Harmony is stressed.]	Open exchange of relevant interpretations. [Group members begin to agree on ways of dealing with one another. Certain norms are established. For example, group members may agree to talk about personal problems (in therapy groups, especially) or to openly express feelings about the behavior of other group members (in encounter groups, especially).]

Table 1   PHASES FOLLOWED IN EXPERIENTIAL GROUPS *(Continued)*

	GROUP STRUCTURE	TASK ACTIVITY
PHASE 4: "PERFORMING"	Functional role relatedness. [Group members accept the roles that others take. Some individuals may concentrate on confronting others, some on providing support, and others on "energizing."]	Emergence of solutions. [Insights begin to emerge concerning the interpersonal processes of the group (in encounter groups, especially), or group members may discover constructive possibilities for individual change (in therapy groups, especially).]
PHASE 5: "ADJOURNING"[a]	Anxiety about separation and positive feelings toward the leader. [Group members frequently express regret about leaving one another and appreciation to the leader for his or her role.]	Termination review. [Discussion of the entire experience. Individuals often talk about what they have learned and how they plan to act on their new insights. The role of the leader and other "unfinished business" may be examined.]

SOURCE: Adapted from B. W. Tuckman, "Developmental Sequences in Small Groups," *Psychological Bulletin* 63 (1965): 384–399; also B. W. Tuckman and M. A. C. Jensen, "Stages of Small Group Development Revised," *Group and Organization Studies* 2 (1977): 419–427.

[a] The "adjourning" phase was not included in Tuckman's original formulation (Tuckman, 1965), but was added in a later review of literature (Tuckman and Jensen, 1977). Tuckman and Jensen acknowledge the work of Mann (1967) and Spitz and Sadock (1973) in the discovery of this fifth phase.

apathetic or resort to discussing trivia in order to circumvent frustration and hostility.

3. Norming. The group might fail to arrive at a substantial level of group cohesion and the establishment of norms for behavior. Frustration from phase two might never be resolved, and the group could break up into subgroups. Such results could occur, for example, if members of a therapy group refuse to discuss personal problems or if members of an encounter group resist giving one another personal feedback.

4. Performing. Failure at this phase might come from a lack of commitment to established group standards. This might be precipitated by the withdrawal of some group members.

5. Adjourning. The omission of this phase is very unlikely if the other four phases have been accomplished. However, the introduction of "new business" at a late point or the inability of the group to resolve some interpersonal issue before running out of time might short-circuit the termination process and leave group members with feelings of incompleteness.

However, even when a group does not successfully complete all the phases, the experience may not be totally worthless for all group members. Individuals may discover how they respond to others emotionally and may receive valuable feedback from others about their own behavior, even though group unity and involvement is not achieved. Likewise, those who withdraw may experience their inability to become involved and resolve to change this tendency in themselves.

When the phases are not completed, however, there remains the possibility that group members may find the experience frustrating and may be unclear about what learning has taken place. It is for this reason that the leader—the therapist or group facilitator—should be aware of the stages which such groups tend to experience. This knowledge may be useful in helping the group have a satisfying and complete experience. Or, in those kinds of groups where the leader is very nondirective and tries not to influence the process in a major way, the information can be used to give group members insight into the process after it is completed.

We may also draw implications for task groups from the information on experiential group processes. You may notice that Tuckman's stages are roughly similar to Fisher's phases for policy-making groups. Forming is similar to orientation in its tentativeness; storming is certainly a type of conflict; norming, like emergence, involves group agreement; and performing, similar to reinforcement, is the process of acting on agreements. The adjourning phase probably occurs to some extent in policy-making as well as experiential groups, although Fisher apparently leaves it out because it does not affect decision emergence and is perhaps less prominent in the kinds of groups he studied. The main difference between the two situations is that the decisions made in the therapy or encounter groups concern interpersonal relations themselves—how the group members should deal with one another on a feeling level—whereas the policy-making group makes decisions on task matters which are external to the group, the decision ordinarily being passed on to another body for further consideration or action.

Although it is possible that the similarity between the two models is more apparent than real, that it consists simply of a superficial likeness of the terms used to describe phases in each model, it seems more probable that something similar to the phases of experiential groups occurs in policy-making groups in diluted form. If we accept the idea suggested earlier in this chapter that groups must work out their emotional relations in order to be maximally effective in achieving a task, then it makes sense that policy-making groups are going through both processes at the same time. In fact, we could also reverse the analogy and say that it is possible that an experiential group, in which interpersonal relations is the focus, must go through phases which are similar to those of policy-making groups, but which also are in diluted form.

SUMMARY AND CONCLUSIONS

The content of this chapter can best be understood in light of an idea which has been repeated throughout this book: namely, that a group is a *system* a self-regulating entity with interdependent parts. From this perspective, the tendency of groups to agree more than disagree can be seen as a system-maintaining activity. People talk more when they are reinforced, and thus each group member is to some degree dependent on others for support. Also, widespread participation helps hold the group together, even though at times this amounts to little more than passive agreement on the part of some members. Likewise, the preponderance of positive socioemotional reactions combined with the gradual "bleeding off" of a lesser number of negative socioemotional responses also serves this bonding function.

While agreement and positive reactions may help the group survive *internally* and make a contribution to the motivation of the members and to the commitment that they feel to carrying out their conclusions, it does not in itself assure that the group will survive *externally*. To succeed in their task function, the members must also achieve a *viable* solution.

In the process of accomplishing the task, the group needs ideational leadership. This means that some people may become more prominent than others. When this process of leadership emergence goes on long enough, when the group devotes itself almost exclusively to the task for an extended period of time, there will ordinarily be strains which cause the group to devote attention to internal relations, temporarily pushing the task into the background. On each occasion when this happens, however, the group must eventually return to its primary function—the task. The system realigns itself and moves on.

Task performance requires that the group regulate not only the balance of task and socioemotional activities but also thinking processes; that is, there must be a certain amount of checking of ideas by disagreement and conceptual modification. This conflict goes on throughout the group interaction, but it is likely to be especially prominent in a conflict phase somewhere toward the middle of the discussion. On the other hand, the group members are likely to begin and end their deliberations with more positive responses to one another's ideas. In this way, both system change and system maintenance are facilitated in the process of idea exchange.

Drawing on the research of Fisher and Tuckman, we have suggested that the phases which characterize policy-making groups (orientation, conflict, emergence, and reinforcement) are rather similar to the first four phases of experiential groups (forming, storming, norming, and performing). Fisher refers to the former process as "decision emergence." The latter might be called "group culture emergence." Since every group has both task and maintenance dimensions, it seems likely that both processes are going on simultaneously in every group. Which set of phases is more prominent or more obvious depends on purpose, that is, whether the group is oriented more toward task or maintenance functions.

The picture of policy-making groups which emerges is one of members as rather cautious decision makers who stress agreement and harmony. Ideational conflict has been viewed as a necessary and important activity, but one which is emphasized less in the total quantity of group interaction. While we believe that the general impression we have created is accurate in terms of most groups, the degree to which agreement predominates over ideational conflict may vary considerably. Those groups which have been studied in the investigations on which our conclusions are based consisted largely of college students who probably did not have a high stake in the outcome of discussion and who may have been stressing their abilities to reach agreement within the somewhat artificial contexts of the studies. We have witnessed other kinds of situations in which disagreement was more in evidence throughout the discussion process, but in which consensus and feelings of satisfaction among group members were nevertheless achieved. In addition, it should be recognized that "natural process" is not the only choice available to groups. When circumstances such as a strong clash of interests warrant the use of a "prescriptive approach," an agenda may be employed to bring about greater control of the decision-making process. This is the subject of the next chapter.

STUDY SUGGESTIONS

1. Sit in as an observer on the meetings of at least three different decision-making groups. How similar or different are their macroprocesses and microprocesses to those described in this chapter?
2. Would you expect to find the kinds of processes described in this chapter at a meeting of labor and management negotiators hammering out a contract or at a meeting of diplomats working on an international agreement? Why or why not?
3. Make several copies of Bales' or Fisher's categories so that you can assign each message in a group discussion to the appropriate category, perhaps using one sheet for each 15 minutes. When you finish, calculate the highest to lowest frequency categories (types of messages) for the group as a whole and for each member of the group. Does this profile allow you to evaluate the meeting you

observed? What does the group seem to concentrate on? What types of contributions does it avoid? Who plays what roles in the group? What would you interpret to be the norms of the group you observed?

4. Record several meetings of a group to which you belong. Select one of these and do a personal analysis of your own role and contribution to the group. Do you make certain kinds of contributions and avoid others? Do you have a wide variety of communicative roles, or a narrow set of them? What sorts of skills should you develop to become a more flexible and constructive group member?

Chapter 10
The Process of Decision Making: Prescriptive Approaches

Although "doing what comes naturally" is appealing to many people, after sober reflection we realize that many if not most great accomplishments—whether in the arts, technology, sports, or even love-making—are the result of some degree of self-conscious attention to methodology. Indeed, in a methods-oriented society like ours it is surprising that we have paid as little attention as we have to devising prescriptions for the improvement of processes of interpersonal and small group communication.

This is not to say, with respect to group decision making, that it will *always* be desirable for the members to concern themselves with their procedures; doing what comes naturally may often be best. Nor is it to say that there is only *one* right way for a decision-making group to proceed. There are a number of alternative strategies for increasing system and order in discussion, and the best approach will depend on the nature of the task a policy-making group confronts. But before any group can decide what plan to adopt, there is a more basic issue to be considered, and that involves the amount of control it is desirable for a group to impose on itself.

FACTORS IN DETERMINING THE APPROPRIATE DEGREE OF ORGANIZATION

When we discuss, should we move from point to point in a systematic way, or should we go wherever our individual thoughts and feelings and the corrective reactions of others take us? The research that has been conducted to date gives us only a little help in answering this question. At this writing, we know of only one study which directly compares structured and unstructured discussion in terms of the quality of the final product. Larson (1969) had different groups use one of three types of agenda or no agenda at all to solve problems for which a "best answer" had been previously determined by experts. He found that groups using two particular agenda plans found the best answer more often than did groups using no agenda. However, the third kind of agenda plan was not more effective than no plan at all, so the results of this study were not conclusive. Even if there were more studies, however, and their results were rather unequivocal, we would not have a definitive answer. We must also consider philosophical outlooks and individual taste affecting the balance we want to achieve—or that is healthy to achieve—between freedom and control.

For example, in preparing for a vacation, many of us reject the notion of planning and prefer to leave decisions about our trip to chance. We want to go where the spirit moves us, stay wherever we find an attractive lodge or inn, wander off the beaten track in hope of finding something unusual and exciting. Often the high point of such a trip, and one that we delight in telling friends about for years afterwards, is a discovery that everyone else missed because they slavishly followed a prearranged plan and never deviated from it.

But following this method can also lead to misadventure. After a long day's journey, we sometimes are unable to find a place to stay. We may run out of gas in an isolated part of the country or find, to our disappointment, that the coffee shop we stumble upon is a "discovery" all right, but one that would never merit a connoisseur's rating. Then we may remember other trips when we followed a recommended itinerary. We may have been irked, at times, by sticking so closely to a plan, but we travelled the most scenic routes and when we arrived at our destination, tired and hungry, a good meal and pleasant room were waiting for us.

This same theme—of conflict between disciplined and spontaneous approaches to problems—also pervades the arts. Some creative artists work consciously and deliberately, others by intuition. A number of painters, dramatists, and musicians say that they work according to a plan, step by step. They have in their mind's eye a rather carefully worked out model of what they are trying to do and are constantly aware of how nearly they are coming to realize their conception in stone or on canvas. However, many equally talented artists follow their inspirations of the moment. One line across a canvas dictates another; a mass of color here requires a balancing mass there; and so on until the painting is finished. If one were to ask sculptors who work according to this principle what they were trying to sculpt, they might answer with only a shrug of the shoulders, for such people do not know where the hammer and chisel will lead. The statue created is not something formed according to a blueprint prepared in advance, but something which is discovered in the stone or the clay.

Fortunately, we do not have to answer the question of freedom and control one way or the other for all situations. Individual circumstances are too highly variant to justify stating formulas for determining whether or not an agendum should be used in every possible case. What we can do, however, is to call attention to some of the factors which you will need to consider in making a decision about the degree of organization to be followed in a given situation.

Time and Size

Among the factors which influence whether or not a group will approach its problem spontaneously are some that are purely administrative in character. If a committee has little time in which to solve a complicated problem, it may wish to adopt a plan of some sort to reduce the time wasted on irrelevant matters. If deadlines are to be taken seriously, then members of the committee will expect and usually accept some restriction on how they contribute to a meeting. When there is no deadline, however, some relaxation in, or complete abolition of, procedural limitations might be indicated.

Also, as the group grows in size, greater self-control as well as greater group control may prove desirable in the interest of keeping order, in providing openings for less aggressive committee members, or in maintaining some connections between remarks. Committees of four, five, or six people can enjoy a freedom from formal procedures that might lead to chaos in a group of 20 or 30 people. The extent to which we accept spontaneity in behavior is somewhat linked to the size of any group.

The Nature of the Problem

The nature of the problem being discussed and the attitudes of group members toward it are factors that should also influence the decision about the degree of control. As problems become increasingly difficult to unravel, more systematic investigation may be necessary. It is a relatively simple matter to follow a conversation about homecoming arrangements or about the hiring and firing policies in a small company. But when groups begin to talk about our foreign policy in the Middle East or try to thread their way through the planning of a complicated budget, the same casualness may interfere with intelligent decision making. When group members are involved with more complex questions, it is difficult for them to make sense unless each contribution is somehow related to the issue being discussed.

The depth of people's emotional involvement in the problem also deserves consideration. When we discuss matters about which we have strong feelings—when there is likely to be a high level of ego-involvement—it may be difficult for members to follow a plan. To control thinking either tends to make the airing of honest feelings difficult or disguises them so that they become more difficult to understand. As the problem becomes more complex, more careful control of the meeting seems to be indicated. Yet, as groups discuss sensitive issues on which committee members have strong, if not violent, feelings, less and less control seems feasible.

The Purposes of the Group

The different motives that prompt people to hold a meeting also affect the degree of planning which the members find helpful. As we found earlier, the members of cathartic groups are likely to find that adopting an agenda is incompatible with their purpose of establishing close interpersonal relationships with one another as a basis for sharing feelings. In a learning group, such as a seminar at a university, where the principal objective is to provoke new ideas, we would also expect to find a high degree of "freewheeling" to stimulate original thinking on the part of students. Decision-making groups, on the other hand, often find that in order to complete their investigation of a problem, they need some sort of guide so they will be certain to give all vital issues the consideration they deserve. At the same time we must remember that feelings are also expressed in policy-making groups. For example, company officials are likely to be emotionally involved in carrying out a reorganization of a large company, particularly when it involves their own position in the hierarchy of administration. We must avoid making too sharp a distinction between what Mortimer Adler called "heart-to-heart" and "mind-to-mind" talk.

Personal Desire for Order

It is clear, both from personal observation and from psychoanalytic writing, that each of us can tolerate different amounts of order and disorder in our lives. This is often evident in the way we respond even to physical objects in our environment. Some people are made uncomfortable by a misplaced chair or a picture that hangs slightly askew, while others seem perfectly at ease in chaotic environments.

This is true of our relations with people as well as with objects. Some people need to "know their place" or to know what procedures are to be followed. They are uncomfortable when the exact role they are to play or the method of discussion is not defined. These group members experience mild to serious anxiety when thrown into ambiguous situations in which they are expected to relate to others in informal ways. Often they are people who prefer to be formally introduced, who like to work under an elected chairperson and secretary, and who feel that procedural rules will allow everyone "to get along better and accomplish more." To a large extent, these reactions reflect a low tolerance for spontaneous human relationships and, according to some, an "escape from freedom." One way of protecting oneself from the need to behave spontaneously is to get the group to operate on the basis of formal rules.

As we have suggested, the justifications for adopting any sort of organizational plan in a group include more than just an emotional need for order. Some demands for control are quite rational and spring from the nature of the problem being confronted or the purposes of the group. Even though there may be no justification other than the fact that the group is composed of people who cannot do without formal rules to regulate their participation, their desire for a plan may have to be honored if the discussion is to succeed. However, the coin has another side. If some committee members have grown accustomed to operating spontaneously and informally, it may prove equally difficult to get them to adopt controls when the situation demands some regulation of participation.

Interpersonal Attitudes

Finally we need to consider the sorts of attitudes group members have toward one another. For example, to disregard the factor of hostility when labor and management begin negotiating after a long and bitter strike is to be naive about human behavior. The anger people feel toward those with whom they disagree, either because of the organizations they represent or because of interpersonal frictions growing out of earlier incidents, cannot be overlooked in deciding procedural questions. It is even more difficult to know what to do when the group is made up of people who hide deep suspicions of one another behind a smoke screen of amiability.

That this is an important factor in deciding on the character of the agenda is apparent from experience in many areas of negotiation. Unfriendly nations almost always insist on establishing a detailed agenda before beginning high-level talks, while nations enjoying friendly relations generally do not. This same rule holds true for talks between different segments of a community, competing corporate entities, and special interest groups of all kinds. It is also illustrated at the level of ordinary social intercourse; people normally are more "cool" or formal with each other when they first meet or after a falling-out. Later, when they get to understand each other better, this formality may be dropped.

In some cases, groups which start out by following a very flexible plan may find that later they must resort to stricter control. This may mean that members have become more aware of the difficulties they face in solving the problem, or it may mean that something has gone sour in their relationships. In either event, whether procedures are set up as a precaution at the outset of a meeting or later as a consequence of interaction among participants, the adopting of elaborate procedural machinery in a group underscores a basic fact—that frank and uninhibited expression is fostered by an accepting and permissive atmosphere. When people do not respect each other, protection through rules or regulations is sometimes necessary.

On the other hand, procedural control may not always be the answer. This is especially true if the hostile feelings experienced are more important to the group members than the desire to solve the problem they share. Participants may express their anger in indirect ways by withdrawing from the discussion or by engaging in cutting remarks. Under these conditions, it is possible that little progress will be made on substantive issues, despite the use of a plan for discussion. Thus, it may be helpful for the group members to clear the air by expressing their reactions to one another in an open and direct manner. Even if the interpersonal hostilities are not entirely resolved, the group can better distinguish ideational from personality and status clashes.

AGENDA PATTERNS: STRATEGIES FOR ORGANIZING GROUP THINKING

Let us assume that the members of a group are aware of the factors that might increase or decrease their need for procedural restrictions and that they have chosen to exercise some kind of formal control over their process. There are several ways that this can be done. The group can appoint a leader to regulate the interaction, perhaps calling on certain people to speak, summarizing the progress of the discussion, and deciding when to move on to a new topic. In effect, the leader determines the agenda by his or her acts. The group can also employ parliamentary procedure, a method which determines the rules by which topics are introduced, proposals are made and modified, discussion of topics is terminated, and votes are taken. In this case, a guide such as *Robert's Rules of Order* or a formal set of procedures drawn up by the group in advance will be employed. A designated leader, or perhaps, a parliamentarian, will be required to interpret and enforce the rules. Finally, the group may develop an agenda, a plan for the steps the group will take. This may or may not entail the use of an appointed leader or parliamentary procedure, depending on what degree of control the group deems necessary.

Parliamentary procedure is especially useful when it is necessary for the group to adopt formal resolutions in order to provide a record of actions taken by the membership. Since the rules are complex and are not ordinarily used in the kinds of small decision-making groups discussed in this book, this approach will not be examined in detail. The advantages and disadvantages of an appointed or elected leader will be examined in the next chapter. So, for the present, we will limit our discussion of the topic of control to the use of agendas.

Suppose that the group members favor the idea of an agenda and that they wish to discuss the pattern of organization and make a cooperative decision about it. What they need to know are the choices they have among various agenda patterns so they can select the one strategy which fits their situation best. It will also be useful for the group members to know what research shows about the effectiveness of each agenda plan. There have been a number of empirical studies comparing various systems of organization with one another. We will cite the relevant evidence when we discuss each of these systems, but we want to alert you to certain weaknesses of these studies: (1) Groups are ordinarily given an hour or so to reach a decision; therefore, agendas which are complex and difficult to learn are probably not given a fair test. (2) The tasks given laboratory groups do not always fit the kinds of agenda being tested. Because of these limitations of research conclusions, we will rely on an amalgam of the available knowledge from research and our own experience and judgment in assessing the usefulness of each type of agendum.

Agenda Based on Reflective Thinking

The most carefully worked out set of recommendations for improving human decision making and, therefore, the one which we shall study in the greatest detail is based on a mode of analytic thinking called the "reflective pattern of thought."

Reflective thinking was first described in a slim volume written by John Dewey which appeared in 1910 and was destined to become something of a classic. It was called, simply, *How We Think*. It was an attempt on the part of this well-known philosopher to distinguish among the various kinds of mental activity in which human beings engage in solving a wide variety of problems. Not only did the author describe how we *do* think—using intuition, reverie, creative imagination—but he also formulated how we *ought* to think. He found that scientists in their investigations of physical and social phenomena have followed a method that has been instrumental in the great discoveries they have made. As Dewey and many others since him have noted, it is not the *results* of science that can be transferred from one field to another, it is the *method* of science. From the records of their achievements he attempted to distill the elements which were a part of scientific thinking and to make them applicable to the solving of social problems. In his opinion, human affairs would be greatly improved if the methods of science were applied to the solving of social, political, and economic problems.

To think reflectively requires both an *attitude* and a *method*. According to Dewey, reflective thinking begins with the "active, persistent, and careful consideration of any belief or supposed form of knowledge in the light of the grounds that support it and the further conclusions to which it tends" (1910, p. 6). This implies that reflection starts with an inclination on the part of the problem solver to find better, more dependable beliefs on which to base his or her actions. It would be useless to follow the pattern of reflective thinking while violating the whole *spirit* of reflection. When people do not sincerely want or urgently need more valid and objective conclusions, reflective thinking is not going to help them.

As to the method of reflection, Dewey states that it is a unique way of thinking. "Reflection," he says, "involves not simply a sequence of ideas, but a *con*-sequence—a consecutive ordering in such a way that each determines the next as its proper outcome, while each outcome in turn leans back on, or refers to, its predecessors" (1933 edition, p. 4). Thus, reflective thinking begins with the desire on the part of the problem solvers to form more valid conclusions and leads to an organization of their thinking so that they will move logically from one issue or one part of the problem to the next.

Dewey finds there are five major steps in this sequence. The best description is found in the original 1910 edition and is as follows:

1. The occurrence of some difficulty.
2. Location and definition of the problem.
3. The formulation of possible hypotheses or solutions.
4. The elaboration of their consequences.
5. Further testing or experimentation.

If we consider each of these steps in turn and modify the terminology, we may see how the pattern of reflective thinking can be easily adapted to the needs of discussion groups which are attempting to solve complicated problems. First we shall take up the steps in solving a full-fledged or "complete problem"; later we shall consider how to modify the pattern of reflective thinking to deal with abbreviated or "truncated problems."

VENTILATION

As Dewey noted, thinking begins when we find ourselves facing a perplexing or confusing situation, when we discover that our present patterns of behavior are not adequate to allow us to reach the goals we desire. A problem may arise out of personal needs that are not being satisfied (an unsuccessful disciplinary rule in the home or failure to make constructive use of leisure time), out of environmental pressures (the need to forestall bankruptcy or to accomplish political reforms), or out of many other sorts of interpersonal, intergroup, or international frictions. The problem may take the form of an "ambiguous situation," where we vaguely sense that "something is wrong," or the form of a "forked road situation," where we face a choice between clearly defined but competing courses of action.

Like an athlete about to participate in a contest, group members need some time to "warm up" to a problem. Participants can make profitable use of this interval to try to formulate in their own minds what is troubling them. By talking over the situation briefly in general terms, committee members can learn whether the people in the group are apathetic, bitter, or belligerent in their attitudes toward the problem, the committee, or both, and can take these feelings into account in beginning their work. A few minutes, or even longer, spent in ventilating feelings can help group members to establish a rapport with one another and to obtain a clearer idea of their goals.

CLARIFICATION

Before an investigation can get under way, the exact problem has to be phrased precisely. (A well-phrased question, it is said, is half answered.) Dewey would say that the emotional state of participants has to be intellectualized; that is to say, the vague feelings people have about a situation have to be objectified and made conscious. This we do, of course, whenever we verbalize a discussion topic.

There are several principles which a group should keep in mind when stating a problem: (1) Narrow the topic so that it can be reasonably handled in the time available, or else expand the time to be devoted to the discussion. (2) Phrase the topic as a question and, if possible, in the form of a simple sentence. (3) Phrase the question in an unbiased manner so that an answer is not implied by the wording. (4) Phrase the question so there are multiple possibilities for conclusions, unless the group is clearly faced with a choice between only two options. Especially avoid wordings which can be responded to with a "yes" or "no" answer.

Additional steps may be necessary in order to clarify a problem sufficiently for effective discussion. Often, agreement will be needed on the limits to be placed on the topic and on the meaning of key terms to be used in the discussion. If a group is to take up the question, "What sort of federal aid should be given to education?", committee members will avoid many communication breakdowns and misunderstandings if, at the outset, they agree on what to include and exclude in the discussion. Is the group to consider aid to elementary or secondary schools, to public or private schools, to colleges or adult education centers? Furthermore, it is often desirable, early in the meeting, to define terms, not only those which appear in the phrasing of the question but also those which will have to be used in investigating the topic. If the problem is "What sort of labor legislation do we need?", participants had better spend some time, before getting too deeply into the discussion, defining terms such as "closed shop," "open shop," "jurisdictional dispute," "lockout," and so on. Some consistency in the use of terms will help members of the group to understand each other better. In short, in the clarification step, group members are trying to answer the question, "What is the specific nature of our problem?"

FACT-FINDING

The third step in thinking reflectively is to gather and assess the information available on the problem. The aim is to find answers to the question, "What are the relevant facts of this problem?" This information may take the form of factual statements or authoritative opinions concerning the history and background of the problem or may concern its current symptoms. We get some idea of how to carry out fact-finding from observing the behavior of those who ordinarily use reflective thinking in their jobs— the doctor in examining a patient, the mechanic in checking an engine, the technician in eliminating trouble in a television set. Doctors, for example, do not jump to conclusions about a patient and begin to operate without making an exhaustive study of his or her condition. They will gather all sorts of information from conversation with the patient, from a careful physical examination, from extensive laboratory tests, and only after carrying out these steps will they later attempt to derive the causes of the patient's discomfort. Similarly, in solving a problem in an industrial plant, a school system, or a family, it is essential that people collect all the available data and assess them before trying to determine the causes of the trouble.

DISCOVERY

In the next step, hypotheses or solutions should be formulated and proposed. In this stage of the problem solving, group members will try to determine, "What are the possible answers to this question?" Note that the question asks for "possible answers," not for a single answer. This means that more than one hypothesis or solution should be suggested. If this is done, groups will avoid becoming committed too early to a single explanation or course of action when there may be many other—and better— ways of dealing with the problem. The wider the group's range of selection, the wiser the final choice is likely to be.

How does a group go about discovering new and better ways of solving a problem? To begin with, intelligent solutions are partly a product of adequate fact-finding. As group members study and isolate the conditions that underlie the problem, they inevitably will begin to think about some of the hypotheses or correctives that may be needed.

The discovery stage of reflective thinking requires some talent for imaginative and original thought. Unfortunately, little is known about the factors that stimulate inventiveness. Those who have made studies of creative imagination say only that it requires a full knowledge of the problem combined with a willingness to discard old patterns of thought and action. Albert Einstein may have had something like this in mind when, in replying to a question as to how he discovered the principle of relativity he replied, "By refusing to accept an axiom." One of the great barriers to the optimum use of human intelligence lies in our intense desire to cling to traditional theories and familiar institutional practices. To draft new hypotheses requires, perhaps most of all, courage.

In this step ordinarily the group should avoid the temptation to evaluate. To suggest a novel solution is, for many people, an open invitation to rip it apart with devastating criticism. Of course, it is essential to evaluate suggestions that are made, but experience seems to indicate that critical thinking and original thinking often progress better when each is handled separately.

EVALUATION
Finally, a group must examine the consequences of accepting any of its hypotheses or proposals. Some assessment must be made to answer the question "How adequate is each hypothesis in explaining the problem?" or "How effective is each solution in correcting the difficulty?" This will require that the suggestions be taken up in turn and the validity or invalidity of each hypothesis or solution be considered. In a problem of policy, the workability of any proposal, in addition to its theoretical soundness, will have to be projected. Out of this evaluation will come a group's decision.

DECISION MAKING
The last step in reflective thinking is accomplished when this question has been answered: "Precisely what decision have we reached on this problem?" It involves nothing more than the verbal formulation of the conclusions reached by the discussants. It is important that groups complete this final step, or they run the risk of leaving the meeting in the belief that the problem has been solved when actually each person may have a different impression of what was decided. The decisions may be stated orally or in written form if that is required.

Thus, the steps in reflective thinking involve a systematic ordering of the processes of investigation so that the group approaches each issue in a logical, sequential manner to reach the decision(s) that they must make. There is one other characteristic of reflective thinking to which Dewey calls attention: Each step in the pattern grows out of preceding steps and also may "reflect" back on earlier stages. The six steps are not independent of each other: The scope of fact-finding will be determined by the limits that are set up in clarifying the problem; the facts lead, in turn, to the hypotheses regarding the causes of the problem and to possible solutions. In addition, later stages may reveal that there are additional terms that need clarifying or may indicate that the limits originally agreed on are too restrictive; that is a group may find itself first going ahead and then returning from one stage to another stage in order to complete a thorough investigation.

When should a group employ the adapted version of Dewey's method as described above? Clearly, it is a rather complex and methodical approach which is not likely to fit every group's needs. We suggest that the steps of reflective thinking are most appropriately used under the following circumstances.

1. *The decision should have important consequences.* What constitutes "importance" is a matter to be interpreted by each group. Because the reflective thinking method can be a rather laborious process, only those groups which deem their decisions important would choose to invest such energy in this type of decision making. Consider the fact-finding stage, for example. The group is called on to assess all the information which appears to be relevant to the problem at hand. This may require sending the group members out to gather facts, after which the evidence must be evaluated. The advantage of the approach in this case is that it calls on the group to touch on all bases in order to avoid a hasty conclusion; the disadvantage is that some directions the investigation takes will not prove fruitful. Therefore, this approach would not be particularly advantageous to those groups involved in making decisions of smaller consequence.

2. *The group should have time to complete all the steps satisfactorily.* Allowing the group members to ventilate their feelings, clarifying the problem with precise definitions, finding facts, discovering all possible solutions and evaluating them—all of these steps take time. Thoroughness, but not efficiency, is the hallmark of this approach, and a group which cannot do each step completely might well adopt some other method.

3. *Each individual in the group, and perhaps the group as a unit, should have some skill and prior training in using the reflective thinking approach.* In one of the early studies of reflective thinking, Johnson (1943) was able to demonstrate with a paper-and-pencil test that individuals differ widely in their abilities to apply Dewey's method. Other studies have shown that the ability measured by this test has important consequences for how well people are able to function in problem-solving discussions. Pyron and Sharp (1963) found that discussants who were rated highly in their contributions to group goals also tended to score high on Johnson's test. And Sharp and Milliken (1964) showed that groups comprised of people who did well on the test produced better final solutions than did those composed of people who did poorly. In short, people who thoroughly understand each step of Dewey's process will do better in decision making than will others. It seems unlikely that a group composed of participants who have never before been exposed to Dewey's ideas will be able to use

the pattern effectively just by going through the specified steps, although such a task might be a learning experience for them.

4. *Finally, the pattern should be used on "full-fledged" problems which require a complete process of reflective thinking.* If, for example, the clarification and fact-finding stages have already been successfully completed by another body of decision makers, it does not make sense that the group expend effort retracing these steps.

Truncated Problems

Groups are often assigned truncated problems which do not involve all the steps described earlier. In these cases the group will have to adapt the procedures to the specific requirements of each task. Some of the common departures from the pattern of reflective thinking will now be considered.

PROBLEMS OF DISCOVERY ONLY

Sometimes groups are assigned problems of attitude or policy that have already been diagnosed and are asked only to suggest ways of dealing with them. After a club has decided what is wrong with its monthly meetings, it may then appoint a committee to suggest some new types of programs. The senior class of a college or high school may name some of its members to a committee to do nothing but outline ways of raising funds for their class gift. An advertising agency may arrange meetings to formulate new advertising plans for one of its clients. In these instances the group is responsible only for proposing a wide variety of solutions from which a choice may later be made. Their agenda need only include three steps: (1) summary of the diagnosis, (2) suggestions for correcting the situation, and (3) editing of the proposals.

One technique, called "brainstorming," has been developed specifically for solving problems of discovery. It is based on the principle, stated earlier by Dewey, that creative thinking and critical thinking are best separated because they interfere with each other. The rules for brainstorming are simple and few in number:

1. Anyone may contribute an idea. Talk out whenever you get an idea no matter how naive it may seem.
2. No criticism or evaluation is permitted. Questions or comments only distract from the purpose of the meeting.
3. The more ideas the better. Even a bad idea may provoke a better one from someone else.
4. Ideas can be edited later. Some suggestions can be combined, others improved on.[1]

[1] *Report of the Proceedings of the Third Annual Creative Problem-Solving Institute* (University of Buffalo, July, 1957), p. 5.

Brainstorming seems to be a simple and practical way of solving a truncated problem which involves only the discovery of new solutions.

PROBLEMS OF EVALUATION ONLY

On occasion, committees and boards are called upon to judge which of alternative policies should be adopted. Problems such as these (e.g., Should the company locate its new plant in Rockford, Oshkosh, or Ithaca? Should my children go to Columbia, Dartmouth, or the University of Michigan? Is the country better off under Republican or Democratic administrations?) force groups to choose among different ideas, policies, or actions. The agendum, in this case, consists of only two steps: (1) summary of available courses of action and (2) discussion of advantages and disadvantages of the proposed solutions.

PROBLEMS OF DISCOVERY AND EVALUATION

Sometimes groups propose new solutions *and* evaluate them. In cases of this type, should groups brainstorm first and then evaluate (the "ideas-criteria" procedure), engage in both simultaneously (the "concurrent" method), or suggest standards for evaluation first and then consider solutions in light of them (the "criteria-ideas" approach)? To suggest solutions first has the advantage of keeping creative and critical processes isolated and might help members who are shy or afraid of being criticized to get into the conversation. The competition between participants in "brainstorming" is also stimulating. (We have found the members of a group to formulate dozens of hypotheses under these conditions when, without this stimulation, virtually nothing was being accomplished.) The simplicity of the method leaves group members free to devote their whole attention to the business of thinking up new ideas.

On the other hand, it may be argued that for some problems the combination of discovery and evaluation can be advantageous. When the question is a difficult one and the solutions likely to be complicated, members cannot simply call out a word or phrase and expect the idea to be really assimilated. "Brainstorming" sessions produce a lot of silly ideas along with some good ones. The chief disadvantage of the concurrent approach is that a group might accept a solution before they have had a chance to review alternatives. The danger that the group will eliminate a good idea too early probably would not be a problem, since the group can always reconsider a rejected idea, and perhaps modify it, if subsequent suggestions prove to be less attractive.

The third, or "criteria-ideas," pattern involves having the group specify what needs to be accomplished before enumerating potential solutions. This pattern seems to have an advantage in terms of efficiency since after listing all the possible solutions, the group can save time by readily eliminating some, but it may discourage group creativity by introducing evaluation too early in the group process.

Research suggests that if the generation of many good ideas is an important goal in discussion, then the ideas-criteria or brainstorming approach is superior to the concurrent approach, according to studies by Parnes and Meadow (1959), Meadow, Parnes, and Reese (1959), and Brilhart and Jochem (1964). In the Brilhart and Jochem study, some groups also employed the criteria-ideas pattern, which the investigators found to be the least effective approach. They concluded that this method was "dubious at best and harmful at worst." Bayless (1967), on the other hand, found no advantage for any of these patterns over the others in terms of the quality of the final solution. The research is not conclusive, but it does suggest that if efficiency is not a very important consideration, a group might as well choose the ideas-criteria pattern, or else the concurrent pattern if brainstorming seems awkward, since more ideas will be produced by these methods than by the criteria-ideas approach.

Patterns Designed for Group Efficiency

Sometimes groups do not have very much time to reach a solution, and yet they are faced with a "full-fledged" problem with no substantial part of the decision-making process handled by others. There may be no time for extensive fact-finding, so that the group members must rely on the facts as stated and on their own general knowledge. There also may be little or no time for ventilation and the elaborate exploration of possible solutions. Such "emergency" problems are not unusual in many circumstances. In the military, a decision may have to be made after an unexpected reversal on the battlefield. In business, a decision to buy or not to buy may have to be made before a competitor steps in. In government agencies or in academia, "higher-ups" sometimes require an immediate decision on such matters as the expenditure of temporarily available funds. One approach in such situations is to direct an individual rather than a group to come up with an answer, because groups are ordinarily less efficient. Unfortunately this sacrifices the advantage of the group's capacity to correct error at the very time when oversights are most likely. Clearly, when a decision must be made efficiently, the group needs some kind of organization to focus its efforts. The question is, what kind?

Larson (1969) conducted a study of four ways of solving a series of problems. Untrained groups of discussants had a limited amount of time to consider four different industrial relations problems previously analyzed by a panel of experts who had identified a "best" solution to each problem. The four agenda plans were: (1) "no pattern" (the natural process approach), (2) "reflective thinking" (a variation of the agendum discussed earlier in this chapter), (3) a pattern called the "single-question form", and (4) another pattern called the "ideal solution form." Larson found the single question and ideal solution agenda to be superior. Groups which used the "reflective thinking" and "no pattern" forms did not perform as well.

THE SINGLE QUESTION FORM

Harris and Schwahn (1961) examined the studies of others in order to determine how successful as opposed to unsuccessful problem solvers approached their tasks. The following pattern for group deliberation is Larson's adaptation of their conclusions:

1. What is the single question, the answer to which is all the group needs to know to accomplish its purpose?
2. What sub-questions must be answered before we can answer the single question we have formulated?
3. Do we have sufficient information to answer confidently the sub-questions? (If yes, answer them. If no, continue below.)
4. What are the most reasonable answers to the sub-questions?
5. Assuming that our answers to the sub-questions are correct, what is the best solution to the problem? (Larson, 1969, p. 453).

The reasons why the single question form is a particularly efficient method of problem solving can be readily seen. (1) This pattern forces the group to narrow the topic and work it into the form of an answerable question and sub-questions. No time is taken for the airing of feelings or exploration of the broad ramifications of the problem. (2) Even if the group does not have enough information to answer the sub-questions definitively, the pattern requires them to make their best guess about the answer to each question. (3) Once the questions are answered, a single solution is asked for. There is no brainstorming of possible solutions. In short, the problem is treated much *as though* it were truncated, most effort being directed toward what would be the clarification stage if the reflective thinking pattern were being used (steps 1 and 2 above).

THE IDEAL SOLUTION FORM

Larson also wrote a brief adaptation of a procedure suggested by Kepner and Trogoe (1965) for systematic decision making by managers. This pattern is as follows:

1. Are we all agreed on the nature of the problem?
2. What would be the ideal solution from the point-of-view of all parties involved in the problem?
3. What conditions within the problem could be changed so that the ideal solution might be achieved?

4. Of the solutions available to us, which one best approximates the ideal solution? (Larson, 1969, p. 453).

Here again, we can see why this pattern is especially efficient: (1) According to this form, the group formulates the problem in the first step. If no one seems to disagree, the group moves forward to consider the characteristics of an "ideal" solution. (2) The criteria are not binding. The group can adopt a solution which merely approximates the ideal. In other words, the problem is again dealt with much as though it were truncated. In this case, the pattern closely resembles the criteria-ideas approach we discussed earlier. The fact that this method discourages the generation of multiple solutions contributes to its efficiency.

THE LESS EFFICIENT APPROACHES

One can also see why the other two approaches studied by Larson are less effective in a situation where a time limit is imposed. The "no pattern" or natural process approach is time consuming because it is not very organized. In particular, the conflict phase often takes time to complete. If the group skips over this phase, the advantage of the natural approach is lost. Decision modification, which usually involves conflict, is also a slow process. Each proposed solution must be examined, and the same solution may reappear several times in different forms before it is finally accepted or rejected.

The reflective thinking pattern is inefficient for the opposite reason: It is very organized and encourages the group to expend time on topics which may or may not be directly related to the final solution adopted. In contrast to the "single question" and "ideal solution" forms, it calls for an analysis of the causes and effects of the problem and also requires a detailing of possible solutions before one is selected. However, note that the group members in Larson's study were inexperienced and untrained, so it is possible that people who were skilled in using Dewey's method would have done better.

SUMMARY AND CONCLUSIONS

In this chapter we have suggested that before a group can settle down to working on its substantive problem—the task confronting it—there is a problem of procedure to be solved. This involves a decision about how much the group should impose its control on the decision-making process.

There are two ways in which groups commonly approach the problem of agenda. Some make a choice by default. They do not consider whether or not to adopt an agendum; they simply start discussing and "let nature take its course." The second way of dealing with the problem of agenda is the one which we advocate: The group should make a conscious decision about whether and how extensively to control its process. We have suggested several criteria for the group to consider in making this choice. The advisability of using an agenda will depend on how efficiently the decision must be reached, the size of the group, the nature of the problem, the purposes of the group, the personal needs for order among the group members, and the interpersonal attitudes of the participants toward one another.

If the group decides that an agenda is in order, they may select one from among the patterns suggested in this chapter. If the group is faced with a problem requiring a highly systematic and cautious approach and if it has enough time, the group members can employ the steps of reflective thinking based on Dewey's method. This approach ordinarily requires some preparation and training for effective performance because the group members must know how to proceed through successive stages of ventilation, clarification, fact-finding, discovery, evaluation, and decision making. Truncated versions of this pattern may be used. In emergency situations, the "single question" and "ideal solution" formats are preferable to Dewey's method or the "natural process" approach. Although one of these patterns may be useful when a central problem is considered, an agenda is sometimes suggested directly by the problem or problems which the group faces, especially in the kind of meeting where many topics and separate "little decisions" must be handled.

The group may decide not to impose a structure on the discussion. It may be immediately apparent that there is no need for an agenda. If they are going to follow that route, they ought to make a quick decision to that effect. Otherwise they may end up spending an inordinate amount of time just deciding what they don't want to do. If they are going to be spontaneous, let them make a quick, spontaneous decision to be so.

STUDY SUGGESTIONS

1. Most decision-making groups give little or no thought to their problem-solving processes but simply "dive in" to their tasks. Why do you think this is so? How realistic do you think it would be to get the groups with which you are most familiar to follow a more systematic pattern of problem solving? How would you go about trying to accomplish this?
2. What do you see as the relative advantages and disadvantages of keeping separate the generating and the evaluating of solutions to a problem?
3. Try to identify a group of specialists who are involved in a problem-solving assignment. Record the flow of topics that they consider. Compare this with a meeting of laypeople also meeting to solve a school or community problem. Are there differences? What are they? What were the consequences?
4. Compare the abilities of two groups within a class or within an organization to which you belong in generating creative solutions to a problem. Give one of the

groups no direction on how to conduct its session, but specify that the other must follow the rules of "brainstorming." Record in each the number and quality of suggestions made. Try to discover if there are differenc s in the number and variety of ideas generated and why.

Part IV
LEADERSHIP
IN GROUPS

Chapter 11
Sources of Leadership

It is likely that every reader of this book has been, or in the future will be, charged with some kind of leadership responsibility. Some may be eager for the opportunity, seeing it not only as a chance to help steer their groups toward the accomplishment of desirable goals, but also as an opportunity to fulfill their creative potentialities. Others may assume leadership more reluctantly, having it thrust on them because their talents, experience, or education are needed by the groups to which they belong or because no one else seems willing to do the job. In either case, to perform effectively it is helpful to understand precisely what leadership is and the ways it operates. As we explore this subject, we will discover that everything presented so far in this book has a bearing on the problem of leadership. In a sense, therefore, this section will serve to review and perhaps bring into sharper focus many ideas which have already been touched on.

THE MEANINGS OF LEADERSHIP

Most of us, when confronted with the term "leadership," tend to think immediately of a single individual—a committee chairperson, a supervisor, a club president, a parent, a teacher, or a military officer—who holds a position of authority in a group. When members come together for discussion, this leader sits at the head of the table, or stands at the front of the room, and presides over the meeting. Our concept of leadership is thus an image of a person who has been elected or appointed to the task of assuming major responsibility for the group's activities. Actually, however, there are three different ways of defining leadership: as ascribed status, as achieved status, or as influential action.

Leadership defined as *ascribed status* conforms to the everyday, common-sense meaning we have described above. It is understandable that most of us view leadership in this way. Ever since we have been old enough to be aware of group relationships, we have been accustomed to the idea of someone's being in charge—be it father, mother, or grandparent in the home; teacher in the classroom; president of student government; minister in the pulpit; foreman; boss; or chairperson of the committee. Hence, when we go to a meeting where discussion is expected to take place, we are likely to assume that someone will have been named in advance to be the individual in charge and that he or she will call the group to order, start and guide the proceedings, verbalize any decisions that are agreed on, and bring the discussion to a close.

There is also a second rather common meaning. Some people think of leadership as *achieved status*. For them, leadership is still a role performed by one person, but it is not necessarily the position assumed by the appointed leader or figurehead. In fact, ascribed status is not necessary in the kinds of groups they envision. Rather, those who define leadership in this way expect to see one person *emerge* as the dominant influence in the group. Such a person *earns* the position; it is not given to him or her from the outset. Presumably, "the leader" is identified by consensual recognition from the group members.

There is still another way of viewing leadership, although it is a much less common meaning than the others. We can think of it as *any action which exerts a significant influence* on the group. With this definition in mind, one sees the "power behind the throne" to be as much a part of the leadership of the group as the person who happens to hold the gavel or occupy the role of emergent leader. The person who cracks jokes to change the serious climate of a meeting or the deviant who continually disagrees to delay actions on a matter is also seen as exerting leadership. Even the silent members, by the uncertainty or anxiety they may create in others or by their contributions to an atmosphere of indifference, exert influence. In short, since every member of the group, if by no means other than mere presence, has some effect on the discussion, every member is regarded as exerting some degree of leadership.

Whether one defines leadership as ascribed status, as achieved status, or simply as influential action has important implications for how small group communication will be viewed and practiced. We regard the action definition as the most useful. In the first place, the different meanings tend to affect what one *perceives* in a discussion. The definitions of leadership as ascribed or achieved status direct one to concentrate on the behaviors of one person. On the other hand, the action definition permits one to recognize the effects of the appointed leader (if there is one), the influence of an emergent leader (if one person is clearly predominant), and also the combined impact of the behaviors of a variety of participants. In short, the definition we prefer tends to open the observer's eyes to a variety of leadership phenomenon and is, therefore, less restrictive.

Second, each definition tends to promote certain value judgments and to encourage certain ways of behaving. If we focus on the appointed, elected, or emergent leader, we are likely to regard a discussion which has no one identifiable leader as a failure. This may cause the group members to search for a single leader when their experience suggests that none is needed. Conversely, the definition of leadership as action may lead group members to value more highly those discussions where influence is shared by several people, and we believe that this more accurately describes behavior in an effective group. At the same time, it does not preclude the possibility that the group may require the services of a designated leader, nor does it suggest that the members should shun the outstanding contributions of one person.

However, as with all ways of viewing the discussion process, there is a certain disadvantage to the action definition. We have chosen to regard as leadership only that member behavior which exerts a *significant* influence on a group, that is to say, action which affects the group as a whole and which has some important bearing on the group's movement (or lack of movement) toward its goals. Thus, for practical purposes, it becomes necessary to isolate certain events as acts of *leadership* and to relegate other actions to the category of *membership* contributions. We may regard the participant who stirs up an argument in one group as having significantly influenced the course of the discussion by this act, whereas in another situation we might consider the same behavior as inconsequential. Thus, the dividing line between what is and is not leadership must be a somewhat arbitrary one, determined by subjective evaluation. On the other hand, the ascribed status definition is by far the easiest one to apply. We can simply ask, "Who has been *named* to lead this group?"

Viewing leadership as achieved status involves a judgment of intermediate difficulty. It introduces the problem of evaluating influence, although this is often resolved by identifying the person who talks most or who is addressed most often by the other group members. Or, we can simply ask the group members whom they regard as the most influential participant.

Defining leadership as the significant influence of individual acts calls on the observer to assess the total context of the discussion and to study the apparent effects of each person's behavior on others. This is all the more difficult because, in many cases, it will not be clear at the time an action is performed exactly what impact it will have in the long run. However, we would argue that this disadvantage is also an advantage: Discussion leadership can be viewed in the broadest as well as in the most accurately descriptive manner.

One other point about the meanings of "leadership" should be emphasized. People often use the term in such a way that it has the positive connotation of helping a group to accomplish its goals. But it is also true that individual actions can lead the group astray. Although an individual who exerts this negative kind of influence may seldom be acknowledged by the other group members as "the leader," such acts are nevertheless important. Thus, the definition of leadership as action is nonevaluative in the sense that it includes those behaviors which may have a deleterious effect on group productivity or social climate.

THE DETERMINANTS OF LEADERSHIP

What *causes* leadership to come about? And what determines the *effectiveness* of leadership? These are questions which have intrigued students of human behavior for a long time. Presumably, if we had the answers, it would be possible to select and train people for leadership and thereby to maximize the chances for group success. Solving the puzzles of leadership has proven to be an elusive task, however. A history of the attempts that have been made, and documentation of the degree of success achieved is the topic of this part of our discussion of the sources of leadership. As might be expected, each effort toward finding determinants tends to be affected by the way investigators have defined "leadership."

The Traits Explanation

For a long time, one of the most popular ideas about leadership has been that there are certain traits possessed by people who become leaders. In other words, some people are "leader types," and others are "followers." Perhaps the persistence of this notion stems from a fundamental premise of the American culture, as Shaw (1976) has suggested:

> In the latter part of the nineteenth century and the first part of the twentieth, the Western world was dominated by an individualistic position which held that a man could become whatever he wished to become, so long as he worked hard and persevered. Thus, the leader became a leader because of his own personal efforts and attributes (p. 274).

Therefore, it is not surprising that the earliest studies of leadership were concerned with identifying the traits of leaders.

It is clear that those who pursued this explanatory approach defined leadership as the role of a single person—as ascribed or achieved status. Thus, studies of leadership traits involved comparisons of individuals who held positions of authority (or, less commonly, emergent leaders) with those who were not acknowledged as leaders. The basis of comparison was some list of physical, emotional, or intellectual characteristics.

Out of the literally hundreds of studies of this type that have been conducted, some general trends have emerged. In physical traits, there is a slight tendency for leaders to be bigger (taller and heavier) and to have a better appearance (physique, looks, and dress) than others. With regard to personality and various abilities, there is some evidence that leaders tend to have a slight advantage over others in certain characteristics. Shaw (1976) summarizes the conclusions of Stogdill (1948) as follows:

> . . .the average group leader exceeds the average group member in such *abilities* as intelligence, scholarship, knowing how to get things done, insight into situations, verbal facility, and adaptability. The leader exceeds the group member with regard to such *sociability* factors as dependability in exercising responsibility, activity and social participation, cooperativeness, and popularity. *Motivational* characteristics are indicated by the findings that leaders exceed other group members with respect to initiative and persistence (p. 275).

Despite these conclusions, the results of these studies do not tell us very much about leadership. In the first place, the findings are rather inconclusive because the correlations between traits and leadership were almost always low. Correlations found in some studies did not show up in others. In some cases, the same traits were positively associated with leadership in certain investigations and negatively associated in others.

A second problem with the research is that there have been very few investigations of relationships between traits and *successful* leadership; that is, the findings tell us a little about what characteristics will help a person to *become* a leader, but almost nothing about traits which will make a person an *effective* leader. These might not be the same at all. The qualities that help a person to get elected or appointed may not be the same as those which make for *good* leadership.

More research might reveal characteristics of effective leaders, but, in light of the past failings of the traits approach, it seems unlikely that much would be uncovered. On the whole, then, it is not surprising that most investigators have abandoned the traits approach and have sought other explanations.[1]

---

[1] An interesting exception is found in Velma Lashbrook's (1975) study of perceptions of group leaders. She found that the person who interacted the most with a majority of the members in each group was seen by others as having certain characteristics: task attraction, character, and extroversion. These perceived traits are roughly equivalent to the categories identified by Stogdill (1948): abilities, sociability, and motivation. However, it is unclear whether Lashbrook's results mean that leaders were those who displayed certain traits or that cultural stereotypes about the traits of leaders caused group members to "see" those characteristics in prominent participants.

The Traits and Situations Explanation

It might seem that the search for traits of leaders was a total waste of time, but actually it accomplished a great deal, even though the findings did not reveal what the investigators expected. In the first place, it did much to discredit the popular myth that a few people are destined to be leaders, while most others are doomed to follow. As Ackerson (1942) pointed out some time ago, the personality profiles of most group members are rather similar. It may be, as he suggests, that the dramatic differences in traits are between those who might be in contention for leadership, on the one hand, and those who are *indifferent*, who neither lead nor follow and who seldom join groups, on the other. In short, it seems likely that in most groups there are a number of people who have "leadership potential."

Another unexpected benefit of the studies on traits was the discovery that *situations* are critical in the determination of who will rise to a position of leadership. For example, in most studies, appearance and physical bearing were found to have at best a moderate or weak relationship to leadership, but in one study of the achievement of rank in the military, these factors were found to be very important (Kohns and Irle, 1920). This suggests that the traits which help a person to become a leader depend on the nature of the group to be led—its goals, the norms for appropriate behavior, the way the task is structured, and so forth. If we extend this idea by implication to the realm of leadership *effectiveness*, the conclusion would be that each group has specific requirements for successful performance which only certain people can meet.

Out of the disappointments of the research on traits came a new theory: Leadership involves a *combination* of traits and situational factors. Although a number of investigators have followed this lead, it is Fred Fiedler whose work is the most widely associated with this approach (see Fiedler, 1968). He tested his "contingency model" in research extending over a 15-year period, examining the operation of over 1600 groups in more than 35 studies. Fiedler was interested in predicting the success of appointed leaders by seeing how their traits matched the situational features of groups. Thus, unlike previous investigators, he was not concerned with the question of who will be appointed or who will emerge as a leader, nor did he study the effectiveness of emergent leaders. However, the "traits and situations" approach could be extended to an examination of those issues.

Fiedler based his research on a single trait—the tendency of individuals to see a large or a small difference between those people they like to work with and those they don't. This trait is measured by means of the "assumed similarity of opposites" (ASo) scale. People are asked to think about past work associates and then to rate the "most preferred co-worker" (MPC) and the "least preferred co-worker" (LPC) on a variety of dimensions (pleasant–unpleasant, friendly–unfriendly, etc.). A person with a high ASo score sees MPC and LPC as rather similar and rates both rather favorably. Such an individual may be characterized as "warm," "democratic," or "human relations oriented." He or she derives satisfaction from having good relations with others. On the other hand, a person with a low ASo score sees a big difference between opposites, tending to rate the MPC favorably and the LPC unfavorably. He or she may be characterized as "cold," "authoritarian," or "task-oriented," and as deriving satisfaction from performing the task.

The contingency model says that the type of person who will be effective in a given group is contingent on certain features of the group situation:

1. *Leader-member relations* refers to the liking and respect that group members have for the leader.
2. *Task structure* consists of specifications for expected outcomes and the way the group is supposed to operate. A well-defined task is structured, while an ambiguous one is unstructured. For example, most action groups have more highly structured tasks than, let us say, those found in policy-making groups which have the job of generating solutions to a problem.
3. *Situational power* is the degree to which the appointed leader has control over the rewards and punishments which can be handed out. For example, an executive who can hire, fire, and promote employees in a certain group would be high in situational power.

According to Fiedler, each of these factors influences the *favorableness* of the work situation to the leader; that is, good leader–member relations, a structured task, and a high amount of situational power all tend to increase the leader's control over the group. As Fiedler points out, however, this list of factors is not exhaustive, since any number of elements may affect the favorableness of the situation. For example, the situation becomes less favorable when the group members are diverse in technical skills or cultural backgrounds.

How do traits and situations fit together to produce effective groups? According to Fiedler's model, the low ASo or "cold" leader will be most effective when the group situation is either highly favorable or highly unfavorable. Under favorable conditions, very little attention to interpersonal relations is needed, and the task-oriented leader does well. When the conditions are highly unfavorable to the leader, it is important that the group be kept strictly on the task, and so, again, the low ASo leader does better.

On the other hand, the contingency model predicts that the high ASo leader will be more effective when the situation is only moderately favorable or unfavorable; that is, warm, people-oriented leaders do better when they have something in their favor but when other conditions are poor. For example, the leader–member relations might be good, but the task unstructured and positional power weak, or respect and liking might be moderately poor in a situation where task structure and positional power are rather favorable to the leader. Under these circumstances, the leader will need to be especially considerate and persuasive to accomplish the group goal.

The practical implication of Fiedler's model is that *traits of leaders should be carefully matched with situations for maximum group effectiveness.* Within the varied business, industrial, and military settings in which his research has been conducted, the model has had considerable predictive strength. On the average, Fiedler's theory accounts for about 50 percent of the productivity of the groups he studied. Considering that no one theory or statistical analysis is likely to account for everything, this figure is rather high. However, before we can accept and act upon the Fiedler model as an explanation of leadership, we must consider two of the limits of this perspective.

First, the traits and situations approach assumes that leadership styles are more or less determined by personality tendencies. While Fiedler would not go as far as to say that leaders cannot be trained to be more adaptive to situations, his perspective tends to deny the open, spontaneous, flexible potentialities of people as systems. Matching traits with situations presumes, to a large degree, that leadership behavior is "locked" into personality.

A second—and closely related—assumption is that situations are comparatively easy to engineer; that is, while people are difficult to change, leaders or group members can be readily shuffled from one group to another, or else task structure and positional power can be altered to fit the leader's personality. The problem with this idea is that experimenting with various group compositions and working conditions can be very costly, and success is by no means guaranteed. There is no assurance that a new combination of group members will create greater liking and respect for a leader. Changing task structure or positional power may create morale problems among those who remain with the leader. In addition, it is not always possible to change personnel and working conditions, especially in those institutions which operate on the basis of democratic principles; that is, people may be assigned to groups because they volunteer or because certain interest groups must be represented. In general, the traits and situations approach applies best to groups within military and industrial organizations.

The Functional Explanation

The functional explanation was developed partly in response to the shortcomings of the previously discussed explanations which give central importance to the traits of single leaders. The assumption of this alternative perspective is that leadership is such a complex, fluid, and dynamic phenomenon that it cannot be explained by any simple list of traits or combinations of traits and situations. In the first place, it places heavy emphasis on the *unique functions* of each group. One way of looking at these functions is to characterize them as the types of groups discussed in Chapter 3; that is, a particular group may take action, arrive at policies, learn about something, give members an outlet for feelings, carry on casual social conversation, or perform several of these purposes. But functions are also more specific. A group takes action on a certain kind of task—mathematical, mechanical, athletic, or whatever. The members make policy for or learn about a particular type of issue or topic, and, at the same time, deal with the group's own particular socioemotional problems. So the specific leadership abilities of group members which are required for effective performance may vary considerably within and across the situations faced by the group.

In stressing the role of the situation in the determination of leadership behavior, the functional approach is similar to the traits and situations perspective. But it differs in that it assumes that the needs of the group are numerous and subject to *change* from time to time. Therefore, it is unlikely, although possible, that one person will be able to perform all the essential functions that a group will have during its lifetime.

A second feature of the functional explanation is that it stresses leadership *behaviors* rather than traits. If a person has certain traits which help him or her to satisfy a function at a particular time, this is all to the good. But what is important is that *someone* or *some people* perform the needed acts. So another important difference between the functional explanation and those approaches which stress the importance of traits is that individual behaviors in groups are not seen as being locked into personality characteristics. People may act in a certain way to perform a certain function because of personality tendencies, but they might just as well rise to the occasion because they see that the group needs a particular kind of contribution, regardless of their usual ways of responding. Thus, people are viewed as open, spontaneous systems, and traits are not considered to be crucial factors.

It is obvious that the functional explanation is more compatible with the definition of leadership as *action* than as ascribed or achieved status; that is, if we focus on how behaviors change with situations, we are unlikely to be interested only in an appointed or elected leader or in the one person who emerges as the most prominent discussant. At the same time, however, we can apply the functional approach to single leaders to see how they respond to certain circumstances or to assess the effectiveness of their behaviors.

The strength of the functional explanation is also its weakness; that is, while it provides a way of looking at leadership in its full complexity, it also makes prediction difficult because there are so many factors to be considered. In addition, because of the relative newness of this explanatory approach and the large number of variables which might be examined, we have only a small amount of research which has employed the functional perspective. Nevertheless, it seems to be the most promising and useful of the three approaches.

From a practical point of view, the functional explanation has two important implications. First, it suggests that *discussion participants ought to be trained to perform acts which will serve a variety of functions*. In advance of a particular situation, it is difficult to say exactly what behaviors will be required at what times. Placing individuals with certain traits in a group might give us a little assurance that various functions can be handled, but, at present, we do not know much about the relationship of traits and leadership effectiveness.

Another way of stating the above principle is to say that *discussants need practice in trying out various behaviors in a variety of circumstances in order to discover what acts fit with different situations*. Cartwright and Zander (1968) explain the reasoning behind this idea in the following way:

> Under specific circumstances, . . . any given behavior may or may not serve a group function. Making "expert information available to the group," which might be expected to help the group reach a goal, can be done in such a manner that it stultifies movement toward the goal. To cite another example of usually helpful behavior, a group of children may be stimulated to self-direction at a time when they are not ready for it and when a more appropriate action would be to suggest a plan of action. Or clowning by a member of a discussion group may be exactly what is needed in a tense moment to relieve strain, but at another time such levity may seem inappropriate or may even block locomotion to the goal . . . (p. 305).

A second practical implication of the functional explanation is that *groups ought not to be rigid about who performs what functions*, even where a single leader is identified. A classic study by Riecken (1958) demonstrates this principle. He tested whether a participant who had established himself as the "biggest talker" in a problem-solving group would gain more acceptance for a so-called "elegant" solution (secretly given to him by the experimenter) than would a "small talker" similarly provided with the answer. Riecken found that:

> When the top man has the insight needed to solve the problem elegantly, the group accepts this solution more than two-thirds of the time; when the bottom man has the same information, the elegant solution is rejected more than two-thirds of the time (p. 313).

Another finding was that the small talker had a better chance of getting the elegant solution accepted if he was helped by the "second biggest talker," who served as gatekeeper and encouraged the small talker.

Riecken's study shows why it is important for the group to draw on the skills of the various group members to accomplish its goal. There were two essential functions which had to be fulfilled in order for the group to find the best possible answer: (a) discovery and expression of the elegant solution, and (b) assurance of a fair hearing for the idea. When the biggest talker had the needed insight, the second function was taken care of fairly readily. But when the small talker was the one capable of fulfilling the first function of idea generation, it became critical that the second function of gatekeeping be served by someone in the group, and this was best done by a prominent member of the group who was not the biggest talker.[2]

THE FUNCTIONS OF LEADERSHIP

At this point, it should be clear to you that we favor the functional explanation of leadership. It allows us to examine how specific *communication behaviors* can be used to meet the unique requirements of each group interaction. However, it is not intended to answer the question, "What causes leadership?" At best, the functional explanation would be that the person who has insight into group needs and the courage to act on that insight has a better chance than others of exerting influence. But as we have seen, the functions of a group are not always fulfilled. Rather, the functional explanation has more to say in answer to the question, "What determines the effectiveness of leadership?"

What are the functions of leadership and what kinds of behaviors tend to contribute to fulfilling those functions? We cannot describe the exact behavior that will fit every conceivable group situation. But we can explain those functions most groups require, and we can describe some behaviors which tend to satisfy each type of need. Various authors have proposed lists of leadership functions (see Cartwright and Zander, 1968, pp. 304–309). We have developed our own set of categories, some of which resemble other lists,[3] and have organized ideas under three main headings, according to whether the leadership function involves creative and critical thinking, procedural matters, or interpersonal relations. A fourth category concerning conflict management, which cuts across the other areas, has been included. Subcategories of functions are listed under

---

[2] A similar principle is illustrated by the Torrance (1954) study reported in Chapter 6, where groups consisting of air force pilots, navigators, and gunners sometimes solved problems incorrectly because they allowed themselves to be more influenced by the higher-status pilot, who was wrong, than the lower-status gunner, who knew the right answer.

[3] In fact, the description of functions presented here predates many other lists. It was originally developed by one of the authors (Barnlund, 1955), and most of the items are the same as those found in the first edition of *Dynamics of Discussion* (1960).

main headings, and examples of behaviors which tend to serve each need are given.

Leadership in Creative and Critical Thinking

CONTRIBUTING FRESH IDEAS

Every group needs new ideas. A congressional committee looking for a solution to labor racketeering, a staff of scientists seeking a defense against intercontinental ballistic missiles, a police department attempting to piece together clues that will lead to the explanation of a crime, economists attempting to unravel the problems of inflation—all look for leadership to those of their number who can provide fresh and promising suggestions. The psychologist's contributions to a therapy group may be mainly to provide the patients with fresh insights into human emotions. The English teacher's role in class discussion may be to expose the students to new ways of looking at a piece of literature. If group discussion is to be a productive enterprise, there must always be present those who can and will open new avenues for exploration.

PROVOKING ORIGINAL THOUGHT IN OTHERS

Quite as important as the "idea person" who keeps pumping fresh leads into a discussion, is the individual who can provoke others to do likewise. It is a sad fact that so few people in our society utilize their full creative potential and that so many need to be stimulated by others before they can become truly productive. When provided with the proper encouragement, they sometimes surprise themselves with the new thoughts they can produce. Therefore, we must not be too easily discouraged when we find ourselves in groups that seem lethargic and uncreative. It may be that through such methods as dramatizing the topic for discussion (perhaps by a vivid description of a concrete case) or through provocative and searching questions, the members of that group can be motivated to operate on all their cylinders. Surely one of the secrets of great teaching is the ability to stimulate original thought in students.

CRITICALLY EVALUATING THE IDEAS OF OTHERS

It is important to remember that unless the ideas which are contributed to a discussion are subjected to critical scrutiny, the group may find itself accepting theories and programs which are full of hidden flaws. One of the dangers of the "brainstorming" technique is that it may encourage people to believe that all they need in discussion is new ideas, regardless of how inane. What the too-agreeable group needs is individuals who can exercise leadership in the posting of danger signals—who can ask such questions as: "How do you know that?" "On what do you base that opinion?" "Would that really happen?" "Are you sure those statistics aren't outdated?"

ENCOURAGING CRITICAL THOUGHT IN OTHERS

No one individual can or should be expected to discover all the fallacies in the course of a group discussion. We need the help of everyone. Yet, as in the case of creative thinking, many discussion participants are not sufficiently accustomed to thinking critically. They fall prey too easily to the glib salesperson or the group member with a "good line." Hence, they require someone to goad them into making discriminating responses. This can sometimes be achieved by playing the devil's advocate, that is, by arguing quite convincingly for a point of view which is unpopular in the group, thus forcing otherwise complacent listeners to come to the defense of their now-threatened prejudices or opinions. Also, by setting an example of friendly but firm criticism, one can demonstrate to others that such behavior is both permissible and valued.

MAKING THE ABSTRACT CONCRETE OR THE CONCRETE ABSTRACT

One of the common causes of unfocused thinking in group discussion is the carrying on of conversation at levels that are either too abstract or too concrete. In the former instance, participants tend to talk in big words and vague generalities, passing each other by without really communicating. In the latter case, the group becomes so involved in petty details and individual cases that it loses sight of general goals and principles. In both instances leadership is needed in either lowering or raising the level of generality. If the discussion is too abstract, one can pull it down from the clouds by asking for examples and illustrations or by injecting figurative analogies. On the other hand, if, the conversation is embroiled in minutiae, one can simply ask: "What is the point of all this?" or "Can we find some general principle at work here?"

Leadership in Procedural Matters

INITIATING DISCUSSION

The obvious first step in getting a discussion group organized is to start the meeting. Whoever does this exerts considerable influence, because the opening remarks may set the tone and direction of the entire conversation. Usually the initiator not only starts the discussion, but also, directly or indirectly, provides some indication of the purposes for which the meeting is being held. In other words, opening remarks tend to carry with them goal-setting implications, just as the driver of a bus who starts out eastbound from Chicago on U.S. 20 raises a presumption that the riders are heading for South Bend.

MAKING AGENDA SUGGESTIONS

Our analogy of the bus ride can also be used to illustrate the inadequacy of opening remarks in determining the entire course of a discussion. There are many places besides South Bend that one can get to by starting eastward on Route 20 from Chicago. In short, the members of the group will have to make further procedural decisions en route as to where they want to go and how they want to get there. In order to make these decisions, leadership in the form of either asking for or offering procedural suggestions will have to be provided. Here are a few examples:

"Where shall we start?"

"I suggest that we first discuss movie censorship, then move on to magazines, and take up television last."

"Shall we just begin with the first item in the report and then take up the others in chronological order?"

"I have a feeling we're getting a little off the track. I'd like to go back to what Bob was saying when . . ."

"You know, we've only got 15 minutes left. Don't you think we had better drop this now and get on to the question of . . ."

CLARIFYING

Thinking is a difficult enough process when we do it in solitude. How much more complicated it becomes when several people try to make it a joint enterprise! Confusion and misunderstanding are almost certain to arise at some points and the leadership services of a "clarifier" may be extremely helpful. As in the case of decisions on agenda, either questions or suggestions can be useful. By someone asking, "I'm lost. What are we talking about now?", the attention of the group may be called to the fact that obstructions need to be removed from the channels of communication. Clarification can be achieved, also, by contributions which point up the relationship between what group members are saying (e.g., "It seems to me that John's plan is similar to the one Bill was describing at our last meeting") or which otherwise provide helpful links (e.g., "Would that be set up the same way as Division X is now?"). Merely requesting others to explain more fully what they mean may also help clarify matters for the entire group.

SUMMARIZING

Another "administrative" problem that arises when groups of people attempt to think together is that as the discussion roves over wide areas of thought, participants tend to forget many ideas that have been proposed or important points that have been made or agreed on. Therefore occasionally it becomes necessary for someone to remind the group of what has been accomplished so that the discussion can be brought back into focus:

"We've had three proposals put before us now—Sam's, Jean's, and Tom's. Are there any others?"

"We agreed at our last meeting that we've got to do something about the congested conditions at the school and that whatever we do we can't exceed the present budget. Where do we go from here?"

VERBALIZING CONSENSUS

An easy way to get rich would be to collect a dollar for every discussion which fails in its purpose because each participant goes away from the meeting with a different idea of what has been decided or agreed on. Frequently members leave the adjourned meeting with such vague ideas of what has been determined that they are incapable of translating their decisions into action. This is such a common ailment among discussion groups because so few people are highly skilled in gathering together the strands of a conversation and making statements which adequately capture the total thinking of the group. To perform this function to the satisfaction of all the diverse elements present requires considerable sensitivity to others as well as a more-than-average talent at verbal expression.

Leadership in Interpersonal Relations

CLIMATE MAKING

The establishment and maintenance of an emotional atmosphere that is conducive to the most productive discussion involves several kinds of leadership services. We would cite first those contributions and actions which help to create a climate of *informality* in the group. This could include everything from the proper arrangement of chairs to suggesting the use of first names or to taking off one's coat. But more important than any of these relatively superficial acts would be the attitude and manner with which one presents his or her ideas when speaking to the group. A cold, impersonal approach particularly on the part of a member who holds a position of high status, can place a group in a deep freeze, whereas a warm and friendly contribution can set an example of ease and informality for others to follow.

Closely related to inducing informality is stimulating *frankness*. Again, this can be accomplished best perhaps by being frank oneself, for such behavior has a way of becoming contagious unless there happen to be rather potent counterforces present in the situation. Frankness can also be increased sometimes by suggesting to the group directly that "we seem to be beating around the bush" and by proposing that "we take off the kid gloves and get down to business."

Providing *emotional support* to other members who are in need of such aid can be another important leadership contribution within the broader category of climate making. Coming to their defense when they are unfairly attacked, helping them to "save face," joining them in opposition to attempted steamroller tactics—all of these actions could add to the maintenance of a permissive atmosphere in which participants would not fear to become involved.

These kinds of emotional support may be helpful in a certain policy-making or learning group, but they might be inappropriate in other situations. Here, as with each of the categories of behavior being described, we must keep in mind that effective leadership depends on the functions of the group. In an experiential group, whose purpose is for individuals to receive feedback from others and to learn about their own emotional responses, it may be unfortunate if someone rushes in to protect those who are temporarily "in the hot seat." Appropriate emotional support in such a situation might take the form of showing people that they are accepted as people despite the fact that some of their behaviors result in negative reactions from others.

REGULATING PARTICIPATION

The fondest hope of a discussant might well be to participate in a group which is so self-disciplined that actions to regulate participation are unnecessary. Unfortunately this is rarely the case. It is the unusual group, indeed, where there is no need whatsoever to draw in nonparticipants, to take or keep the conversation away from overtalkative members, or to restore unity when the discussion splinters into subgroups. Thus, from time to time, someone in the group may need to say something like, "I think Bill had a comment to make a moment ago," or "Shouldn't we hear from everyone on this issue?"

ENCOURAGING OTHERS BY LISTENING

Closely related to climate making and regulating are those behaviors which encourage people to continue contributing once they do feel free to speak and are able to get into the conversation. This involves active listening—showing others that their remarks are attended to. For example, good listeners may rephrase comments of others in their own words, perhaps asking if this is what was intended. In addition, when a listener follows the comment of another by interjecting his or her own idea, it is important that the previous comment be acknowledged by means of a transition statement or a direct response, rather than by an abrupt change of topic. For example, the succeeding speaker may say, "I see your point, but I think there is another fact to be considered."

INSTIGATING GROUP SELF-ANALYSIS

We have found, at a number of points throughout this book, that the most effective answer a group can find to some of its problems may come through a process of self-analysis—a "discussion of the discussion." When this is needed, somebody in the group must become aware of it and instigate the process. To do so, either by proposing self-analysis to the group or simply by plunging in and starting to analyze without first asking the group's consent, is to exert an extremely important influence.

Helping to Manage Conflict

We have omitted from our three general categories of leadership functions and have left to the last a kind of contribution which does not respect the boundaries of classification we have set up—namely, helping the group to deal with conflict. This should serve to remind you once again that classifications and categories, though often helpful in setting forth descriptions, are always artificial, for managing conflict involves elements of all three categories. Effective mediators may be idea leaders who propose new solutions which neither of the parties to a dispute had thought of. They are surely leaders in procedural matters—clarifying, summarizing, and separating out what is agreed on from that which remains in dispute. Finally, those who fulfill this function must be diplomats *par excellence*— remaining on good terms with all parties to the conflict and helping to span the emotional gaps between them.

THE ROLE OF NONVERBAL COMMUNICATION IN LEADERSHIP

The examples given in the previous section consisted of verbal behaviors. This is partly due to the fact that illustrations of what people say in discussions can be accurately expressed in written form, but what people do nonverbally is more awkwardly and less efficiently described in words. In American English, we do not as yet have a precise and widely understood vocabulary for the nonverbal components of interaction. Nevertheless, nonverbal behaviors comprise a major element in leadership contributions. Some investigations have shown that the perception of leadership is affected at least 50 percent by visual cues. For example, a person who "acts like Clark Gable" will be seen as potentially much more influential than one who "acts like Wally Cox" (an actor who played a mild-mannered teacher on the television program "Mr. Peepers").[4]

Nonverbal contributions play an especially important part in leadership in interpersonal relations. For example, it is not always necessary that

[4] See Gitter, Black, and Goldman (1975) and Gitter, Black, and Fishman (1975).

people paraphrase or show by other kinds of verbal responses that they have heard what another member has to say. Some group participants show they are listening simply by maintaining eye-contact with those who are speaking and show that they understand what is being said by nodding or responding with appropriate facial expressions. Some people scan the group to see how others are reacting to what is going on. Although such behaviors are not always perceived as "leadership contributions" by those who are verbally oriented, the consistent use of these subtle signals often exerts a significant influence on group interaction.

Nonverbal behaviors also play a part in idea and procedural leadership, usually in coordination with verbal messages. For example, people who are perceived as influential tend to gesture more than others (O'Connor, 1972). Presumably this lends an element of dynamism to their ideas. Also, as compared to less prominent participants, those acknowledged as leaders tend to address a large share of their comments to the entire group rather than to individuals (Bales, 1950). This means not only that they verbally indicate when remarks are intended for the group as a whole, sometimes using the plural pronoun "we," but also, and perhaps more often, that they look around briefly at each other when they are making comments. Imagine, for example, a person making a procedural suggestion by saying: "Are we in agreement on this point? Could we move on to another issue?" This comment will be much more effective in getting responses from others if it is accompanied by a sweep of the head and eye-contact with all others than if only one or two people are addressed. Conversely, in most situations, a comment made with a shrug of the shoulders, barely audible voice, and downcast eyes does not have much chance of making an impact on the group. A well-conceived observation may fail to meet group functions if it is not accompanied by appropriate nonverbal behaviors.

THE RELATIONSHIP OF STATUS AND FUNCTION

We have said that the functional approach is more consistent with the definition of leadership as action than with those of ascribed or achieved status. The focus is on behaviors as they fit situations; but this is not to say that status and function are unrelated. To the contrary, status is one of the elements of the group situation which influences the effectiveness of any particular membership contribution in meeting functions. Status in most groups may be described not merely in terms of one person who holds a special position, but rather in terms of relative positions in a *hierarchy*. In some situations, such as that found in a group of military personnel of different ranks, prestige is ascribed in advance. In other groups, the relative status of the members emerges as they interact and become more or less influential. In either case, the impact of "what one does" is likely to be affected by "who one is."

In the first place, an individual's position or degree of authority in a group may make it easier or harder for him or her to perform certain leadership functions successfully. For example, it is extremely difficult for a person such as a boss or teacher, who possesses considerable power over other members of the group, to draw nonparticipants into the discussion without making them feel coerced into speaking. A peer can perform the same function much more gracefully. On the other hand, there are some leadership functions, such as initiating discussion or verbalizing a consensus, for which possession of relatively high status in the group is almost a prerequisite. We have observed a number of meetings where attempts by low-status members to initiate a new phase of the problem or to articulate a group conclusion have been ignored, while high-status people, saying virtually the same thing a few minutes later, have met with acceptance. This would suggest that there is a quality about starting a discussion and drawing it to a close which tends to be regarded by most groups as the prerogative of only "duly constituted authorities."

Status not only determines the ease with which particular functions of leadership may be performed, it may also affect the motivation which an individual will feel to take the initiative in assuming leadership responsibilities. For group members to come to the support of another individual whom the group is about to drive over with a steamroller ordinarily requires that they be sufficiently secure in their status to take this risk. Similarly, participants who are unsure of themselves and of their acceptability to the group are less likely to provoke creative thinking through the injection of radical ideas than are those who know that they cannot or will not be ostracized for originality. Some of the research that has been done by Bales (1955) and his colleagues suggests that discussants who provide a group with leadership functions in our categories 1 (creative and critical thinking) and 2 (procedural matters) are likely to arouse some hostility from other group members who may regard them as taskmasters. If this be true and if group members sense it, the performance of those functions is likely to be avoided by individuals whose status in the group is already shaky or who cannot tolerate being disliked.

SUMMARY AND CONCLUSIONS

Leadership may be viewed as the power exercised by the one individual who is elected or appointed to the office of group leader (ascribed status), as the role of the most influential group member (achieved status), or as any *action* by a group member which exerts a significant influence on the course of a discussion. Whichever one of these definitions people favor will have implications for how they perceive and evaluate the discussion process. For example, if they adopt the ascribed status perspective, they may fail to notice influential contributions on the part of those not named as leader or may react negatively to someone other than the designated leader who seems to take over. The definition of leadership as action seems to be the most useful because it aids one in perceiving influence of all kinds, whether it comes from a designated leader, an emergent leader, or anyone else in a group.

Over the years, many theorists have tried to explain how leadership emerges and how it can be made effective. The three most prominent explanations are: (a) that leaders are people with certain traits, (b) that traits interact with situations to determine who will be an effective leader, and (c) that whatever behaviors meet the needs of a group at a particular time will provide the best leadership. The third or "functional" explanation seems to be the most promising because it attempts to deal with the full complexity of leadership phenomena, although research using this perspective has only just begun. Research on the first or "traits" explanation shows that there is no single list of personal characteristics which are highly predictive of individual influence. Studies of the second or "traits and situations" approach suggest that traits are more useful in predicting effectiveness when information about the leader's popularity, the degree of task structure, and the power given to the leader are known. However, despite its advantages, this perspective is limited in applicability to those circumstances where there is a single designated leader and the group situation does not change over time. Also, unlike the functional approach, it does not take into consideration the possibility that leadership within the group can change hands or that various functions can be handled by different members.

Leadership functions can be classified roughly into three broad areas: influence in creative and critical thinking, influence in procedural matters, and influence in interpersonal relations. The first category includes specific actions such as contributing fresh ideas, provoking original thought in others, critically evaluating ideas, encouraging critical thought in others, and making the abstract concrete or the concrete abstract. Leadership in procedural matters encompasses initiating discussion, making agenda suggestions, clarifying, summarizing, and verbalizing consensus or agreement. Influence in interpersonal relations includes such functions as climate making, regulating participation, encouraging others by listening, and instigating group self-analysis. Helping to manage conflict cuts across all three general categories and serves to remind us of their interrelatedness. Most effective leadership behavior in each of these areas involves an appropriate combination of verbal and nonverbal acts.

Finally, note that status and function are mutually dependent in the exercise of effective leadership; that is, there are some functions which are best served by those who are high in status, while others are best performed by those who are not so prominent in the group hierarchy.

STUDY SUGGESTIONS

1. List all of the leadership functions (whether included in this chapter or not) for which it is useful to have high status in a group so as to perform them effectively. Then list all of the leadership functions for which high status seems unnecessary (or actually detrimental) for performing them effectively. Compare the two lists and try to determine why some functions seem to require high status in order to be performed effectively and others do not.

2. It has been observed that most people have a psychological need to think of leadership in terms of ascribed status and that it would be difficult for them to accomodate themselves to the concept of "influential action" advocated by the authors of this book. Do you agree with this? If so, why?

3. Form a group without an appointed leader and give it a task to do or problem to solve. Observe and record every contribution that you believe serves a leadership function. What makes them appear to be leadership? Are they concentrated in a single person, two persons, or more? Do some contributions provide only a single type of needed assistance, but others several?

4. Observe the appointed or elected leader of several groups to which you belong and try to see to what extent each leader encourages the sharing of leadership functions. How do the leaders do this? Which leaders excel at it? Does the membership of the group make a difference? Does the task matter or the time available for completion of the task? How do group members respond to sharing leadership functions? How do the leaders respond to others taking over their functions?

Chapter 12
Philosophies of Leadership

In the previous chapter, we reviewed some ways of defining leadership and explained some causal factors which affect the exercise of influence. We also described the kinds of behaviors needed to fulfill the functions of groups. These are the sources of leadership, the raw materials of influence. But lists of behaviors and explanations of cause and effect relationships do not in themselves tell people how to lead. There are also *value judgments* to be made. For this, group members need a *philosophy* of leadership. Specifically, they need to answer two questions: (1) What is the proper *locus* of leadership, that is, who should have the responsibility for leading? (2) What *style* of leadership—democratic, autocratic, or nondirective—is the most desirable?

THE LOCUS OF LEADERSHIP

Ideally, how should a group distribute its functions among the membership? Should authority be given, as it usually is, to an appointed leader? Should the group plan on the emergence of a single leader? Or, should the group avoid acknowledging any one person as the leader? Each of these approaches tends to correspond to one of the three definitions of leadership given in the previous chapter: as ascribed status, achieved status, and action. Yet, in adopting the broadest meaning—any action which significantly influences the group—we have left the way open to examine any of the three approaches to assigning responsibility.

Each approach has certain advantages and disadvantages. Before reviewing these criteria for choice making, however, we should say something about the third alternative, which may be called "the leaderless group." Here, no one is named as leader, but all are expected to share the job of leading. Most people are so familiar with the idea of appointing or electing a single leader, or acknowledging one person as the emergent leader, that these approaches need no explanation. The leaderless group is not as familiar. Or is it? Many of us may not have recognized the countless times we have participated in leaderless groups without knowing it. A dormitory bull session, a serious discussion at the office, a group of workers solving a mechanical breakdown in a piece of machinery, a class subdivided into project committees—all may be operating unconsciously without acknowledged leaders. Whoever sees a better way of running the meeting will propose how the group should proceed. Others may modify the original suggestion. Soon a consensus emerges, or the idea is dropped and the group moves on. There is no distinction between participant and leader, for each member plays both roles at various times. A person may be in the center of an argument at one moment and an arbitrator at another. On one occasion he or she suggests a solution to the problem and later helps to integrate the proposals of others. One person opens the meeting; another may close it.

The following description of a leaderless meeting may make the concept more concrete:

> The members straggle into the meeting room in groups of one to four. Casual conversations fill the air until apparently all who are coming have arrived. Social talk may continue for a short while, perhaps longer than it would if a single leader were present to call the group to order; but soon one of the members who has business to present will speak up and state his problem. Others will respond. If two or more begin to talk at once, the ones with the least motivation will stop and perhaps even say, "Go ahead," to the one who seems most eager. Conversation will continue until the issue is resolved by someone who can verbalize a summary to which the rest of the group give their assent. If a conflict arises over a point which the majority are interested in pursuing, but which they do not have time to explore fully, someone who is not too deeply engrossed in the issue will interject the suggestion that time is getting short and that the group had better settle the matter by a vote or else postpone it to another time. . . . When the customary closing time approaches, someone will say, "Let's go home." If he voices the sentiments of

the majority, people will begin to get up and leave. If he has interrupted something in which the majority are interested, he will be ignored (Haiman, 1953, p. 321).

Later, if someone were to ask, "Who was the leader?", it would be difficult to answer because no one was recognized as such.

The argument over the proper locus of leadership is complicated by the fact that many people confuse the "leaderless" group with the "leader*ship*less" group. And this distinction is one over which many critics stumble. As we see it, no group activity, from playing sand-lot baseball to negotiating a labor contract, can go on successfully without leadership. To coordinate any mutual undertaking requires somebody to do the coordinating. But in the leaderless group the behavior we call "leading" is so widely shared, so diffused throughout the membership, that to designate a single leader is inaccurate. The group follows whatever person *at that moment* is sensitive enough and skillful enough to meet its needs. A jazz combo is an excellent illustration of distributed leadership. To operate without a leader is not really as foreign to our experience as the word is to our vocabulary. The difference between a leaderless and a led group lies in the locus of authority—in one group it is concentrated in a single individual who has special status in the group, in the other it is shared by many people of equal status. However, both leaderless groups and those with a designated leader may, or may not, have effective leader*ship*.

Those who "read between the lines" of the description above will detect that we generally prefer the leaderless group. But actually, none of these approaches has an absolute advantage over the others. This is illustrated in a study by Wheatley (1966). He compared groups with three different kinds of nominal leaders: (a) a supervisor, who regulated the process in a manner similar to many appointed leaders; (b) a participant, who acted much like an emergent leader; and (c) a nonparticipant, who remained silent and thus forced the group to share responsibility. Group members were least attracted to the supervisory group but were only moderately anxious in that condition. They liked the participant best but talked least with that kind of leadership. They talked the most but also tended to be the most anxious with the silent leader.

Choosing the locus of leadership depends partly on the group situation. In fact, this decision is influenced by the same factors examined in Chapter 10, where we discussed the issue of whether or not a group should employ an agendum. Generally, if a large amount of control is needed, a group will function best with an appointed or elected leader and least well with a leaderless format. The choice also depends on the values of the participants. If stability and predictability are preferred, it is likely that the first choice will be the nominal leader group; the second will be the emergent leader group; and the third will be the leaderless group. If participation, flexibility, and creativity are highly valued, the order might well be reversed.

Advantages of the Nominal Leader Group

Official, centralized leadership, the most familiar pattern, has not survived for so long a time without having many advantages. To begin with, having an officially recognized leader satisfies the desire for a figurehead, someone to look up to. In this sense, naming a chairperson fulfills both a functional and symbolic purpose. Sociologists recognize this factor when they note how frequently someone is elected as leader who not only meets the requirements of the office, but who has sufficient glamor to serve as a sort of substitute father/mother-image. One of the strongest arguments for the English monarchy is that the King and Queen serve as a living embodiment of the values of the British people. This need for a symbol, for someone who represents and embodies the group spirit, may be present even in the small group.

Also, the members of an organization know more clearly where they stand when there is an appointed or elected leader. If everyone is responsible for leadership, it may mean that no one is really responsible. The fluid, unstructured relations in the leaderless group are confusing. Members do not know what is expected of them. Berkowitz (1955), who studied the behavior of college students in experimental situations and executives in business and industry, found, among other things, that group members seemed to want a designated leader and reacted negatively to those who competed with that person for leadership. Likewise, Damusis (1972) has reported that observers of groups give unfavorable ratings to people who talk more than a designated leader. Knowing where one stands may improve communication, because committee members will know what channels exist and will use them with some regularity. External details such as arranging for meetings, preparing reports, scheduling activities, can be handled most efficiently if someone is unmistakably in charge. When decisions are necessary, people will know to whom to look.

There are real advantages, too, in a division of labor. Why not have the most skillful member of a group do the leading and let the rest concentrate on what they can do well? The principle of specialization has worked well in industry and has led to great efficiency and economy of effort. No one interested in winning ball games would substitute a guard for a quarterback or an outfielder for a pitcher. The effectiveness of any committee would seem to be enhanced by putting an experienced and well-qualified leader in the position where he or she can do the most good.

It is true that appointing a leader means some concentration of authority. But is this necessarily bad? With one person in charge group discipline should be easier to maintain. When the leader states a consensus, regulates participation, or rules irrelevant talk out of order, there will be no long, drawn-out argument or bickering over his or her action. Of course, the conformity that is achieved may be only on the surface, but at least order is preserved. Even in self-governing organizations, such as college dormitories, it is often necessary to make some *one* person finally responsible for maintaining rules and regulations. When everyone is a part-time cop, friendships are constantly strained. It is sometimes important, too, to be able to fix responsibility for action. A corporation must be able to hold someone accountable for the failure of its policies. If changes in a factory lead to higher profits, administrative officials want to reward the person most responsible. If a school board makes a decision outside its legitimate authority, citizens must be able to criticize or remove the offending person from office. And, if no one is a leader, who will act as spokesperson for the group, announce their decisions, publicize their activities, or represent them before affiliated organizations?

Furthermore, designated leaders who take their job seriously can act impartially in any crisis that develops. A certain "distance" helps the leader to keep perspective. A chairperson may be able to detect, more easily than others, when the group is getting off the track or when hidden motives are obstructing its operation. Instead of being drawn into conflicts as a partisan, he or she is able to function as an arbitrator or referee.

The advantages of the nominal leader group are not automatically realized, of course. There is some danger that power will be abused, that the leader will throw weight on a preferred side, frankly or subtly. If this happens, the consequences may be disastrous, for the nominal leader's influence is disproportionate to that of the other members. If this power is abused, more harm than good may be done. If not, this kind of leader can assist the group by helping people to be more objective and by separating essentials from nonessentials. Thus, the elected or appointed leader should be chosen carefully with an eye to his or her qualifications, skills, and emotional reactions.

However, it may not be enough to consider the talent or inclination of potential nominal leaders. There is evidence to suggest that the status of such leaders is also important. Kardush (1968) conducted a study in which "status congruent" and "status incongruent" groups were compared. The congruent groups were each led by a graduate student, while other roles were assigned to upper- and lower-division college students. The lower-division student was named leader in the incongruent groups. Task performance was most effective when the high-status person was also the leader. One implication of this finding is that nominal leaders ought to be persons whom others will regard as deserving of the position. Yet, in selecting a leader when there is a conflict among high-status people for the position, groups sometimes compromise and settle for an individual with lower status and, perhaps, fewer qualifications.

Some would argue that the dangers of the nominal leader group are not great, that procedural decisions are of little importance. The really vital decisions involve the topic under discussion; the way in which the group operates, within limits, is a matter of little consequence. Hence, procedural responsibilities may as well be turned over to some individual in the group in order to permit the rest to concentrate on the problem at hand. Leaders who take themselves too seriously or who abuse their position can be deposed; of course, this applies only to democratic groups which elect their leader.

On the whole, those who favor an elected or appointed leader feel that it is the most productive, most efficient, and most satisfying way to conduct group meetings.

Advantages of the Emergent Leader Group

In some groups, one person emerges to become the *unofficial* leader. This might occur in a group with a nominal leader, but it is more likely to happen when no one has been designated as the holder of that position. As we have pointed out in the previous section, group members often resist a person who seems to challenge the nominal leader; in addition, the official leader may be threatened by someone who seems to usurp power.

In the long run, however, the critical factor is the shared "philosophy" of the group members—their feelings on the proper locus of leadership—whether or not there is a nominal leader. Some theorists believe that the rise of one person to the highest status position is more or less inevitable, at least in any effective group (see Fisher, 1974). However, we believe that the emergence of a single leader does not necessarily occur; rather, it must be *permitted* and *encouraged* by the group membership. Admittedly, in this culture there is a certain bias in favor of the notion that "every group must have its leader," but this expectation is not always held by discussion participants. In fact, when members disagree on this issue, a protracted and unresolved "leadership struggle" is likely to ensue.

A group in which members share the belief that someone should achieve the status of leader is an "emergent leader group." Assuming that a leader is "found," there are certain advantages to this kind of arrangement. Most of the benefits are similar to those of the nominal leader group. Group members "know where they stand"; there is someone to discipline the discussion; and there is a good chance that the acknowledged leader can inject some objectivity into the proceedings by means of his or her position. There is even a better chance that the most skilled member will become the leader since the group does not have to choose the leader before they see that person "in action" in the particular situation they face.

In addition, there are certain advantages over the nominal leader group. Unless the status hierarchy becomes set and inflexible, the emergence process can be repeated each time the group faces a new situation. Not having named a leader officially, there is less loss of face for the leader when someone new takes over. Even if changes in leadership are resisted, deposing the leader is usually easier than in the nominal leader group. Also, group members cannot readily object that the leader has risen to power unfairly if the position has been achieved by means of interaction with the entire group rather than by the votes of the majority or by appointment by an outside source. So the dangers of ascribed leadership are lessened.

Still, the emergent leader group is not without its limitations. In the first place, it is not certain that one person will rise to the top. The group may flounder while waiting for someone to take over, each member resisting the responsibility of leadership. Second, who has the ultimate responsibility for the group's actions is less clear than in the case of the appointed or the elected leader. While it is one thing to lead the group in discussion, it is another to act as spokesperson to outside groups. And higher authorities have no one to whom they can look as the official group representative.

Finally, there is one feature of this kind of group which is difficult to categorize as either an advantage or a disadvantage, since, depending on the group situation, it can be beneficial or detrimental. Because the emergent leader seldom has a prescribed function, he or she is seldom limited to the categories of procedural leadership and conflict management. On the other hand, the elected or appointed person, because of being "apart" from the group, often feels forced to take on that role.

The potential advantage is that the emergent leader can contribute in a variety of ways and is not boxed in by a narrow definition of the position. Furthermore, there is evidence that emergent leaders are more satisfied with the decisions reached. For example, in a study of supervisory and participant leaders by Paul Hare (1955), "the supervisory leaders who were specifically told to stay out of the discussion had little chance to influence the group. They tend to have the least agreement with the group . . . after discussion" (p. 558).

The possible disadvantage is that the emergent leader may be expected to fulfill too many functions. It is questionable whether one person can effectively serve roles as procedural disciplinarian, objective overseer of conflict, idea leader, and socioemotional helper, all at the same time. If one or more of these functions is slighted, other group members may not be willing to fill the gap, even though they are capable, especially if they feel "put down" in the leadership struggle which often precedes the emergence of the leader.

Advantages of the Leaderless Group

The leaderless group is like the emergent leader group in that influential actions come from the membership and not from a designated chairperson. But there the similarity ends, because the premise of the leaderless group is that leadership will be shared among the various participants. One leader may emerge for a brief period of time, but the question of influence remains open throughout the group's deliberations. Seldom will one person attempt to handle all essential functions, even during a single meeting.

Because this kind of group is distinctive in outlook, it is natural that its advantages are unique. First of all, the leaderless group draws on the total talents of its members. The motive behind appointing a committee of any sort is that several heads are better than one. If it is true that through discussion more information, more experience, and more inventiveness are brought to bear on the *substantive* problem before the group, will this principle not hold true also for the *procedural* problems of the group? By having a number of alternative leads to choose from and by discussing their merits, the group will be able to function better than it would under the wisest control of a single person. In view of what we know about the effects of hidden agenda upon the course of a discussion, it is clear that the technical problems of working together cannot be dismissed as being of less concern than the objective problem before the group. Too sharp a distinction between the external and internal tasks seems unjustified.

Sharing in the leadership of a group will often lead to greater involvement in its deliberations. As all participants assume more responsibility, they will be likely to attach greater importance to the group and their own roles. Chairpeople of committees usually take the work of a group more seriously than do other members because of the larger role they have in it. Giving greater influence to committee personnel may increase their stake in the outcome of the deliberations.

Avoidance of specialization of roles may also increase a group's survival power. The military platoon in which all responsibility for decisions is assigned to one member does not develop the leadership resources for dealing with emergencies when that one person is lost as a battle casualty or replaced through reassignment. Similarly, the committee that becomes dependent upon its chairperson or emergent leader will most readily fall into chaos when that person is absent or fails to function.

The leaderless group, according to its advocates, is also healthier for people because self-discipline is more effective in the long run than discipline imposed by one person. As Robert Bales has found in his studies of small group interaction, any member who takes over task leadership is likely to arouse hostility toward himself or herself. When leadership functions are shared, people are more inclined to regulate their own behavior. This reduces the need for group restraints and makes people less disposed to use someone as a scapegoat for their own shortcomings.

In addition to these distinctive advantages, the leaderless group improves in some ways on the emergent leader group. We have said that appointing or electing a leader tends to cause specialization of the leadership role and reduces the contributions which can be made by the person in this position. This denies the group part of the potential services of the person who may be its most valuable member and also reduces the satisfaction of the leader. The emergent leader and leaderless groups both avoid this problem, but it is also true that satisfaction with the decision is likely to be more widespread in the leaderless group than in the emergent leader group since all members get a chance to participate more. In addition, the leaderless group does not have the potential disadvantage of relying too heavily on the emergent leader to fulfill critical functions. If everyone shares the responsibility, no one will be kept from contributing worthwhile points for fear of encroaching on the leader's domain.

No way of allocating leadership responsibility is without its drawbacks, of course, and this applies to the leaderless group as well as to the other approaches we have discussed. As we noted earlier in citing the study by Wheatley (1966), anxiety may be greatest in the leaderless group. There is no figurehead or single emergent leader to provide group members with a sense of security. Conversely, if apathy sets in, it is possible that no one will have the motivation to fulfill needed group functions. In addition, it is even more difficult to assign responsibility than in the emergent leader group. However, assuming that tension levels in the beginning of a discussion can be tolerated or will dissipate later, that there is a fairly high degree of concern among the participants, and that there is a sufficient pool of skills among the membership to meet the group's needs, the leaderless group has considerable potential for creative problem solving.

Combinations of Approaches

A group need not be locked into any one of the three alternatives we have examined, although considerable skill and insight may be required to use a combination of approaches successfully. The nominal leader can make it clear that he or she will handle certain organization tasks (calling meetings, turning in the final report, etc.), but that help in fulfilling various functions, including leadership in procedural matters, is sought. Thus, the group may be able to enjoy the advantages of an emergent leader or a leaderless group and still have a figurehead and spokesperson. Also, co-leaders might be named to lead the group. Or a trio of leaders, one functioning in the area of creative and critical thinking, one in the area of procedural matters, and one in the area of interpersonal relations might divide up leadership in the group.

One widely used approach is that of the "leader in reserve." In this case, even though someone is formally designated to lead the group, he or she acts only as needed, usually when no one else serves a given function. In fact, the leader in reserve can coexist with another designated leader, an emergent leader, or an otherwise leaderless group. Such an approach is often used in educational settings where the objective is for group members to learn about a certain topic or about discussion itself. It may also be employed in other places, such as business and industry, when the leader wants group members to work out things for themselves, but lends his or her expertise on occasion.

Frequently, the leader in reserve operates as a kind of balance wheel, serving a variety of functions. If the group is sufficiently involved, he or she will do nothing to stimulate it. If it is moving forward on the task, the leader will refrain from directing its thinking. If a reasonably constructive climate exists, he or she will not interfere. Such a person will sometimes hesitate to exert leadership, even when the group is in trouble, allowing the participants a chance to develop their own solutions to problems before stepping in. But if a problem goes on too long and no one is doing anything about it—if the participants are too partisan, too abstract, or unclear on objectives—the leader will try to help out by making suggestions or interjecting ideas. This role obviously requires experience and perceptiveness on the part of the leader. If he or she jumps in too soon, the purpose of allowing people to decide for themselves is lost. If the leader waits too long to intervene, it may be too late to improve the situation.

Sometimes, the role of the leader in reserve is restricted to fulfilling special functions. For example, a teacher might serve as a resource person, providing information on certain topics. Or, a committee member with special skills in handling conflict might be asked to provide direction only at particular times when help seems especially needed.

STYLES OF LEADERSHIP

A *style* of leadership consists of a pattern of behavior involving a number of different influential acts, all having a common theme. Behind each pattern is a set of assumptions about the needs of the situation or the ways people respond to leadership. There are many ways to Rome, and many ways to lead. One can command, persuade, suggest, or psychologically manipulate. Broadly speaking, however, there are two main styles—autocratic and democratic—and most of the others are subtle variations of these two.

At first glance, it may seem as though styles are determined by the locus of leadership. In a general way, it is true that democracy is more likely to prevail as we move from the nominal leader to the emergent leader and on to the leaderless group. But, as we shall see, it is possible for a single leader to behave democratically, and for a person sharing leadership with others to be nevertheless quite autocratic in style.

The Autocratic and Democratic Styles

The choice of leadership style will be affected by what the influential person perceives the problems of the group to be. The person who uses the autocratic style assumes, at least initially, that full participation is either *unfeasible* or *undesirable*. From this person's point of view, it may be unfeasible because time is limited, the group members are inexperienced in working on the task at hand, or because of some other feature of the group situation. Full participation may be deemed undesirable because people in general, or at least the people involved in this particular group, are regarded as incapable of making certain choices themselves. In addition, the leader may wish to retain power for himself or herself.

On the other hand, the individual who employs the democratic style assumes that full participation is both feasible *and* desirable. It may be thought to be feasible in the immediate situation because the group has time to reach a cooperative decision, because there is sufficient diversity of knowledge and skills within the group to solve the problem, and so forth. Full participation may be seen as desirable because the group members are regarded as having the maturity and motivation to make choices and because the leader thinks that each person should have an equal opportunity to influence decisions.

Growing out of these assumptions are two different ways of behaving. For example, White and Lippitt (1968) describe these contrasting styles as they were used in a particular study of leadership in boys' clubs (p. 319):

Authoritarian	*Democratic*
1. All determination of policy by the leader	1. All policies a matter of group discussion and decision, encouraged and assisted by the leader
2. Techniques and activity steps dictated by the authority, one at a time, so that future steps were always uncertain to a large degree	2. Activity perspective gained during discussion period. General steps to group goal sketched, and when technical advice was needed, the leader suggested two or more alternative procedures from which choice could be made

3. The leader usually dictated the particular work task and work companion of each member

3. The members were free to work with whomever they choose, and the division of tasks was left up to the group

4. The dominator tended to be "personal" in his praise and criticism of the work of each member; remained aloof from active group participation except when demonstrating

4. The leader was "objective" or "factminded" in his praise and criticism, and tried to be a regular group member in spirit, without doing too much of the work

We can make the difference between autocratic and democratic influence in the face-to-face discussion group more concrete if we examine how each style would affect the exercise of leadership functions in the areas specified in the last chapter. In view of the fact that earlier we indicated that leadership might rest in one or all members of the group, we will henceforth use the term "leader" to refer not only to individuals who hold positions as ascribed or emergent leaders, but more broadly to anyone who exerts a significant influence within a group.

INFLUENCE IN PROCEDURAL MATTERS

The difference between autocratic and democratic influence is most clearly seen in the control of procedure. A meeting that is organized openly and collaboratively stands in sharp contrast to one in which choices are limited, or in which no provision is made for alternative procedural arrangements.

Framing the agendum is the first, and one of the most critical, leadership decisions. The specific topics to be considered and the order assigned to them can greatly affect the outcome of the meeting. A person who wishes to dominate the discussion is likely to prepare an agendum privately, rather than publicly, and may not allow others an opportunity to amend or revise it. In some cases he or she may not provide any opening at all for a discussion of group procedure. Democratic group members who wish to contribute to, but not dominate, the planning of a meeting will refrain from imposing their own prearranged plan on the group. Or, if they prepare a draft of an agendum, they will invite others to amend, rewrite, or discard the plan if it seems wise to do so.

Opening a meeting will often bring out the autocratic or democratic tendencies in group members. The person who starts a discussion by arbitrarily stating, "First we will take up the cost figures" or "Where do you all stand on the honor system?" does not encourage or even permit others to have a voice in organizing group thinking. On the other hand, the person who opens a meeting by asking, "How should we go about discussing this problem?" or "Do any of you have ideas on how we should proceed?" does invite others to participate in planning. Even more helpful, and as democratic, is the person who raises the question of procedure and also offers several alternative plans. Such actions not only alert others to the leadership problem they face but also contribute to its solution without cutting off those who may have better suggestions. One of the most difficult problems in the management of discussion is to keep the group moving from point to point without stalling somewhere or getting off on unnecessary tangents. Group thinking is managed autocratically when someone stops discussion of an issue by announcing, "That's irrelevant!" or "we're off the track!" (Some caution must be exercised in interpreting these phrases, since vocal inflection and emphasis can greatly change the meaning. An extremely democratic person, as well as an autocrat, might say "We're off the track," but the former would mean, "In my opinion, we're off the track", and the latter would mean, "We *are* off the track." The speaker's past behavior and general attitude will have to be considered as a clue to his or her present intention.) Any time the group is suddenly catapulted into a new issue without knowing how it got there, it is probable that someone led it there arbitrarily. However, the person who asks, "How does this tie in with our topic?" alerts the group to the problem of relevance and asks for clarification without redirecting attention to a new point. The answer to the question of relevance is a particularly elusive one because it is so difficult, even for experts in group work, to agree on what is relevant and what is not. This fact alone should make arbitrary leadership in this area suspect.

Summaries must be made and agreements verbalized before the work of a group can be terminated. Under autocratic influence, the ideas discussed in the group will be filtered and edited to suit the person who summarizes them. Certain opinions will be repeated accurately, others forgotten, still others reworded in an effort to bring them into line with those of the speaker. Sometimes the sentiments of individual members, or the underlying attitude of the whole group, will be completely overlooked. Or a person may cover up distortions through artful use of language. However, we must be careful not to conclude too quickly that a summarizer is autocratic. It is difficult to phrase a good summary, and many abuses are due to lack of skill, not intent. Some idea of the motive of the speaker can be obtained from his or her readiness to invite revisions in statements or to qualify the conclusions drawn. It may then be clear that accuracy, not manipulation, is intended.

Sometimes the time factor is used to control the direction and depth of group thinking. The autocratic person may allow the group to consume most of its time on minor points and then inform them that only 20 minutes remain in which to reach a conclusion. A democratic leader would make the group fully aware of its time limits and how they will affect the discussion and perhaps suggest some shortcuts. If this is not done, there is the danger that someone will use the lack of time to bludgeon others into approving or disapproving of ideas simply because the deadline demands it.

Whenever members slow a group down, or speed it up, or direct it this way or that, without obtaining the free consent of the participants, they are exercising arbitrary and autocratic control.

INFLUENCE IN CRITICAL AND CREATIVE THINKING

The difference between the two styles is more difficult to detect in the area of substantive thinking than in procedural matters because autocratic control is likely to be submerged in the ideas themselves and, thus, would be more subtle. To some degree, as Sargent and Miller (1971) have found, it is reflected in the amount of talking a person does; autocrats tend to dominate conversations more than those who are democratically inclined. Some indication of the style being used may be seen in the way ideas are phrased. Leathers (1969) found that certain kinds of remarks which would be consistent with the autocratic style were disruptive of group interaction. An example would be the "high-level abstraction": "Don't you think this is basically a matter of historical dialectism?" "Don't you think Reagan is really a Jeffersonian Philistine?" Other participants tended to react to those comments with confusion, tension, and withdrawal. Likewise, Leathers found that interaction was disrupted by statements of "unequivocal person committment": "Let me make my point clear. I don't think we have a shred of evidence to show that Reagan has done anything which requires action by the university." "I say Reagan is a slave to the rich—I don't see how anyone can disagree with that." In contrast, the democratic leader is more likely to express ideas in an open-ended but clear fashion, using qualifying phrases like "One possibility is . . . " or "According to some information I found . . . ," and to go on to report the data and give concrete examples.

Perhaps the difference between the styles in the area of critical and creative thinking is clearest in the way leaders voice their responses to the ideas of others. For example, the autocrat is more likely to employ "dismissal reactions": "That just isn't so!" "It simply won't work!" "That's the most stupid thing I've ever heard!" Or, he or she may try to bring compliance by labeling ideas of others in very positive or negative ways as "reactionary," "atheistic," "monopolistic," "Christian," "materialistic," "dictatorial," or "democratic." These kinds of linguistic devices occur less often in the comments of a person using the democratic style.

Likewise, each style tends to go with certain ways of dealing with a conflict of ideas. The autocratic style is most consistent with the strategies of *avoidance* and *suppression,* which we discussed in Chapter 8. When others express ideas with which the autocrat disagrees, he or she may lecture about the importance of unanimity, suggest that others are being unreasonable, or make references to supposed threats from outside authorities. The person who uses these tactics does not always have to be in a high-status position in order to exert influence. One low-status member we once observed won his point by repeatedly suggesting that "the administration is very much opposed to this." Since he was the only one who claimed to have a private line to the source of power his statements had a devastating effect on the decisions that were reached.

On the other hand, the democratic style is more consistent with conflict management strategies of *prolongation* and *collaboration*. Democratic leaders may encourage conflict by saying, "I think it's good that we're getting all these diverse opinions on the table." They may ask open-ended questions which are likely to bring out ideas opposed to their own views, and they may even express positions with which they disagree in order to have ideas discussed.

Despite the examples we have given here, it is often true that the autocratic and democratic styles cannot be identified by the way a person expresses a single idea. A democratically inclined person may sometimes be blunt. Autocrats sometimes appear to be open to the ideas of others, even though they have a clear picture in advance of how things should turn out. Sir Winston Churchill, in response to a reporter's charge that he was an autocrat, is said to have replied, "I'm not an autocrat, I simply believe that after due discussion my cabinet ministers ought to agree with me." It is sometimes necessary to carefully examine a pattern of behavior over time in order to detect the underlying motives and actual style of the leader. For example, people who seem to listen to others but agree only with ideas which strengthen a certain position and who disagree only with those ideas in favor of other positions which can be most readily refuted are behaving autocratically. On the other hand, democratic leaders often confront opposing ideas directly, but they also tend to concede points and modify their positions.

INFLUENCE IN INTERPERSONAL RELATIONS

Autocratic influence in regulating participation can take many forms. Those who monopolize a conversation are, by the very act of talking so much, forcing others to remain silent. On the other hand, when active members insist that nonparticipants express an opinion, they also prevent noncontributors from choosing to stay out of the discussion. A remark such as "We ought to hear from everyone on this," democratic as it sounds, is actually quite coercive. There are also indirect—nonverbal—methods of controlling participation. Turning away while someone is speaking, snickering, gesturing approval or disapproval, are all attempts to impose certain habits of communication on others. Even the group member who seldom talks is sometimes guilty of autocratic behavior in this area.

Is it possible to bring about better communication in a group and still do it democratically? It may be difficult, but it is possible. When a person communicates effectively—listens empathically, avoids interrupting, speaks to the entire group, expresses himself or herself frankly—that person encourages but does not force others to behave in certain like ways. Or when members become aware of communication barriers in the group and bring them to the attention of the rest of the members, they make it possible to discuss the difficulty openly without imposing standards on others. Also, it is possible to ask another for an opinion without putting the person on the spot or compelling an answer. For example, one might simply say "Joe, do you have anything further to add?" rather than "What's your opinion, Joe?"

When we turn to democratic and autocratic influence in other areas of interpersonal relations, climate making in particular, we are dealing with a subtle phenomenon. Feelings of warmth and acceptance, or of coldness and rejection, are conveyed very largely by nonverbal messages. The way we dress says something to others. Our gestures and posture communicate our personality. Just as a formal arrangement of magazines on a coffee table says, "Do not touch," so the wrinkling of a brow, the tightening of lines around the mouth, or the nervous drawing in of a breath may say, "Let's not talk so frankly. I am getting uncomfortable." Conversely, a quieting pause or a look of acceptance may establish rapport and understanding.

The climate in any group is also a product of many kinds of remarks. On a hot day, the person who tells everyone to "Take off your coats" forces everyone to conform, including the person who suspects his shirt is embarrassingly wilted, while the question, "Do you want to take off your coats?" is noncoercive (especially when it comes from a low-status person). A discussion of housing may be forced to a personal level if someone belligerently announces what his house cost, implicitly demanding that others be as confidence-sharing as he is. The list of ways in which we influence interpersonal relations is endless, but the principle is clear: Any attitude, action, or statement that makes it difficult for others to respond spontaneously and autonomously is not democratic.

Of the two styles described above, the democratic pattern will usually have more positive effects, at least in those group situations where discussion, mutual influence, and creative problem solving are appropriate. There is some evidence that the autocratic style fosters greater productivity, at least in such tasks as solving arithmetic problems (Shaw, 1955) and doing clerical work (Morse and Reimer, 1956). However, most studies have also shown that group members were more satisfied with their work and with interpersonal relations in democratically led groups (Cf. Preston and Heintz, 1949). When it is important that the group members be committed to decisions in order to carry them out successfully, satisfaction with the group product is especially important. In addition, most of the studies which show increased productivity for autocracy involve groups which work together for only a brief period of time. Negative feelings about a group will tend to influence productivity in the long run. Also, extended use of the autocratic style may have disastrous effects on social climate. In Lewin, Lippitt, and White's (1939) classic study of boys' clubs, autocratically led groups were characterized by hostility, aggression, and scapegoating, and the quality of the products was inferior to that of the democratically led groups.

In general, the democratic style seems more consistent with the aims and potentialities of discussion as a means of decision making. However, we are reluctant to say that this pattern is always preferable. In the first place, inexperienced leaders may have trouble performing effectively in the democratic role. Referring to one of his own studies, Shaw (1976) reports that:

> . . . both the most and least effective groups had democratic leaders; there was relatively little variance among autocratic groups. It is easy to issue orders, but difficult to utilize effectively the abilities of group members. If a leader doubts his ability to be an effective democratic leader, then he is well advised to play the autocratic role (p. 279).

Second, there are situations which call for a strong hand. Examples from certain military organizations and social institutions which deal with delinquent children come readily to mind. In other cases, where democracy would ordinarily work better, there may be times when the group is floundering and in need of some autocratic control.

Autocratic and Democratic Belief Systems

Thus far in our discussion of leadership styles, we have tried to describe autocratic and democratic behaviors without referring to *types of people*. It is feasible that styles of leadership can be donned much like different kinds of clothing. For example, a person could be an autocrat at home on certain issues of child rearing, and a democrat at work when deciding how to approach a given task. And yet, most people are probably inclined more to one style than the other, and some individuals appear to use a certain style *consistently* regardless of the situation. This phenomenon was conceived of as a personality syndrome in some of the early research (see Adorno, *et al.*, 1950). More recently, these tendencies have been explained as *belief systems* (see Rokeach, 1960).

When autocratic or democratic orientations are viewed as beliefs about the nature of human beings, two distinct sets of assumptions emerge. In the sphere of business management, these have been referred to by McGregor as Theory X (the autocratic orientation) and Theory Y (the democratic approach):

Under Theory X, management makes the following assumptions about human behavior:

1. The average human being has an inherent dislike of work and will avoid it if he can.
2. Therefore, most people must be coerced, controlled, directed, and threatened with punishment if management is to get them to put forth adequate effort toward the achievement of organizational objectives.
3. The average human being prefers to be directed, wishes to avoid responsibility, has relatively little ambition, and wants security above all.

Behind this conventional theory, there are several additional beliefs—less explicit, but widespread:

4. The average human being is inherently self-centered and indifferent to organizational needs.
5. He is by nature resistant to change.
6. He is gullible, not very bright, and the ready dupe of the charlatan and the demagogue.

Under Theory Y, management makes the following assumptions about human behavior:

1. The expenditure of physical and mental effort in work is as natural as play or rest.
2. External control and the threat of punishment are not the only means for bringing about effort toward organizational objectives. Man will exercise self-direction and self-control in the service of objectives to which he is committed.
3. Commitment to objectives is a function of rewards associated with their achievement.
4. The average human being learns, under proper conditions, not only to accept, but to seek, responsibility.
5. The capacity to exercise a relatively high degree of imagination, ingenuity, and creativity in the solution of organizational problems is widely, not narrowly, distributed in the population.
6. Under the conditions of modern industrial life, the intellectual potentialities of the average human being are only partially utilized.
7. The essential task of management is to arrange organizational conditions and methods of operation so that people can achieve their own goals best by directing their *own* efforts toward organizational objectives.[1]

There is some evidence to suggest that there are various personality traits associated with each kind of orientation. Rosenfeld and Fowler

[1] This summary of McGregor's point of view is excerpted from Goldhaber and Goldhaber, (1973), pp. 266–267. Also, see McGregor (1960).

(1976) gave subjects a battery of psychological examinations and the Sargent and Miller Leadership Questionnaire, a scale designed specifically to measure autocratic and democratic orientations of individuals to group situations (Sargent and Miller, 1971). They found that autocratic leaders, whether male or female, tended to be "aggressive," "revengeful," and "desirous of being the recognized authorities in their relationships." However, it is interesting that male and female democratic leaders were rather different in personality. They conclude:

> Whereas democratic males were characterized as forceful . . . [and] analytical . . . democratic females were characterized as open-minded and nurturing. The democratic male may appear to group members as analytical and thereby aloof, while the democratic female may appear to be warm and affectionate (p. 324).

The results suggest that autocratic leaders may be rather consistent in style, but that there are at least two ways of performing the democratic style which correspond to cultural sex roles—the (male) task leader and the (female) socioemotional leader (see Bales and Slater, 1955). It should be noted, however, that these findings do not mean that either sex has a monopoly on either set of attributes or skills.

To the degree that the autocratic and democratic styles are tied to deep-seated beliefs and enduring personality tendencies, flexibility in the performance of leadership functions is limited for individuals. And yet, the person who has democratic leanings seems to have a certain advantage in this regard. In describing the study by Rosenfeld and Fowler above, we noted that the democratic orientation may take two forms, males being directed more toward task accomplishment and females toward interpersonal relations. As people become more androgynous, less governed by rigid sex roles, it may be that individuals of either sex will be able to perform either type of democratic role. There is also evidence that people with democratic tendencies are more able to adapt their behavior to varying situations calling for either authoritarian control or democratic permissiveness (Rice and Chemers, 1975).

Recognizing the repercussions of the consistent use of either style and practicing a new style can be helpful. We have already said that the autocratic style is easier to acquire. There is also evidence that people can be trained to employ the democratic style.[2] It should be noted that there is a tendency for individual leaders who have learned the democratic style to regress toward older autocratic patterns when they return to organizations which are autocratically run (Fleishman, Harris, and Burtt, 1955); that is, the surrounding system affects the style employed within groups. But as Lippitt (1949) has shown, the effects of training last longer if the group is trained to work democratically *as a team*. In short, while belief systems and personalities may function as stumbling blocks to effective leadership,

[2] See Barnlund (1955) and Flieshman, Harris and Burtt (1955).

especially in the case of the less flexible person with autocratic tendencies, there is reason to believe that people can be trained to perform either style as the situation requires. In most circumstances, the democratic style will work best, especially if all members of a group know how to use this approach.

Variations in Styles

In this chapter, we have tried to isolate the styles of leadership (the method of influence) from the question of locus (who will influence). But it is obvious, in some cases, that the two are closely related. People occasionally behave autocratically in a leaderless group, giving orders or coercing others, but this is difficult to sustain when leadership is shared. The group must be willing to allow the emergence of some person (or a coalition of people) if the autocratic style is to be employed extensively. The single leader, especially the nominal leader, has the opposite problem. The more the leader "leads," the more likely it is that he or she will be using autocratic style.

One solution to this dilemma is for the nominal leader to employ a *combination* of styles, varying behavior according to the issue at hand. On some issues, the leader assumes it is his or her right or obligation to be autocratic, while on other issues he or she functions in a democratic fashion. For example, an executive may retain the right to hire and fire, first receiving "input" from others, but making the final decision alone, while at the same time allowing decisions on job assignments to be made democratically. This is a difficult solution to implement successfully because issues may overlap and some group members may feel that they don't know where they stand if a leader switches back and forth between the two styles. That is, if the boss can hire and fire, the group members may wonder how free they are to decide on issues of job assignment. Often however, if it is clear in advance how issues are to be handled, group members will feel that they know where they stand and confusion will be minimized. (In fact, these decisions can be made democratically.) Of course, it is also important that the leader keep these understandings clearly in mind, and the person with democratic personality tendencies will find this easier to do.

What if the nominal leader wishes to be *consistently* democratic? Such a person may believe that there are no situations (at least with respect to the particular group in question) which justify autocratic leadership, and that, in the long run, it is best to deal with every topic or decision through full participation. Yet, this person may find himself or herself in a position of leadership responsibility. A solution to this problem is to be found in a variation on the democratic style known as "nondirective leadership" (see Chapter 7). This method derives from nondirective counseling procedures. Therapists who use this approach refrain from controlling, advising, or directing the client. They do this for a number of reasons: First, they recognize the tremendous influence they have on the client because of their position and training; second, they do not want to coerce other people into living by their standards; third, they believe that every person has the potential for becoming autonomous and mature if given time and support.

By following in the footsteps of the nondirective therapist, an officially designated leader can work toward sharing leadership responsibilities with the members of the committee and cultivate in them the skills they need. In spite of the position of such leaders, they can refrain from offering direction at critical junctures in the life of the group. They can withhold leadership, sometimes allowing the group to flounder, so that participants will develop their own motives for leading. On some occasions they may alert the group to its problems but refuse to solve them. On other occasions they will offer so many alternatives in response to the group members' requests for help, that the participants will still have to make their own decisions.

One thing such leaders will not do, however, is default from leadership. Laissez-faire and nondirective leadership are different breeds altogether. Laissez-faire leaders do nothing at all, either because they do not know what to do or because they do not care. The nondirective leader works hard. Such leaders listen intently to what is being said. They try to understand what people are saying to one another—both consciously and unconsciously. They will try to relay back to the group what they believe the members are feeling so that they will become more sensitive to their own impulses. As one of the patients in a group psychotherapeutic session remarks in the book *Fortunate Strangers*, "there's a great deal of difference between do-it-yourself and a relationship in which another person says, in effect, "Try it and I will help you explore the unknown and yourself" (Beaukenkamp, 1958, p. 125).

Here again, we return to the question of the locus of leadership to find a parallel. The leader who uses the nondirective style is also a "leader in reserve." The difference is that when the leader in reserve enters the discussion, he or she may do so in an autocratic fashion (making decisions, giving orders), in a directive but democratic manner (suggesting ideas or procedures), or in a nondirective mode (voicing feelings expressed by others, interjecting observations on the group process).

SUMMARY AND CONCLUSIONS

We have said that group members need more than factual knowledge about the variables which affect leadership (the subject of the previous chapter). They also need to know about philosophies of leadership so that they can make value judgments intelligently.

One kind of choice involves the *locus* of leadership—the question of *who* will be expected to do the leading. Responsibility can be assigned to a nominal leader, who usually functions primarily in the area of procedural matters; it can be delegated informally to an emergent leader, who tends to fulfill several functions; or it can be shared by all members of a group. In addition, there are various possible combinations of these approaches, including the role of the designated leader who stays "in reserve" until needed by the group.

The other kind of choice concerns the *style* of leadership. Regardless of the locus of responsibility, those who exert influence may do so in an autocratic fashion (controlling procedures, pressing for the acceptance of certain ideas, cajoling others to behave in particular ways, and sometimes coercing and manipulating others), or they can behave democratically (suggesting procedures, proposing ideas, and encouraging certain kinds of interpersonal behavior). Although some individuals use one style or the other rather consistently because of their beliefs about human nature and personality tendencies, there is some evidence that people can be trained to use either style. Such flexibility is probably easier to achieve for the person who is democratically inclined. In addition, variations on these styles are possible, including combinations of both behaviors—democratic on some issues and autocratic on others—and a particular style in which a designated leader behaves democratically in a "nondirective" manner.

Although the locus of leadership and styles of leadership can be considered separately, they are not totally independent. While the autocratic style can exist with any of the three approaches to delegating responsibility, it flourishes when there is a single nominal leader and is progressively more difficult to employ as we move to the emergent leader group, and, most especially, the leaderless group. The reverse is true for the democratic style.

In deciding on the locus and style of leadership, group members should be aware of the total group context and of philosophical alternatives. We cannot give you a blueprint for successfully handling the problem of leadership in every possible situation. Partly this is because there are so many combinations of factors which might come into play in any one context, and partly we are reluctant to make choices for you because it is necessary to make value judgments in weighing the merits of each locus and style. However, we can suggest what factors may be involved and how they might influence choices.

In general, *the greater the need of the group members for direction, the more importance attached to efficiency in performance of the task, the larger the group, and the greater the external pressures for quick decisions, the more attractive centralized and autocratic leadership becomes.* A small committee of close friends may work well without a chairperson because many of the problems of leadership-competition for the floor, communication breakdowns, the need to summarize diverse ideas—do not arise. As a committee grows in size, diffused leadership becomes more and more difficult and finally impossible. A sinking ship, a burning theater, and military rout are situations that call for a single, powerful figure. By the same token, we should remember that we spend very little of our lives on sinking ships or in burning theaters, and *any decrease in the pressure for decisions should favor more diffused and democratic leadership as a way of preparing for future emergencies, promoting good interpersonal relations and satisfaction among group members, allowing for personal growth, and encouraging creative thinking.*

STUDY SUGGESTIONS

1. Do a brief survey of a number of groups that regularly meet to handle various types of problems. (Good sources for information on existing groups might be campus or local newspapers, bulletin boards, activities calendars, and so on.) Select several that are as diverse as possible. What kind of leadership would you expect to find at these meetings or in these groups? Make predictions about the degree of centralization and style of leadership in each group. Then visit the groups to confirm your expectations. Which ones do not conform to your predictions and why?

2. Many discussion groups have nominal leaders who occupy positions of power and authority in relationship to the group members—a teacher in a classroom, a boss at a conference with employees, or the President of the United States at a cabinet meeting. Do you think that a leader can successfully establish ground rules for such a group so that it can function as an emergent leader group or as a leaderless group? What difficulties would you expect might be encountered in such an effort?

3. It has sometimes been argued that to speak of "democratic leadership" is to indulge in a contradiction in terms—that to the extent one leads, no matter how openly or tentatively, one is acting autocratically. Do you agree? Why or why not?

Part V
IMPLICATIONS OF THE DISCUSSION PROCESS

Chapter 13
The Self and Groups

If you have been reading the chapters in this book in the order they are presented, you may have been asking yourself all along, "What does this have to do with me?" This is a natural question—so natural, in fact, that if you thumbed through the Contents before you began reading, you might very well have picked this chapter to read first. In a sense, it is both one of the first and one of the last topics to be considered when examining social interaction. Similarly, when one enters a group, he or she is likely to be wondering, "Who am I in this group?" The individual's self-concept is involved in the way he or she relates to others.

As the term is ordinarily used, "self-concept" refers to "the way a person consciously perceives himself or herself." Argyle (1967, 1969) identifies three dimensions of self-concept:

1. One dimension is the "ego-identity" or "self-image." This is the way a person structures self-perceptions, and it consists of all the traits, qualities, roles, attitudes, and habits that people use to describe themselves.

2. The second dimension is "self-esteem," the overall evaluation that one assigns to his or her self. It may be described as "the degree to which I am praiseworthy" or "the degree to which I accept the way I am." We would add that in addition to the general feeling of self-worth, a person may vary in self-esteem from one part of the self-image to another; that is, he or she may feel good about some role performances, attitudes, and so forth, and not others.

3. The third dimension is the "ego-ideal," the way the person would *like* to be. As Argyle (1967) says, "This may be based on particular individuals who are taken as admired models, and who may be parents, teachers, film stars, or characters from literature. It may consist of a fusion of desired characteristics drawn from various sources" (p. 118).

Self-concept and communication are related in two ways. First, how we see ourselves influences the way we communicate with others. For example, a person who has high self-esteem about his or her performance in groups will behave differently from one who has low self-esteem in the same context. Second, and conversely, communication influences self-concept; that is, it is largely through the process of interacting with others that we develop our self-concepts.

CHANGES IN SELF-CONCEPT

There are several ways that alterations in self-concept can occur. Most authors stress the role of social situations and other people in the growth process. For example, Argyle (1969) suggests the following:

1. *Role-playing.* The individual may find himself or herself performing a new social function—"father," "mother," "group leader," etc.

2. *Feedback.* Others may tell the person how they see him or her, or they may give indirect feedback in the form of approval or disapproval of the way a person is behaving.

3. *Comparison with others.* A person may decide that he or she is either better or worse than he or she thought, depending on who is available for observation and comparison.

4. *Imitation.* The individual may copy someone who provides a model for the way that individual would like to be.

Obviously, these ways of change can work together. A person may receive positive or negative feedback for a new role he or she has played, and this role performance might be acquired by imitation. A parent may give feedback to a child by comparing him or her to a sister or brother.

Some authors have suggested that an individual can become the source of his or her own change. That is, people are not solely dependent on others in forming a view of the self; they can influence their own perceptions. Methods such as meditation, introspection, and using "the power of positive thinking" are all ways of changing self-concept. For example, people who use techniques of "visualization" (Samuels and Samuels, 1975) or "psycho-cybernetics" (Maltz, 1960) *imagine* themselves performing effectively in certain social circumstances. They play out scenes *in their minds* as they would like things to happen. They can also anticipate everything that could go wrong, visualizing themselves handling each problem effectively. As a result, according to the proponents of this approach to self-help, the individual develops a more positive self-image and also performs more proficiently in the actual situations.

THE SALIENCE OF SELF-CONCEPT

Michael Argyle argues that "the self does not affect all behaviour: it influences behaviour in situations which are 'ego-involving' " (1969, p. 357). We would qualify this position by saying that self-concept *always* affects behavior, but sometimes it is more influential than others. Conversely, at those times when self-concept is highly salient, the person's self perception is especially subject to influence from others.

Argyle (1969) suggests several conditions which make self-concept especially salient for the individual (pp. 373–378). First, awareness of the *presence of an audience*—being monitored by one or more people—heightens consciousness of self. Second, *assessment by others* produces a similar effect. An example of this would be a job interview. Third, *conditions of individuation* (as opposed to "de-individuation") increase awareness of self. For example, being in a crowd or dealing with unresponsive strangers in a bureaucratic setting promotes de-individuation. Being the "odd person out"—the only female, the only nonblack, etc.—creates a tendency toward individuation. Finally, experiencing *penetration* by others, when another or others see beyond the public self to a more private aspect of the person, also makes self-concept more salient. This can occur by accident, as when a crisis situation unveils aspects of personality not ordinarily seen by others. Or, the person may make a choice to self-disclose, as when feelings are discussed with a close friend, a therapist, or an experiential group.

In addition to the above situational factors, Argyle also discusses the notion that there are individual differences which affect the saliency of the self. People who experience anxiety about social situations feel more "exposed" or "observed" than do others; they feel they show more because they can't help it. Others frequently self-disclose on purpose; they are "exhibitionistic" or "open."

In short, Argyle's analysis suggests that anything which causes an individual to feel that attention is focused on his or her social performance brings the self-concept into play in a significant way. Therefore, it is easy to see why self-concept is so often discussed in the context of dyadic communication. Since each partner in a dyad is the sole object of response of the other, the potential for feeling "assessed," "individuated," and "penetrated" is greater than in the multiperson group. Of course, multiperson groups provide a larger potential audience, but they do not provide the constant surveillance characteristic of the two-person interaction.

On the other hand, it can also be seen that these conditions exist in multiperson groups, particularly at certain times. One of these occasions is the first meeting of a group. The exact roles of the participants are unknown, and individuals may devote considerable energy to the task of making a good first impression. This is especially true if the participant is a newcomer to an established group. Later, self-concept becomes highly salient whenever the individual feels *singled out*—as a leader, a deviant, or simply the object of group attention. At these times of individual prominence in the group, the effect of the reactions of others on a person's self-concept may be rather powerful. While there may be more instances where the self is salient in dyads, the cases where it is salient in groups may be very significant because any unified response from several people carries special force.

There is one other circumstance beyond first meetings or situations in which the individual is singled out where the multiperson group may have a strong impact on self-concept. That occurs when membership in the group is very important to the person. This group identity can become a rather permanent part of the self-concept which is carried by the individual into other contexts; that is, even when not with the other group members, the person may think of himself or herself as a member of a certain fraternity or sorority, an official of a certain organization, or a representative of a certain prestigious group.

IMPORTANT GROUPS

Nearly every group makes certain demands on individual members. In Chapter 6, "Group Culture," we referred to this process as the "maintenance of group norms." Some norms, or standards for behavior, place expectations on all members of a group. Others accompany roles that individuals are supposed to play. Whether a person *internalizes* these norms, incorporating them as part of the self, depends on the susceptibility of the individual and the importance he or she attaches to the group.

No doubt there are certain groups in everyone's life in which the conditions of saliency of self are not very strong. The person feels ignored or chooses to withdraw, is little concerned about the evaluations of others, reveals little about self, and is generally apathetic toward membership.

But the point that groups do play an important role in self-concept can be illustrated by examining some especially significant groups.

For almost everyone, the family is the first group experience. Obviously, it is especially significant to the development of self-concept because it coexists with the early, formative years. Parents, and perhaps siblings, supply the individual with important information about who he or she is. Although people tend to grow away from the family influence as they get older (at least in American society), some rather permanent effects on self-image and self-esteem are usually made. For example, individuals begin to form impressions about whether or not they are "lovable," "responsible," "intelligent," and "strong."

Later in life, most people become a part of a new family group, at first as a member of a romantic dyad, and then often as a parent. When children come along, the individual may become aware for the first time that the relationship of parent and child is one of reciprocal influence. The offspring as well as the marriage partner provide an important audience before which the parent plays out a new role while also affecting the self-concept of the others in the family. It is in recognition of the dynamic relationship of the family and the self-concept that family (as opposed to individual) therapy has become an important clinical practice.

As a child grows older, the breadth of group involvement increases, and the family loses some of its power. At first, the new group may consist of friends who live on the same block; the child learns by imitation and comparison as he or she discovers the expectations other families place on their members. Later, significant group memberships may include a circle of close friends at school, a street gang, an athletic team, a fraternity or sorority, a tight-knit group of work associates. And the evolution of the self-concept continues.

The significance to the self of each of these various kinds of groups depends in large part on the value the individual places on membership. Social psychologists have drawn a distinction between two kinds of groups (see Siegel and Siegel, 1957). *Membership* groups are those in which the person has a sense of belonging. *Reference* groups are those in which the person aspires to attain or maintain membership.

Since one actually interacts with others in his or her membership groups, such affiliations are likely to have some influence regardless of the importance of the group to the individual, but reference groups are probably especially significant in their impact on self-concept. Low self-esteem may result if the individual does not obtain membership in the groups to which he or she aspires. On the other hand, admittance to membership in a reference group will ordinarily cause an increase in self-esteem, at least at first. If the other members of the reference group seem to value the inclusion of the person, self-esteem may soar, but, if not, self-esteem may be affected negatively in the long run.

In some cultures, reference groups are all-important to the development of self-concept. In fact, as Delores and Robert Cathcart (1976) have pointed out, in Japan there is virtually no distinction between one's group memberships and one's perceptions of self. The individual obtains his or her identity from certain basic groups, especially the extended family, which include not only the nuclear family but other relatives as well, and the work group—the organization which serves as a larger "family" for the employee. The Japanese are unlikely to have a "circle" of casual friends outside such group ties.

In the United States, this is clearly not the case. Reference groups may be important, but they are not the only associations in which the self-concept can be anchored. In this culture, it is as though each person were assigned a constant task of deciding "Who am I?". Americans pursue this task in a variety of ways—selecting friends and marriage partners, seeing a psychotherapist, reading books on self-improvement. But a significant, and virtually inescapable, part of this process involves joining and interacting in groups. Much more than the Japanese, Americans are in a position to be influenced by many groups.

MODELS OF SELF-CONCEPT

Thus far, we have discussed self-concept as though everyone saw his or her self in the same terms. The fact is, however, that there are different ways of conceptualizing the self-concept. In this section, we will present three basic models of the structure of self-concept, each identified with the name of a theorist who has proposed a way of describing the self. Just as there are different theories of the self depending on who is doing the theorizing, you may find one of these models more acceptable than the others, or you may conclude that a combination of approaches is necessary to describe your own personal view of the self.

Gergen's "Many Masks" Model

The American social psychologist Kenneth Gergen attacks the popular notion that we have "a single, basic self to which we can be true," as well as the idea that it is healthy to have such a central identity. Rather, he suggests that it is normal for people to play many roles in everyday life, even in a single day. What is more, he proposes that the "healthy, happy human being" is one who wears many such masks (see Gergen 1972).

The structure of Gergen's view of the self can be inferred from his writings. It is presented in diagrammatic form in Figure 9. There are a number of spaces in this diagram, each representing a general role which a person might play, with specific examples of each category labeled within each space. Keep in mind that this diagram is presented for illus-

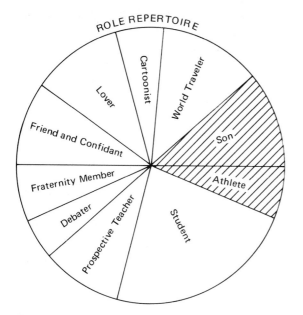

Figure 9 Gergen's "many masks" model. (*Note*: The shaded area indicates a
hypothetical "here–and–now" situation in which two roles are played at once.)

trative purposes only. An actual person would be unlikely to have exactly
this sort of picture in his or her head, and, in most cases, there would be
many more roles in the individual's view of self.

The varying sizes of the slices represent the importance which each
role might assume for a hypothetical person. For some people, let us say a
college athlete planning to become a professional football player, one role
might occupy a major "slice" of the self. While Gergen doesn't deny the
possibility of central tendencies—roles which overlap other roles in various particular situations—he feels that these aspects of personality have
been overestimated in their impact on an individual's behavior.

The effect of the self-concept on communication at any one point in
time, the "here-and-now," is illustrated by the shaded areas of Figure 9.
Ordinarily, a person would see himself or herself in one or more roles on a
particular occasion. We have shaded in two roles, which would represent
the self-concept of a person whose father and mother might have come to
watch him play a tennis match. However, it would not be possible for the
person to play all roles at once, so it would not make sense to shade in all
areas. Some roles could be played together, but only with great difficulty
because of inherent contradictions between the expectations for role performance. Such situations might occur when a person tries to be both
"mother" and "daughter" as she brings a child to visit with grandparents,
or when a person invites two very different kinds of friends to a social

event and tries to perform contradictory roles as "wild party person" and "polite conversationalist."

For Gergen, changes in the role repertoire take place when the social situation changes. In the short run, this might simply mean that the person plays a role for which he or she receives positive feedback, finds himself or herself making a comparison to a person with certain qualities, or performs a task which calls on him or her to exhibit certain qualities. In the long run, the possibilities for the role repertoire might change. For example, when a student graduates from college and takes a job as a teacher, the classroom situation is likely to suddenly and dramatically change his or her role perspective. These changes in the self-concept could be represented in Figure 9 (although we have not done so) by inserting a slice in the pie to represent the adoption of a new role, or by removing a slice to represent the elimination of a role from the repertoire. Gergen also implies that the flexible person, who can play many social roles effectively, is likely to think well of his or her self in general, since the ability to adapt readily to new social situations and to discover "new selves" tends to enhance self-concept. The more masks the person can don successfully, the higher the self-esteem.

Although Gergen says that there are cultural forces which encourage individuals to seek a central, inflexible identity, in some ways his model is likely to have particular appeal for Americans since it stresses adaptability and change. If one accepts Gergen's model as an accurate description of the structure and functioning of self-concept, there are certain implications for the relationship between one's view of self and group participation. Potentially, the ability of each person to adapt to the expectations of the group are great. The person can see self as "leader" at one time and "follower" the next, depending on how he or she reads what is appropriate to the situation. The degree to which the person is able to adapt effectively to the role requirements of the group situation depends on what William Wilmot (1979) calls "the residual self," the residue of past experiences the individual has had with playing similar roles. A person who has been encouraged by his or her past experiences with a certain role will find it easier to adopt that role in a new group. If this description seems positive, another implication of the Gergen view of self may seem negative. It also implies that most people are inclined to be conformists. While they have the potential to fulfill group expectations, they may find it difficult to play the role of the deviant, even if that is what the group needs.

Argyle's "Core- and Sub-Identities" Model

British social psychologist Michael Argyle (1967, 1969) has a view of self-concept which is similar to that of Gergen in that he sees the individual as playing many roles, but it is different in that Argyle's model also includes

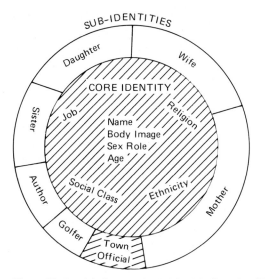

Figure 10 Argyle's "core and sub-identities" model. (*Note*: The shaded area indicates a hypothetical "here-and-now" situation in which aspects of the core and one sub-identity are operant.)

a central, constant element in the self. Figure 10 shows the relationship of these two parts of the self in diagrammatic terms. The "core" consists of those characteristics of the individual which are not situation-bound; they are potentially salient in every social encounter. The most basic of these characteristics are the person's name, body-image, sex role, and age. Frequently, the core identity also includes the individual's job, social class, religion, and race or ethnicity. However, whether these latter factors are part of the core image depends on whether the person considers these to be central to self-identity. Each might be either a core characteristic or a "sub-identity." "Sub-identities" are like Gergen's masks. They are roles that a person plays with a characteristic style in varying situations. Examples might be "mother," "sister," "golfer," and "town council member." Each core and sub-identity has certain qualities attached to it—a "confident" woman, a "loving" mother, a "devoted" sister, and so forth.

Argyle also posits the existence of an "ego-ideal." This feature of the self-concept resembles the ego-image in its structure, except that it represents the kind of person the individual would *like* to be, not necessarily the person he or she really is. Self-esteem in Argyle's model grows out of the relationship of the ego-image and the ego-ideal. The closer they are to one another, the higher the self-esteem; the farther apart, the lower the self-esteem.

On any particular occasion, self-image affects communicative behavior in two ways. These are represented in Figure 10 by the shaded areas. The core characteristics are always relevant. In addition, one or more roles will also be employed. Thus, a person for whom religion is a core aspect of identity may see himself or herself as a "Christian," "Jew," or "Moslem" in all circumstances and, in addition, will adopt a role (or roles) which fit(s) the social situation—"town official," "sister," "friend," "employer," etc.

Changes in the sub-identity aspects of self-image occur in much the same way as they do in the Gergen model. Situational roles become more accepted when they are reinforced by repeated role-playing, feedback from others, and comparison with and imitation of others. Over time, some sub-identities which are no longer used disappear from the self-image, while new ones may be acquired. Changes in the core identity take place more gradually, however, and some elements may never change once established. Change may take place over a period of time until at some point the person regards himself or herself as "middle-aged" rather than "young." A program of exercise may gradually change the body-image from "flabby" to "athletic." On the other hand, a self-perception of being "Jewish" or "black" may remain constant throughout the person's life.

Argyle's model suggests a view of the relationship between self-concept and group participation different from that of Gergen. Since sub-identities, like Gergen's masks, allow a certain amount of flexibility, a person may play numerous roles within the group situation. However, his or her behavior may be somewhat more predictable than the "many masks" model implies, since there will tend to be certain constants in performance owing to the core-identity.

The core will impose some limits on the degree to which the individual will adapt to situational demands. Whenever the direction of the activities of the group touches on these more permanent aspects of self-concept, there will be a tendency for the person to fall back on established ways of reacting. For example, a woman who sees herself as "liberated" may react strongly to any indications of sexism in the group. In this way, the person who has a strong core identity is both less flexible and less conformist than one who does not.

Rogers' "True Self" Model

American psychotherapist Carl Rogers has a view of the self which is distinctively different from that of Gergen or Argyle, although he does discuss some themes found in the writings of each of those theorists (see Rogers, 1961). Like Gergen, he sees the person as being constantly in a state of change, but not so much in response to external demands as to inner feelings. Like Argyle, he believes that each person has certain important central tendencies in the self which operate across situations, but these are not quite the same as a "core identity." Rather, they are values which the person determines for himself or herself, an "internal locus of evaluation," and not a response to role expectations of others.

For Rogers, the "true self" consists of the inner experiences of the individual. In the short run—the "here-and-now"—these experiences consist mainly of the *feelings* the person is experiencing. They change not only from situation to situation, but also from moment to moment. The most immediate answer to the question "Who am I?" thus may be "I am the anger I am experiencing now," "I am the sadness I now feel," or "I feel joyous." In the long run, there is also a more nearly permanent true self for Rogers. This may take the form of repeated patterns of feeling states. Thus, the individual might say, "I am a person who tends to get angry when others do not treat me as an individual," or "I am a person who sometimes feels anxious when I am in a new social situation." The more permanent parts of the self may also be described as values which the person has established for his or her own behavior. For example, speaking for himself, Rogers makes the following statements of self-evaluation:

> In my relations with persons I have found that it does not help, in the long run, to act as though I were something I am not. . . . I have found it of enormous value when I can permit myself to understand another person. . . . Evaluation by others is not a guide for me (Rogers, 1961, pp. 3–27).

Rogers also recognizes another element in the self-concept—one which is in conflict with the true self. This "false self" consists of "facades," roles the person plays which do not reflect inner feelings and self-evaluations. Rogers quotes the statement of a client in therapy which illustrates this kind of facade:

> I somehow developed a sort of knack, I guess, of—well—habit—of trying to make people feel at ease around me, or to make things go along smoothly. There always had to be some appeaser around, being sorta the oil that soothed the waters. At a small meeting, or a little party, or something—I could help things go along nicely and appear to be having a good time. And sometimes I'd surprise myself by arguing against what I really thought when I saw that the person in charge would be quite unhappy about it if I didn't. In other words I just wasn't ever—I mean, I didn't find myself ever being set and definite about things. Now the reason why I did it probably was I'd been doing it around home so much. I just didn't stand up for my own convictions, until I don't know whether I have any convictions to stand up for. I haven't been really honestly being myself, or actually knowing what my real self is, and I've been just playing a sort of false role (Rogers, 1961, p. 109).

Although these are the words of a person in therapy, they have a familiar ring, since most everyone has experienced playing a part which is not really believed.

Rogers' concept of facades resembles Gergen's "roles" and Argyle's "sub-identities." Although Rogers has not dealt directly with this issue in his writings, it appears that his concept is not identical to theirs. It seems possible for a person to play an expected role which is not in conflict with inner feelings. For example, Rogers himself is a psychotherapist, and apparently he feels comfortable with performing a role in which he is accepting and empathic toward his clients. He notes, however, that if he does not like his client, he feels it is important to say so, since deception is not helpful either to the client or to himself. Therefore, a role does not necessarily have to be a facade.

Rogers' view of the self cannot be diagrammed as readily as that of Gergen and Argyle. However, an approximation is presented in Figure 11. In the center is the true self, the on-going experience of the person which consists of feelings and values. The irregular shape of this central area indicates the process nature of the true self. Around the outside of this area are "authentic roles" and "facades" or inauthentic roles. These are indicated with broken rather than solid lines, suggesting two ideas: (1) A particular role performance could be either authentic, or it could be a facade. (2) The boundaries of roles are permeable, since a person could step outside a role to reveal inner feelings whenever these are not consonant with the expected behavior.

For Rogers, change in the self-concept occurs as the person learns to trust inner feelings and throw off facades. When this happens, the individual is free to discover feelings of which he or she was previously un-

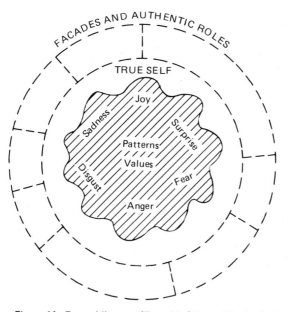

Figure 11 Rogers' "true self" model. (*Note:* The shaded area indicates a "here–and–now" situation in which the person is acting on inner feelings and values and not playing a role.)

aware, and patterns and values emerge from this process. This change is facilitated when the person not only becomes aware of inner feelings, but also acts on them by communicating honest responses to others. The adding of authentic roles or new ways of behaving comes as an incidental by-product of this process of self-discovery. Likewise, self-esteem rises as the individual finds that he or she can act on and trust inner feelings and evaluations. Doing away with facades enhances feelings of personal strength, freedom, and well-being.

It should be recognized that Rogers tends to be prescriptive, while Gergen and Argyle are more descriptive. The discovery of the true self is an ideal, and there are probably few people who are always aware of their inner feelings. Still fewer always act on the basis of those feelings. Nevertheless, Rogers' view suggests certain connections between the self and group behavior.

Rogers describes the person who operates on the basis of the true self as being "congruent" (1961, pp. 338–346). There are two levels of congruence. On the first level of "experience and awareness," the congruent person knows his or her feelings, while the incongruent person does not. On the second level of "awareness and communication," the congruent person lets others know those inner feelings, and the incongruent person does not. It is possible for a person to be congruent on the first level and not on the second, but not vice versa; that is, one can be aware of feelings without communicating them, but it is not possible to communicate, in a clear and unambiguous fashion, feelings of which one is unaware. Most people are probably congruent at some times and incongruent at others, on one or both levels, but there may be wide variations among people in the frequency with which they are aware of and act on the true self.

The person who is often congruent on both levels is likely to exert a significant influence on a group's socioemotional climate because he or she is inclined to express feelings freely. Such a person builds trust with others because it is easy to tell where he or she stands. What is more, according to Rogers' theory, congruency is "catching." Congruent communication behavior on the part of one person tends to cause others to become more congruent—to be more aware of their feelings and to act on them. Conversely, incongruent behavior leads to more incongruency; that is, a person who is unaware of his or her feelings or who deceives others about feelings tends to promote the same behavior in others.

In addition, to the degree that the person communicates here-and-now feelings, rather than responding in terms of the role expectations of others, that individual is less predictable than others, less conformist, and more likely to be a deviant. However, since such a person is inclined to be more aware of his or her own motivations than the average person, he or she is not likely to deviate for the sake of being deviant.

We believe that the discussion participant may find it helpful to review the models of self we have examined here in order to better understand one's own behavior in groups. Some people will find that one model describes their personal view of self better than the others. Although we have presented models which include major ingredients found in the self-concept of many individuals, we do not believe that it is imperative that you make a choice among these alternatives. A combination may make more sense for a particular person.

In addition, we have not presented all of the possibilities. The list of models could be expanded. For example, Vargiu (1974) proposes a view of the self which includes elements similar to those of the Gergen and Rogers models, although his perspective is significantly different. He sees the individual as having many roles, although he does not picture these as being locked into social situations as much as does Gergen. Examples of these roles are "the challenger," "the seducer," "the nuturer," and so forth. In a particular situation, these parts of the self may compete for emergence, much as though a group discussion were being carried on within the individual to choose a leader for the moment, and one or a combination of selves may become dominant for the time being. Vargiu also envisions a central part of the self which regulates the activity of the various selves. This kind of core self may be called "the chooser." While the social situation may influence which self emerges, the individual is also capable of making choices and, thus, of exercising control over his or her own behavior.

We suggest that you examine these various models as a way of gaining self-insight. Observing one's own behavior in groups, and perhaps developing a combination model or an original model of the self which is personally meaningful, can be a worthwhile exercise.

SELF AND GROUPS: THE MEETING OF SYSTEMS

As we have said earlier, both persons and groups can be viewed as communication systems. In order to survive, groups must achieve a delicate, complex, reciprocal interaction between these systems. The group is nothing until the individuals with their limitations, potentials, and self-images come together. Out of the knowledge and impulses they bring, a group begins to form. As it develops, it too takes on the aspects of a system with its own internal structure and integrity and creates the context in which the self systems are influenced and shaped. What a group becomes is a complex outgrowth of the way people relate; what a person becomes, in part, is a complex outgrowth of the groups to which he or she belongs.

In many groups, the two types of systems can complement and feed one another. In such groups, the individual has a chance to exercise his or her potential for change and growth. New behaviors can be tried, and responses from others can be assessed. In return, the group itself becomes more creative by encouraging the expression of diversity within its ranks. But to some extent, these two tendencies—toward individual and group development—are always at war. What is good for the individual is not always good for the group. For example, the leadership role which may benefit a person most may not be the one which is most needed by the group. On the other hand, if the group loses the allegiance of its members, it declines in effectiveness. So a balance must be achieved between the self-concept needs of the individual members and the collaborative efforts required for group action.

SUMMARY AND CONCLUSIONS

The self-concepts of individuals are affected by group interaction. Alterations in the self-image may come about when a person plays a new role, receives feedback, draws comparisons between the self and others, imitates certain people, or introspects about self. Change is especially likely to take place in "reference" groups—those groups in which membership is particularly desired. Self-concept also influences the way people behave in groups, especially at first meetings and at other times when the individual feels singled out.

Several theorists have developed models of the self-concept. Gergen's "many masks" model proposes that individuals perceive "the self" as the situational role they are playing at a particular time. Argyle's "core- and sub-identitites" model adds to Gergen's concept by suggesting not only that people see themselves in roles which fit particular circumstances, but also that certain basic features of a person's self-image always affect behavior, regardless of the situation. Rogers' "true self" model sees the person's feelings and on-going perceptions as being the essence of the self. Thus, it is possible for people to behave in a way which is congruent with the self or incongruent, in which case the person creates a false role, or "facade." Individuals may find that one of these models, or a combination, best describes the way they see themselves. A study of these alternative ways of conceptualizing the self can give people insight into their own behavior in groups.

STUDY SUGGESTIONS

1. Using one or more of the theoretical models of the "self" described in this chapter, try to draw a profile of yourself, the critical groups to which you belong, and the roles or behaviors that typify your performance in each group. Then evaluate the degree to which you are able to be the "self" you would like to be in each group. Are you able to move closer to your "ideal self" (or one or more of your "ideal selves") in some groups more than others? What is there about each group situation and your orientation toward it that influences how your self-concept is revealed in the group?

2. Construct three models of your self based on one of the figures in this chapter (Figures 9, 10, or 11). Let one be a model based on your "self" ten years ago, one as you currently see yourself, and another as you believe you will be in ten years.

3. Are you the same "self" in your relations with your mother, your father, your work group, an activity group (sports, music, theatre), or a classroom group? If not, why not? If so, why so? Does consistency in your behavior indicate rigidity? Does inconsistency in behavior indicate conformity?

Chapter 14
Uses and Abuses of Discussion

Why discuss at all? Perhaps an individual who has the responsibility for making a decision should spend time investigating the facts and reaching a conclusion alone rather than talk to others. Perhaps the individual with a personal problem should learn to meditate rather than seek out others with whom to share feelings. Or, at any rate, even if it is not always possible to work things out alone, perhaps far more use of individual problem solving could be made. Certainly, one hears such arguments from time to time. It is not surprising, in a culture which values individualism as much as Americans do, that for some time there have been critics who strongly question the efficacy of group discussion. Since we have obviously taken a very different position by suggesting that the use of groups is not only widespread but also essential to the healthy functioning of our modern society, it is appropriate that we now face the critics.

THE CHARGES AGAINST GROUP DISCUSSION

Traditional arguments against discussion follow two major lines. The first is that groups are overrated and overused as instruments for solving problems, making decisions, or working out ideas. The second is that group discussion—or "groupthink," as the American sociologist William H. Whyte once dubbed it—produces bland conformists who sacrifice their individual ideas to interpersonal rapport. With the growth in popularity of various kinds of experiential groups, a new and rather different criticism that groups may be used to encourage "narcissism"—the abandonment of responsibility for other people in favor of individual expression—has now been voiced.

The first charge, that group discussion is overrated and overused, was popularized by Mr. Whyte in his best-selling book of the late 1950s, *The Organization Man*. Whyte argued that the American business world is group-ridden and that conferences are called incessantly, frequently for no good reason and with no visible results. About all they succeed in doing, according to Whyte, is kill the spark of initiative and creativity that individuals might have and reduce all problem solving to the lowest common denominator. An expression of this point of view is the cliché: If you want to kill an idea, the best way to do it is to give it to a committee. Although Whyte's criticisms were limited to the world of commerce, very similar criticisms have been made concerning the increasing use of group discussion as a method of teaching.

The second traditional argument, that the growing interest in group activities is part of a cultural trend toward conformity and a loss of individuality, was most vividly developed in David Riesman's book *The Lonely Crowd*, another best-seller of the 1950s. Mr. Riesman portrayed middle-class urban America as a nation of "other-directed" people, each person carrying a very sensitive radar set designed to pick up cues from his or her contemporaries which serve as guides to thoughts and actions. During the time when Mr. Riesman's thesis was so popular, some critics even suggested that Americans were but a short step from the brainwashing processes cultivated, largely through the use of group discussion, by the Chinese communists.

Today these traditional charges against discussion are expressed less strongly, or else the condemnation is less sweeping. Perhaps the critics have simply become resigned to the fact that groups are here to stay. But it may also be that more Americans have begun to accept the idea expressed by Phillip Slater in his book *The Pursuit of Loneliness*. He suggests that the American culture has long frustrated a basic need that people have to feel a sense of community and involvement with others. In any case, individualism continues to be highly valued in our culture, and it is not surprising that the traditional criticisms of discussion have reappeared in somewhat different forms.

Both issues have recently been revived but cast in a new light by psychologist Irving Janis in his book *Victims of Groupthink*. It is significant that Janis uses Whyte's term "groupthink" but applies it to a phenomenon which occurs in some groups at some times and not to all groups, as did Whyte. Janis is not concerned about the long-range effects of the trend toward reliance on groups in our society, but instead calls attention to the fact that pressures for conformity sometimes lead to very bad group decisions on important matters. He cites a number of "fiascoes" of decision making in the executive branch of our government, including the disastrous Bay of Pigs invasion of Cuba of the Kennedy administration and the escalation of the Vietnam War under President Johnson. According to his description, there were individuals who had serious doubts about the plans being formulated and who did not express these views for fear of upsetting the feeling of cohesiveness and certainty emerging in the group.

However, Janis also cites instances of very good group decisions, most notably the development of the Marshall plan for aid to Europe after World War II and the handling of the Cuban missile crisis in 1962, which resulted in Soviet withdrawal from establishing missile bases close to the United States. In these cases, Janis says, certain precautions were taken which avoided the traps of "groupthink."

Thus, to some extent, Janis' ideas echo the older arguments that groups are "overrated and overused" and that they lead to conformity. But he also sees equal or greater dangers in giving decision-making powers to one person. He is more concerned that those who use groups as a means of deliberation will not be aware of their potential misuses, and he sees the tendency toward conformity which exists to some degree in all groups as an obstacle to be overcome.

A new breed of group, sometimes labeled "encounter" or "sensitivity training," has stimulated a new kind of criticism. We will refer to these collectively as "experiential groups." If you have never participated in one of these groups, the following description of what ordinarily goes on may help to show you what the critics are attacking:

> When people sign up for such an experience, their goals are often somewhat fuzzy, but they know that in some way the group experience is supposed to improve their self-awareness and their skills in interpersonal relations. Typically, they go away somewhere for a weekend or even a longer period of time, although they might instead meet for several hours a week on a continuing basis. In some cases, the "leader" or "facilitator" withdraws from the discussion at an early point, allowing the group to flounder a bit in getting to know one another; in other cases, he or she may introduce exercises designed to get people acquainted with one another. Either way, the leader will subtly or quite overtly direct conversation away from trivial information or intellectual exchanges toward the expression of feelings. This may involve individuals telling about personal problems they have experienced outside the group, or it may focus on the reactions which participants have toward others within the group. If the goals of this experience are realized, the group members eventually develop strong feelings of affection for one another and are able to express and examine their emotions rather freely. Ideally, the in-

dividual leaves the group with a new feeling of confidence in his or her feelings, impulses, and perceptions. Of course, when the group's goals are not achieved, it is also possible for the individual to leave with a feeling of confusion or unresolved emotion.

Many of the criticisms which have been leveled at such groups are similar to the traditional arguments against discussion groups which we have already described. It has been suggested, for example, that experiential groups seem to offer a painless and easy way to find "joy,"[1] ignoring the long and difficult struggle which is necessary for a person to really change his or her life for the better (Blanchard, 1970). Some have noted that the positive effects which such groups seem to have on most participants are short-lived, while there may be harmful effects on some individuals. It also has been proposed that the groups may have an "anti-intellectual" influence because they place such a high value on emotional expression while discouraging and disparaging attempts to analyze the motivations of one's self or others. Along this same line, it has also been suggested that the increasing use of sensitivity training methods in the classroom may be inappropriate to academic pursuits (Birnbaum, 1969). All of these objections are reminiscent of the "overrated and overused" charge of earlier days, although they are directed toward the use of groups for purposes of emotional expression rather than policy making or action.

Although the "conformity" charge is less often applied to experiential groups, it has been suggested that the increasing use of such activities as a teaching or training device in schools and business organizations may pose a threat to rights of privacy and thus may endanger individuality (Cottle, 1975). Whether such groups have the effect of creating a "sameness" among participants seems to depend on the kinds of people who participate and the goals of those who direct groups. The use of methods similar to those of encounter groups for purposes of religious conversion, for example, is probably deserving of the charge of conformity. More commonly, however, it is the methods themselves and not the final outcomes which have been likened to "brainwashing." For example, Brewer (1975) has criticized EST (Erhardt Seminars Training) on this ground. In fact, it has been suggested that encounter groups and similar experiences may create people who are *too* individualistic.

In an article in *Harper's* (October, 1975) on "The New Narcissism," Peter Marin has proposed that experiential groups produce effects which are quite different from conformity. According to Marin's analysis, by "getting into" one's own private feelings with the encouragement of other

---

[1] *Joy* was the title of a popular book by William Schultz which was published at the height of the encounter group era (1967). It described numerous nonverbal exercises designed to aid group members in the discovery of feelings.

group members, the individual becomes more and more convinced that perceptions of the world are wholly subjective. Happiness or unhappiness is not something that happens to you, according to this credo, but rather it is something which is chosen, consciously or unconsciously. People who accept this point of view begin to take more responsibility for their perceptions, feelings, and actions, but in so doing, they also come to believe that all others should do the same. Thus, concern for the plight of the poor and oppressed can be easily discarded by those who are better off, says Marin, in favor of the comfortable philosophy that you "create your own world."

AN APPRAISAL OF DISCUSSION

With so much heated expression of views receiving popular attention for such a long period of time, there must be some provocation. Has group discussion been used or abused in ways that would justify the charges leveled against it? Is it, indeed, a process which naturally lends itself to abuse? What, if any, values does it possess? And are they sufficient to warrant our promoting it as a method of learning, decision making, and self-examination? In answering these questions we feel it necessary to respond in guarded terms. This is not a simple, black-and-white issue, and one cannot talk about it intelligently without specifying conditions and qualifications. Still, we do not want to evade our responsibility or to hide our enthusiasm for discussion. We do propose to support the view that *in general*, and *under most circumstances*, group discussion is a valuable method for conducting human affairs.

More specifically, we believe that under most circumstances it is a more effective decision-making method than the determination of policy by one person or by a small elite. We believe that under most circumstances it has more impact as an educational tool than lectures, films, or other one-way means of communication. We believe that under most circumstances it is a more productive means of developing and evaluating solutions to problems than is solitary cogitation. However, we are unwilling to claim the superiority of discussion in *all* circumstances where a task must be performed. Although we would maintain that two heads are *generally* better than one, it depends on the situation for discussion, including whose heads one is talking about.

We would also add that we believe it is usually better for people to express their feelings to others rather than to hold them in. In fact, the frustration of this need in our modern society is one of the reasons why such activities have become institutionalized in the form of encounter and therapy groups. When properly conducted, these experiential groups also can help individuals achieve better self-understanding and effectiveness in dealing with others. In the long run, the experiential group is not an end in itself. Individuals should become better able to do outside the group what they learn to do within the group. We realize, however, that these benefits are not automatic, that the expression of strong feelings is more appropriate to some contexts than to others, and that participation in experiential groups does not always have desirable effects.

In the remainder of this chapter, we will examine the potential values of group participation and the necessary conditions for the realization of those values. Each of these topics will be considered for two kinds of groups. First, we will examine the more traditional use of discussion for the accomplishment of tasks, with emphasis on learning and policy-making groups; then, we will explore the use of discussion for the facilitation of personal growth in experiential groups.

Values of Task-Group Discussion

First we turn to assessing the group which has a specific task to perform. In Chapter 3, we discussed the concept of "the continuum of types of discussion groups" (see Figure 2, p. 43). To the left of the continuum are those groups which focus on the goals of individuals—casual and cathartic groups. Experiential groups fall in the "cathartic" category. To the right are the task groups, those which stress group goals of policy making and action. In the middle are learning groups. Since those groups in the center and right of center stress the creation of quality products—whether these be learning on the part of students, development of effective policies, or efficient performance of specific tasks—it is natural that the criteria for their evaluation will be different from those of other types of groups, and thus we consider them separately.

Discussion makes it possible to bring to a topic a wide variety of information, insights, talents, and critical faculties.

It is not without good reason that the cliché, "Two heads are better than one," has been so often repeated. There is considerable anecdotal evidence as well as experimental research to document the proposition that many problems can be solved more effectively by the interplay of several minds than by people working alone. When discussion does not take place, costly errors can be made. We know of one company which invested a large sum of money in new space for its office—complete with new desks, new telephone lines, and other modern equipment. Responsibility for the arrangement of the new office had been placed in the hands of efficiency experts who did not take the trouble to consult the women who actually worked at the desks. The entire plan eventually had to be scrapped and the office rearranged at considerable expense because one detail had been overlooked. The new placement of telephones made it im-

possible for the secretaries to carry out a well-established office custom—
reaching over and taking each other's calls when one of them stepped out
of the office.

However, we need not rely on casual observation alone to demonstrate that discussion, by its utilization of a variety of insights, can increase
problem-solving effectiveness. In an experiment conducted by Barnlund
(1959) some years ago, comparisons were made between people working
individually on problems in logical reasoning and people working in
groups. All conditions, such as time and personnel, were held equal. It was
found that group solutions as a result of discussion were distinctly superior
to those of the *best* individual member of the group when working alone.
They were also superior to group solutions which were arrived at merely
by combining individual judgments via majority vote.

One of the features of group discussion which makes it superior, in
most situations, to individual performance is the sharing of original ideas.
But another important element of interaction is that members can check
one another's thinking. We quote directly from the study cited above
(Barnlund, 1959):

> Knowledge that one's opinions were to be shared publicly made group mem-
> bers more cautious and deliberate in their own thinking. The necessity of ex-
> plaining a conclusion forced many students to be more self-critical. Errors
> that might have been committed privately were checked before they were
> communicated to others.
> Groups had greater critical resources than individuals working alone. . . .
> Even the poorest members contributed significantly to the quality of the
> group product. Remarks that went no deeper than "I don't understand" or
> "That's absurd" often saved the group from error by forcing them to justify
> their opinions and in so doing disprove their own conclusions (pp. 58–59).

The idea that groups generally perform better than individuals on a
variety of tasks is so widely supported by research that we cannot cite all
of the studies here. Shaw (1976) has reviewed a large number of investigations which show that interacting groups are better at making physical
judgments and at detecting lying or truth-telling in witnesses, that they
perform better at highly structured tasks such as word puzzles and arith-
matic problems, and that they are able to brainstorm more and better solutions to problems requiring creativity (see Shaw, pp. 58–70). Two principles seem to be operating to produce these results: (a) individuals are
able to correct errors and oversights when they can interact with others;
and (b) group members stimulate one another during the discussion process so that they come up with better ideas. This demonstrates the idea
discussed in Chapter 2 that groups are *systems*; they are equal to more
than the sum of their parts.

Therefore, it is not true, as John Steinbeck asserts in *East of Eden,* that "nothing was ever created by two men." If what critics like Steinbeck mean is that there is no such thing as a "group mind" and that ideas cannot be generated in the ether between individuals, we would have to agree. Ideas can only come from people. The issue is whether more and better ideas come from them when they are involved in interacting with others than when cogitating in solitude. On this ground, as we have seen, the Steinbeck generalization is fallacious.

QUALIFYING CONDITIONS

Yet we are not prepared to go to the opposite extreme and maintain that group thinking is always superior to that of an individual. There are a number of qualifications that need to be made.

First, we cannot expect discussion to produce a variety of insights from a group of people who are so much alike in their backgrounds, abilities, interests, and opinions that they largely duplicate each other's views. For discussion to be worthwhile, there must be at least some degree of heterogeneity among the participants. On the other hand, too much heterogeneity can also negate the effectiveness of group action. If there is a wide divergence of attitudes among the members and insufficient unity in goals or values, there may be repeated deadlocks. Discussion may also go awry because of too great a gap in knowledge among the participants. Unless the members of a group are somewhat equally well-informed and of relatively comparable intelligence, the result will either be a conversation dominated by the most able (which becomes a monologue rather than a discussion) or a meeting in which the more capable people are pulled down to the level of the weakest contributors.

Another qualification is that to argue, as we have here, that discussion produces gains in critical thinking presumes discussion *at its best*. But we must not overlook the fact that there are certain kinds of group situations in which critical facilities are lowered rather than heightened. There is a considerable body of research literature which suggests, contrary to the popular notion that groups tend to be conservative, that when individuals think about a problem on their own, they are less likely to make a risky decision than when they interact with others in groups. This phenomenon has been called "the risky shift."[2] While the shift to risk does not always occur in groups (see Clark, 1971) and may represent a rational decision which grows out of interaction (Miller, 1970), this tendency does present a potential problem.

Earlier in this chapter, we referred to the phenomenon which Janis calls "groupthink"—the uncritical acceptance by group members of rash decisions which emerge from a growing consensus and a desire to main-

[2] For a review of the literature pertaining to the risky shift, see Shaw (1976), pp. 70–77.

tain cohesiveness. The process by which this occurs involves the proposal of a risky solution, the lending of support by prominent group members, and the use of social pressure to discourage others from disagreeing. While this may happen with some frequency in groups, especially in those faced with making an emergency decision, it is by no means inevitable. In fact, Janis proposes some ways of avoiding this danger. These include: designation of a "devil's advocate," whose job it is to challenge and test emerging solutions; and the assignment of separate groups to work on the same problem simultaneously, coming together to compare ideas after each has arrived at an independent conclusion.

Finally, assuming that the pitfalls of "groupthink" can be overcome, the value of interaction can be lost if a group is too large for unrestricted communication to take place. In order for discussion to be most fruitful, the group must be small. Some experts place the maximum as low as 8, although our experience would indicate that as many as 15 or 20 *skilled* participants can work together effectively. Even with larger groups it is possible to organize meetings to provide at least some degree of two-way communication and thus to derive at least partial benefits from the variety of people present. Panel discussions in which a cross section of the audience comes forward to talk informally with each other in front of the rest of the group or meetings in which a large gathering of people is subdivided into smaller units which talk for a while and later report their ideas to the general assemblage are but two possibilities for large-group interaction (see Simons, 1966). Generally, however, a group larger than 15 or 20 does not reap the maximum benefit of discussion.

Discussion creates greater motivation, interest and involvement in learning and decision making.

Every one of us has probably had the experience of feeling that we can stay with a job much longer and work harder if we have company. The social satisfactions derived from interacting with other people seem to make the task less onerous. Sometimes a job which is quite boring when undertaken alone can be fun when done with others. Likewise those who have sat in classes conducted by the discussion method have surely noticed how much more quickly the time goes by than when listening to a lecture. This is due to the fact that there are many more sources of stimulation and human interest in a discussion—a variety which even the most outstanding lecturer would have difficulty in matching. In the Barnlund (1959) experiment it was found that subjects:

> concentrated more intently on the assigned problems after being appointed to a group than they did when solving the problems individually. Group members found themselves more and more deeply involved as they pro-

posed, and were forced to defend, their ideas. Participants identified with their own groups to such a degree that when some members became fatigued, others urged them to continue working (p. 58).

One can cite other studies which have demonstrated that when there is greater interaction in a group, there is higher morale and deeper personal involvement among the participants.[3] But the point is so clearly supported by everyday human experience that elaborate proof hardly seems necessary.

In this value of discussion lies one of the answers to the critics who charge that nothing is ever created by a group. If we understand that a group consists of nothing more than individual human beings, it is clear that if they are creative when alone, there is no reason to assume that they cannot continue to be creative, and perhaps even more so, when exposed to the stimulation of other people. Indeed, we could name some individuals who had never known what it was to do truly creative thinking until they were prodded into it by group interaction.

QUALIFYING CONDITIONS

Still, we will agree that, for certain kinds of work, interaction with others may be more of a distraction than a productively motivating force. Although students will usually do better in studying together for an examination involving questions that ask for relationships and interpretations, interaction will be less useful if the test calls for the memorization of lists of terms.[4]

In addition to the nature of the task, there are other considerations which might nullify the normal motivating power of group discussion. People need solitude as well as comradeship, and often some of us do not get enough of the former. Thus, rather than enjoying work on a problem with others, we might find it attractive to solve it alone. Individual temperament is another variable. It may be that people who assert that groups are poor vehicles for creative endeavor are simply expressing their own temperamental aversion to working creatively with others. *For them* it might be true that "nothing was ever created by two men," but this does not make the generalization valid for all people.

Last, people sometimes feel less responsible for solving a problem and, hence, less involved when working with others than when working alone. They take the attitude that in a group "somebody else will do it" and play a passive role themselves. If they had to do the job alone, they would not be able to shunt it off on someone else. In other words, buck-

[3] For instance, see Bavelas (1951) and Horowitz (1954).
[4] Even in this case, however, there may be exceptions. Perlmutter and De Montmollin (1952) found that people do better in memorizing nonsense syllables when they work in groups than when they study alone.

passing rather than greater interest might result from some discussion situations.

Discussion provides an opportunity for dealing with strong feelings and with conflict.

The release of tension is a rather self-evident value of group discussion. Human beings inevitably build up emotional strains and find relief in being able to air their feelings to others. Even if they are not able to eliminate the cause of their frustration, it helps just to tell somebody how they feel. It is probable that a good portion of the benefit derived from group psychotherapy lies in the opportunity for people to share hates, fears, and anxieties with others and to discover that they are not alone in their feelings. Similarly, to the extent that members of task-oriented groups inject personal concerns into a discussion, that meeting will provide some of the values we are here considering.

Sometimes there is nothing that can be done about a situation which causes feelings of frustration. Sometimes emotional reactions are based on a misunderstanding of the conditions which affect one's life, and discussing these confusions with others can lead to clarification. In these cases, discussion serves as a safety valve for individuals and for the groups, organizations, and communities to which they belong. However, in other situations, the expression of grievances can be the first step toward bringing about change. Writing letters to remote authority figures is seldom a satisfying activity, but sharing complaints with others and perhaps taking joint action can be.

QUALIFYING CONDITIONS

It is quite possible for a group to indulge so heavily and so often in catharsis that the participants no longer use it as a safety valve or as a means of initiating productive conflict. It may become the game which Eric Berne has called "Ain't it awful?" If complaints are never carried to the level where something can be done about them, this activity can become a way of avoiding action. In addition, when the sources of frustration lie within the group itself, constant bickering can prevent the members from moving ahead on the task. In particular, the private, personal feelings that people have for one another need not be aired unless such feelings are interfering seriously with the work of the group or with the effectiveness of certain members. A task group is seldom a good vehicle for therapy.

Discussion produces more internalization of decisions and learning.

One of the most basic problems confronted by any society—from the family to the nation—is that of securing understanding and acceptance of social norms and policies from all of the members of the group. Perhaps the most significant claim we can make for the superiority of discussion over one-way communication is supported by its accomplishments in this area. When members of a group have an opportunity to participate in decision-making processes, they feel more identified with decisions, understand them more fully, and are more apt to support and abide by them than if policies are handed down to them ready-made from above.

These generalizations have been tested repeatedly and found valid in a wide variety of experiments, not only in the psychologists' laboratories, but in real-life settings as well. Among the classic pieces of research in this area are the work of Coch and French (1948), Levine and Butler (1952), and Lewin (1943). Coch and French, for example, experimented with three different procedures of decision making affecting a conversion to new work methods in a factory: no participation, participation through representatives, and total participation by all people to be affected by the changes. The investigators discovered that with each degree of increase in participation, the effectiveness of the change was markedly improved.

Likewise, members of learning groups are more likely to master ideas which they have had a chance to discuss than if they study alone. For example, in an early study, Barton (1926) found that students learned algebra better by working in groups than by working individually. As Shaw (1976) concludes, after reviewing a number of investigations, "the results of studies of individual vs. group learning are remarkably consistent in showing that groups learn faster than individuals . . ." (p. 68).

QUALIFYING CONDITIONS

Although most of the critics of group discussion will readily admit its superior effectiveness in producing change in the participants, they find this very value to be a cause of alarm. We must confess that, to some extent at least, we share their concern. They point out that since discussion is so penetrating in its influence it can become a powerful weapon of the hidden persuader. Shrewd manipulators of ideas and of people may pervert the discussion process in such a way that the participants think they are making decisions for themselves when in fact the outcome has been predetermined. Hence, the ideas which they internalize and make their own have been imposed on them without their knowing it.

Yet, we cannot condemn discussion itself for this abuse of its purposes. Rather, we must see to it that ever-increasing numbers of people are trained in small group communication so that they will be able to detect this kind of perversion when it is attempted. There is no danger inherent in the fact that a group decision is effectively internalized—*as long as* those affected have truly had an opportunity to participate in the formulation of the decision and as long as that decision remains open to further exploration and review.

Some critics deny that discussion is the most effective way of bringing about internalization of decisions and information. They suggest that charismatic figures, such as John Fitzgerald Kennedy or Martin Luther King Jr., can gather more support through one-way communication than can a group through means of discussions. Certainly the existence of these examples cannot be denied. Outstanding organization leaders, in all walks of life, succeed in rallying impressive support and loyalty from their followers, who appear to commit themselves rather wholeheartedly to the causes being advocated. Likewise, we can probably all cite instances of an exceptionally vivid lecture or series of talks which have had a great influence on us, just as we can think of discussions which have had no influence at all.

On the other hand, you should recognize that a following achieved through the power of a personality, if not accompanied by discussion and understanding of the issues, tends to be ephemeral. If loyalty is to the leader rather than to the cause, when the leader is gone or when disenchantment sets in, the organization of the movement tends to disintegrate. In a learning situation, this kind of reverence for a teacher, though it may produce some skilled actors, writers, or musicians, more typically develops second-rate imitators of the teacher's style rather than creative independent human beings. In short, when there is little or no opportunity for the development of self-direction, one cannot count on the changes induced in people to last for long. This brings us directly to the final value of task-group discussion.

Discussion develops the abilities and creative potentials of the members of a group.

Not least among the advantages of discussion is what it does for the individuals who participate in it and, thus, indirectly for the group as well. By taking an active part in the decision-making or learning processes which affect them, people are able to exercise and develop whatever creative potentialities they may have. Undoubtedly, in recognition of this principle, many parents and teachers encourage young people who are a bit shy or withdrawn to join group activities at school or in the community. The assumption here is that this experience will help draw them out as individuals.

QUALIFYING CONDITIONS

This value depends on discussion being properly conceived and conducted. Groups can, and some groups do, suppress individuality and creativity. We have already observed how great the pressure toward conformity in a group can be, particularly when such a high value is placed on maintaining friendly relations that anyone who is "different" is cut down to size.

Anyone who has come up through an American high school or college knows what the social pressures are against being "too smart." We would merely repeat again that the kind of atmosphere in which this sort of thing happens is not an inevitable result of group discussion. It can, and in fact is more likely to, occur in a group where real discussion does not take place.

Conditions Necessary for Effective Task-Group Discussion

The values of discussion which we have named above, especially as they apply to decision making, depend largely on certain preconditions of democracy. In discussing these necessary conditions, we will stress parallels between the society as a whole and the small group. While policy-making groups will receive emphasis, some principles apply to other kinds of groups as well, including learning groups.

FULL DELIBERATION

We have said many times in this book that discussion as a means of problem solving requires time. Individuals can usually make decisions more quickly. One of the developments of the last several decades that strikes directly at the foundation of democratic processes is the trend toward increased dependence on what can be called "emergency" decisions. The slower methods of discussion are unsuited to solving crisis situations. When social problems go undetected until the last moment, when there is not sufficient time for proper investigation, when relevant data cannot be gathered, or when external pressures prevent the careful study of alternative courses of action, not only democracy, but *rationality itself*, becomes impossible. Yet there is no escaping the fact that we live in a push-button world. A civil war in Africa, a shift in world markets, a rise in oil prices, a borderline skirmish in the Middle East—these can change the course of world affairs overnight. "Brinkmanship," the art of crisis diplomacy, rules out cooperative deliberation.

The growing reliance on emergency decisions is not limited to world politics. Our personal lives have also been affected. Families are peremptorily transferred from one part of the country to another to carry out corporate plans. In the course of a few days, dozens of family decisions must be made concerning living quarters, school, furniture, personal commitments, etc. In industry, a manufacturer changes a product slightly or reduces cost by introducing a technological change, and competitors must retool or redesign their product within weeks. In a matter of months, quiet farmland is converted into a new and busy community and suddenly schools, fire departments, and police protection are needed. Each of these emergencies creates a demand for action, immediate action. Talk is decried; action sanctified.

Emergencies often play into the hands of those who want to get their own way. The naked use of power is generally frowned on in our society, but this moral stricture is removed when action is desperately called for. So a political figure, a company president, or a parent may find it serves his or her purpose to let events get out of hand in order to justify arbitrary decisions. Sometimes, of course, leaders are not really aware of doing this. They are simply uninformed about the conditions required for democratic decision making. Such actions will be counteracted only when citizens, children, students, and workers realize that one of the costs of self-government is to take an interest in problems and demand discussion of them long before they have become too critical to talk about.

OPEN DISCLOSURE

It is often assumed that security—for an individual or a nation—is best guaranteed by withholding from others critical facts concerning present actions or future plans. Those who are informed about any matter have a natural advantage in making decisions over those who must act in ignorance of the facts. This is most obvious in the case of military decisions. A nation hopes to protect itself from attack by keeping the enemy in the dark regarding its current military strength, the development of new weapons, or the present deployment of its forces. In foreign affairs, it occasionally seems equally desirable to cloak diplomatic or intelligence maneuvers in secrecy.

And yet, the citizens of a government or the members of a policy-making group who are told that the source of certain information cannot be revealed to them may find themselves at a distinct disadvantage in trying to reach a rational decision. They must then rely on whoever claims to hold this information rather than check for themselves. Secrecy can also work in rather covert, subtle ways. For example, the chairperson of an academic department may simply "neglect" to reveal information to faculty members until questioned on the matter, so group members need to know what to ask before they can find out. However, despite the various strategies which are used to promote secrecy, as more and more people insist on their right to know and openly censure those who are discovered to violate this principle, secrecy as an obstacle to discussion can be greatly minimized.

DECENTRALIZATION OF POWER

The symbol of democracy has long been the town meeting where banker, clerk, homeowner, and bus driver have gathered to talk over such problems as enlarging the school, putting in new curbstones, improving the local water supply, or replacing fire equipment. The town meeting is a lovely symbol, but one, unfortunately, that scarcely corresponds to the kind of democracy most of us know in the twentieth century. Very few of us have ever witnessed—much less participated in—a town meeting.

Our problems today, the really important ones at least, are almost never matters of local concern. The village militia has given way to a national defense effort involving millions of men and women and billions of dollars. The individual farmer who once decided how to plant acreage now participates in a federal crop control program. Social welfare measures for a large and aging population have become necessary on a national scale.

Thus, it is obvious, at least on a national scale, that a certain degree of centralization of power is essential. In theory, the smaller the decision-making unit, the greater the chances for decentralization, for sharing of leadership. And yet, there is a tendency for larger systems to influence the operation of those systems which they encompass. For example, in the academic community, federal granting agencies influence the priorities of colleges and universities, which tends to influence the way administrators deal with schools and departments. Where power is centralized in the hands of a chancellor, vice-chancellors, and a few deans, administrators may prefer to handle all business matters "through channels," communicating only with "authorized people." In turn, this gives power to department heads or chairpeople who act as official representatives.

The solution to the problem of overcentralization is for people to work around hierarchical structures. On the governmental level, this means increased use of citizens' lobbies and grass roots politics. We know of one case where a successful movement to stop the winter olympics from coming to Colorado because of environmental considerations was begun with a group meeting of a few concerned citizens. In organizations, the use of ad hoc committees and the establishment of face-to-face contacts cutting across formal lines of power can help. Within small groups, chairpeople can encourage the sharing of influence among the membership, and leaders who try to gather power for themselves can be deposed.

AVOIDANCE OF OVERSPECIALIZATION

A democratic society is threatened by the increased specialization of modern life. The issues of a few generations ago were, for the most part, concrete, uncomplicated, and familiar. The average farmer, storekeeper, or artisan was well prepared to dispose of community problems, for common sense, supported by a modest amount of information, was sufficient. But each advance in science, education, and technology has resulted, as the saying goes, in our knowing "more and more about less and less." The farmer must rely on the work of the expert in soils, genetics, chemistry, and conservation. The general practitioner in medicine has been replaced by the internal specialist, surgeon, orthopedist, gynecologist, dermatologist, obstetrician, and so on.

The relationship of this phenomenon to centralization can be readily seen. The bigger the organization, the greater the need for specialization.

It is in response to this trend that more and more books, such as B. F. Schumacher's *Small Is Beautiful*, argue for a return to human-sized enterprises like small businesses and farms, where individuals or groups of a few people can oversee operations efficiently. To do this effectively, they must rely on their own abilities to gather information on a wide range of topics.

Where does all of this leave ordinary citizens who wish to inform themselves and act with intelligence on public affairs? Consider some of the public issues the citizen faces: Are atomic energy plants safe for the communities in which they must be located, or should we embark on a crash program to develop solar energy and other forms of power? Should wage and price controls be enacted in order to combat inflation? Should taxes be reduced drastically, or will the impact of social services be too great? There are always experts who claim to have the answers, but their recommendations must be carefully evaluated. This has led many critics to wonder if democratic techniques are adequate to meet this challenge.

Policy-making small groups often face similar problems. In light of the many decisions they must make, should they hire an efficiency expert, assign jobs to individuals and give them full power to take action, or allow someone higher in the organization to make difficult decisions? Each abnegation of responsibility by the group loses the advantages of interaction and collaborative action.

Part of the answer is that individuals must keep themselves informed about the issues which affect them within groups, organizations, and society. But even more basically, they need to be broadly educated, not just on various subject matters, but on ways of evaluating evidence and of learning to cope with new and unforeseen problems.[5] Sometimes, they will need to draw on the advice of experts and consultants, but they must also know how to obtain information from such people and how to discuss issues intelligently with others in groups.

INVOLVEMENT

The last, and most important, threat to democratic institutions comes, not from the existence of hostile foreign states or even from antidemocratic forces latent in our own society, but from the personal attitudes of the private citizen. The danger is not external so much as it is internal. Similarly, the greatest problem which any decision-making group may face is that of apathy.

The precondition of involvement relates to all of the other necessary conditions of democracy which we have discussed. Part of the problem lies with leaders. Apathy becomes more likely to the degree that they

[5]A strategy for educating people in this way is described by Postman and Weingartner in their book *Teaching as a Subversive Activity*.

deny participation, fail to reveal information, centralize power in themselves, and restrict the activity of others to narrow specializations. But, on
the other side, those citizens or group members who allow such conditions
to exist are assuring their own continued feelings of helplessness. So we
come full circle. The saying, "the buck stops here," applies not only at the
top but all along the line.

We began this section by saying that the conditions for effective task-
group discussion which we would examine apply mainly to policy-making
groups, but that there are some parallels to learning groups as well. In the
case of the classroom teacher, do the same principles apply? Is it not true
that the teacher who restricts participation, who refuses to negotiate the
nature of assignments, who limits students to the use of assigned materials,
is behaving in antidemocratic ways and is, thereby, limiting the potential
effectiveness of the discussion process?

We must confess that we have known some effective teachers who
were rather thoroughgoing autocrats. This kind of teacher seems to operate best under certain conditions: the subject matter is highly structured
and requires considerable discipline to acquire; the students are strongly
motivated to learn; and, above all, the teacher is highly respected and perhaps liked. (You may wish to compare these conditions with those described under the "traits and situations" approach in Chapter 11, which
called for the cold, task-oriented type of leader.) In this kind of situation,
effective learning can take place in the absence of democratic procedures.
But it seems likely that the discussion method, as we have described it in
this book, will have limited use. Techniques of lecturing and question-
and-answer dialogue would seem to be more appropriate.

Values of Experiential Group Discussion

The experiential group, as we have explained it earlier in this chapter and
elsewhere in the book, has goals and activities very different from those of
the task group. The focus is on interpersonal relations and personal
growth, and not on external products. The stages of group development
are somewhat different (see Chapter 9). Group norms call for more emphasis on self-disclosure and less on the intellectual exploration of ideas.
And, as one might expect, the advantages and dangers of experiential
groups, which we examine below, are distinctive.

*Experiential group discussion tends to bring about increased sensitivity
to one's own feelings and the feelings of others.*

One of the main purposes of experiential groups is to get people to
express their feelings. This is accomplished by various means, including
encouraging people to verbalize reactions to themselves and others and in-

ducing them to participate in nonverbal exercises designed to aid in the discovery and expression of emotions. If this is done, as it should be, in an atmosphere of acceptance, participants are given an opportunity to try out behaviors of self-disclosure which they might feel reluctant to attempt in other situations. This process tends to become contagious, so that expressions of emotion by some group members cause others to become aware of their own feelings, and then to express them, and so on, in a circular fashion. Thus, sensitivity to one's own feelings and the feelings of others are closely related.

We have seen this process occur (and have experienced it ourselves) so often that we take it to be self-evident, at least as a potential outcome of experiential group interaction. It has also been documented in a number of studies. Because of the private and subjective nature of this phenomenon, most investigators have relied on self-report data. Examples of some of the comments made by group participants are provided by Bebout and Gordon (1972):

> I learned to listen—to recognize that everyone has feelings, fears, personal worth. . . . I have learned that other people have feelings and that I cannot come through to them without treating them as such. . . . It provided for me an atmosphere where I was encouraged and at times forced to examine my own emotions and face them honestly (pp. 109–110).

Bass (1962) had participants fill out scales on emotional responses at various points in a group interaction lasting ten days. Feelings of "depression" and "anxiety" rose and then fell over the course of the meetings, while "pleasantness" and "social affection" remained on a high level throughout and increased toward the end.

QUALIFICATIONS

Becoming more aware of feelings should have a therapeutic effect on most people. But some groups concentrate so heavily on the *expression* of emotion, that sensitivity to the feelings of others is neglected. When individuals leave the group, this may result, at least for a time, in their pressing feelings on unsuspecting people without regard for the needs of others. This is part of the "narcissistic" effect described by Marin (1975).

There is some evidence that learning about emotion is to some degree ephemeral. Lieberman, Yalom, and Miles (1972) report the following results of their study:

> Whereas at termination, the ratio of high to low evaluations [of the effect of the group experience] was 4.7 to 1, the comparable ratio six months later was 2.3 to 1. Of sixteen participants judged by the research staff . . . as having received high impact immediately after the group, only nine retained their change fully (p. 129).

These authors also add:

> The picture is not wholly one of "backsliding," however: Of thirty-one participants judged as having changed a moderate amount just following the group, eighteen maintained their change, six lost it, and seven added to their change, deserving the label of late bloomers (p. 129).

These qualifications bring us to another issue: the effect of experiential groups on the communication behavior of participants once they leave the group.

Experiential groups tend to enhance skills in dealing with others.

Some enthusiasts in the experiential group movement believe that this type of activity is justified on "existential" grounds; that is, since participants have the benefit of knowing what it means to experience emotion and growth potentials, they need not apply that new knowledge in relating to other people outside the group. Others, however, argue not only that experiential groups *should*, but also that they *do*, train people to become more skillful communicators.

Experiential groups seem well-suited to developing certain kinds of interpersonal skills—disclosing information about self, taking risks in telling people about feelings, learning how to build trusting relationships, giving direct feedback to others. Bryant and Trower (1974) have found that people tend to rate themselves in distinctively different ways on two types of social skills. One cluster of behaviors may be described as "extroverted skills"—approaching people for the first time, acting as a host or hostess, carrying on a casual social conversation. The other cluster consists of "introverted skills"—getting to know someone in depth, talking to a friend about feelings, helping another to work through a problem. Experiential groups seem to help people most with this latter type of interpersonal behavior.

Several studies have reported improvement of individuals in a variety of communication skills. For example, Himber (1970) found that teenagers who participated in experiential groups said they were better at expressing themselves and making friends. Some investigations have shown that changes in behavior for participants were evident to other people in their home environments. Bunker (1965) found that training affected risk-taking and self-control in positive ways which could be detected by others. Valiquet (1968) observed that co-workers rated those who had returned from experiential groups higher in collaboration, assertiveness, and interpersonal skills. Thus, most respondents reported changes that are related to behaviors which contribute to close personal relations, although some are relevant to skills on the job and in other less personal contexts.

QUALIFICATIONS

While many, if not most, people need to work on their ability to form intimate relationships, other kinds of social skills are also important. In fact, those who have trouble initiating contacts with others may have difficulty in finding those people with whom they can develop close ties. Michael Argyle (1969) has suggested that role-playing, self-observation on videotapes, imitation of socially adept models, and other forms of "skills training" may be more effective than experiential groups in enhancing general social adjustment.

At this point, there is not enough evidence to resolve this issue. Argyle, Bryant, and Trower (1974) have been able to demonstrate that people diagnosed as having severe problems in relating to others may benefit more in the long run from brief skills training sessions than from more extensive exposure to traditional psychiatric treatment. Whether this principle applies to the average person and to those who participate in experiential groups rather than in psychiatric sessions has not been investigated extensively. However, Pyke and Neely (1970) found that both skills and sensitivity training improved performance in small groups, but they did not find a difference between these two approaches. So, at present we do not know to what degree alternatives to experiential groups might be more advantageous for some individuals.

One of the problems with experiential groups to which we have already alluded is that the effects of training tend to "wear off" after the group is over. In addition, a person who has recently returned from one of these groups may behave in ways which are considered inappropriate by others in certain contexts. Open disclosure of feelings may be accepted in a private setting (although not by all people) but rejected at a dinner party. Thus, individuals who have recently acquired new skills may need to learn when and how to use them. An interesting approach, used by some professionals in this field, is to have follow-up sessions in which participants get to process their experiences on the "outside" and to practice adaptations to everyday contexts. In this way, some of the advantages of both skills training and experiential group participation can be enjoyed.

Experiential groups tend to enhance the self-concepts of participants.

Although there has not been a great deal of research on this issue, the available evidence suggests that most people feel better about themselves—have higher self-esteem—after this kind of experience. For example, Burke and Bennis (1961) and Gassner, Gold, and Snadowsky (1964) found that people saw less discrepancy between their self-image and their ego-ideal after participating in experiential groups. This is one of the outcomes of such groups which does not seem to dissipate after the experience. Lieberman, Yalom, and Miles (1972) found that the impact on self-esteem was one of the most powerful effects they observed, and that changes toward increased self-esteem persisted six months later. Bebout and Gordon (1972) discovered that improvement in self-image actually continued to accelerate from the end of the group experience to a follow-up period several months later.

QUALIFICATIONS

Despite the beneficial effects on most participants, there are a certain number of "casualties"—people who suffer increased psychological stress as a result of participating in experiential groups. Several studies have reported this effect, although there is no agreement on how many people may be harmed. In a study of 209 participants, Lieberman, Yalom, and Miles (1972) report a figure of 9.4 percent, one of the highest estimates. They comment:

> The level of disturbance ranged from severe to moderate; one participant had a psychotic episode during the group, another suffered a severe depression with a forty-pound weight loss. Others suffered decrements in self-esteem, felt less trust in others, exhibited increased withdrawal from others. Still other members expressed increased fear of harm from others or a heightened sense of hopelessness or despair over whether they could break through some of the problems they had brought to the encounter group (p. 132).

On the other hand, in a study of 1133 participants, Bebout and Gordon (1972) concluded that:

> it is extremely rare that a member indicates his group as a cause of seriously increasing his problems (less than 1 percent of the time judging from negative comments). In fact, with the available data, we have not been able to identify a single bona fide clinical casualty resulting from a group, though many egos are bruised and lives changed (p. 109).

While several studies report that people are more likely to seek psychotherapy after participating in experiential groups, Lieberman, Yalom, and Miles (1972) point out that only a third of such people in their study were casualties. They say, "for some, entrance into psychotherapy focused on problems that antedated their participation. . . . Others discovered aspects of themselves in the group which they wanted to work on further, so for them entering therapy can be seen as a continuation of growth" (p. 133).

Experiential groups seem to be here to stay. However, as we have seen, the positive effects do not always occur, and there are certain risks for a minority of the participants. This raises a question: Under what circumstances are the chances for the potential benefits maximized and the dangers minimized?

Conditions Necessary for Effective Experiential Group Discussion

Because of the very personal nature of experiential groups, there are few parallels to the societal level, so we will not attempt to draw analogies to larger groups in this section as we did in discussing the conditions for task-group discussion. However, we can point out that there is a certain relationship between the present-day American society and the experiential groups within it. These groups serve a need to redress imbalances in our society toward overintellectualization and ververbalization. People might not need training in recognizing and expressing their feelings if they lived in a culture where self-concepts were rooted in stable social roles and where emotional self-control was not so highly valued. We do not mean this as a condemnation of our culture, but simply as a reminder that there is a price to pay for a highly individualistic orientation. In addition, experiential groups provide social support systems for people who have become lonely and alienated in an impersonal society. This may be a poor substitute for *on-going* relationships in a family, peer group, commune or subculture. But it can be a way of developing within individuals the skills needed to foster and improve those kinds of relationships. On that hopeful but sobering note, let us consider the conditions necessary for successful experiential groups.

COMMITMENT TO PERSONAL GROWTH

In any college catalogue, there is one prerequisite which could be listed for every course: a desire to learn. Motivation is all the more important in experiential groups because active participation is essential. Surprisingly, however, there is little research on this factor, perhaps because most participants are volunteers whose expectations are likely to be similar to the goals of those who conduct such workshops (see Bebout and Gorden, 1972, p. 87).

However, commitment to experiential group activities can be endangered in various ways. In some cases, participants are required or pressured to attend such groups as part of their jobs, even though this is inconsistent with the emphasis in experiential groups on spontaneity and self-directed change. Thus, participants may enter with negative attitudes and the desire to "resist." In some situations, the error is in the opposite direction; more is promised than can be delivered, so participants are highly motivated but also likely to experience disappointment and discouragement. For example, advertisements for experiential group programs sometimes imply that radical personality changes can be achieved. However, the research shows that this seldom occurs (see Shaw, 1976, pp. 352–353). In addition, any factors which tend to undercut the supportive and non-threatening nature of the group situation may also cause motivation to deteriorate (see Bennis and Schien, 1965). If the groups are conducted in a classroom situation, as they sometimes are, this could mean the presence of a teacher who has the power to determine grades. In other circumstances, it could mean simply that participants know one another outside the group, so the protective element of anonymity is lost.

SCREENING OF PARTICIPANTS

While the positive benefits of groups are more likely to be realized when participants are committed to realistic goals, negative outcomes can be largely avoided by screening out participants who are potentially disruptive or prone to psychological harm. These people should be directed to other kinds of help. Screening procedures may include the use of written statements from individuals about their past history of emotional problems and their present motivations for participation, batteries of psychological tests, and brief group sessions held over a period of weeks prior to the more intensive experience (see Stone and Tieger, 1970). Reddy (1970) has suggested a number of kinds of individuals who should be eliminated from participation in groups comprised of people from the general population: (1) those with psychotic tendencies or drug addictions; (2) "narcissistic" individuals who tend to monopolize groups, but without personal benefit; (3) people who are likely to behave in a highly deviant fashion; and (4) participants with histories of psychosomatic illness.

COMPETENT LEADERSHIP

The role of the designated leader is especially important in experiential groups. Although there is some evidence that leaderless counseling groups can have positive effects (Seligman and Desmond, 1973), the uncertainty of the benefits and, especially, the risks of casualties in experiential groups virtually dictate that there should be someone in every group who has a certain degree of responsibility for the outcome and who is competent to lead. There are two aspects of competence. The first is that the leader be well-trained. As Sheridan (1973) has shown, it is not enough to be experienced in such groups; a person should also be trained specifically as a facilitator. Massarik (1972) suggests that this involves conceptual knowledge about group dynamics and related fields, technical skills, and training experience (under the guidance of a skilled co-trainer).

The other aspect of competence is what Massarick calls "humanness"; this quality may be, at best, only partially amenable to training. Leadership style may be so ingrained in personality, that candidates for leadership training must themselves be screened. Lieberman (1972) and his colleagues have shown that the style of the leader is extremely important as a determinant of the outcome for participants. He reports that "energizers," those who specialize in intense emotional stimulation, produce the most positive changes in participants, but also have the greatest number of casualties and dropouts. "Impersonals" (distant, aggressive stimulators), "laissez faire" leaders (passive observers), and "managers" (highly controlling procedural leaders) had an overall negative impact. Of those three, the managers were clearly the worst. The leaders who had the best balance in terms of producing high-learners and few casualties were the "providers" (who stressed caring and made suggestions for personal change) and the "social engineers" (who emphasized learning about group processes, but also gave some emotional support).

SUPPORTIVE ENVIRONMENTS

This is the most difficult condition to meet because those who conduct and participate in experiential groups have little control over this element. In the broadest sense, it means a supportive society—one which has a belief in and a commitment toward individual perfectability. In a specific sense, it refers to the understanding that families, friends, and associates of experiential group participants either show or fail to show. It is difficult to retain changes which are not supported by the systems to which individuals return once they leave the experiential group.

Nevertheless, there are some ways that individuals can exert some influence on their home environments. Lieberman, Yalom, and Miles (1972) report that high-learners, those who were especially "turned-on" to the group experience, "tended to be encounter-mode converts and often were ardent proselytizers who attempted to guide others into encounter groups" (p. 131). There are undoubtedly limits to the degree to which others can be persuaded to join such groups or even to be sympathetic toward them, but participants can be prepared for the shock of "reentry" and also can be taught methods of "translating" their experiences to others, so that rejection of their new behaviors can be avoided or reduced and individuals can have time to adapt skills learned in the experiential groups to everyday situations.

SUMMARY AND CONCLUSIONS

We began this chapter by citing some of the charges against discussion. The traditional arguments are that it is overrated and overused as a method of decision making and learning and that it is part of a general trend in our society toward conformity. The more recent version of these charges is not so sweeping but rather contends that discussion produces poor decisions when strains for cohesiveness and conformity combine to produce "groupthink." The traditional arguments have also been applied in new forms to a comparatively recent phenomenon, the experiential group. In addition, some critics have argued that this kind of group promotes "narcissism"—a self-indulgent disregard for other people and for social issues. We have countered these various criticisms by arguing that the negative outcomes of discussion occur only when the process is misused and certain conditions are not met.

All of the reasons presented in this chapter in favor of or against task-group discussion seem to turn ultimately on the question of what kind of discussion and what kind of group atmosphere one is talking about. Where the group is composed of excessively homogeneous or heterogeneous people, where there are wide gaps in knowledge between the participants, where the group is too large for unrestricted communication, where group pressures toward conformity are strong, where personal interests are irreconcilable, where the nature of the problem requires uninterrupted concentration, where periods of privacy are too rare, where self-indulgence is rampant, or where manipulators remain hidden—under such conditions there is good reason to fear that group discussion will do more harm than good.

On the other hand, where both common purpose and divergent backgrounds are present, where individual differences are respected and encouraged, where the solving of the problem can benefit (as most can) from the interplay of many minds, where the participants can, with good reason, trust one another—under these conditions task groups provide many values. They make it possible to bring to a topic a wider variety of information, attitudes, insights, and talents. Participants can check each other's thinking processes. There is greater motivation, interest, and involvement in learning and in decision making. Discussion provides a safety valve for emotional tensions and a way of initiating productive conflict. It also produces more internalization of decisions and of learning. Finally, it develops the abilities and creative potentials of the members of a group. These advantages of task-group discussion are very dependent on the existence of full participation, open disclosure, decentralization of power, avoidance of overspecialization, and involvement of participants. Without these prerequisites, the effective use of democratic processes is difficult and sometimes impossible.

We have also examined the advantages and limitations of experiential group discussion, an activity which is closely related to learning groups because of its stress on changing behavior, but which is rather different from the policy-making group in its emphasis on emotional expression. Participants in this kind of group tend to gain in sensitivity to their own feelings and the feelings of others, in the development of certain social skills, and in a sense of self-worth. However, it is also true that the impact on emotional sensitivity is sometimes short-lived, that individuals may have difficulty in applying new skills to outside situations, and that some people suffer psychological harm as a result of participating in experiential groups. The values of this kind of group can only be maximized when participants are committed to personal growth, when people who might be harmed by the process are screened out, when leaders are well-trained and suited by personality and style for this kind of helping behavior, and when participants are prepared to cope with social environments which may be unsupportive of changes they have experienced.

The gap between task and experiential groups can be easily overemphasized. We remind you of a principle discussed throughout this book—that every group has both a task and a socioemotional dimension. Regardless of the purpose of the group, neither should be stressed to the complete neglect of the other. There is always the danger that the small task group, in responding to needs for production, efficiency, and emergency decisions, may fail to develop human potentials and member satisfaction, eventually destroying its base. On the other hand, too much preoccupation with impulse, emotion, and adjustment can make experiential groups little more than mere playgrounds for relational recreation, neglecting their potential impact on the work-a-day world. Both needs, for task accomplishment and satisfactory personal relations, for goal-setting and the analysis of process, must receive attention in any human communication system.

STUDY SUGGESTIONS

1. Try to recall the most satisfying group interaction in which you have ever participated and also the most disastrous one. Would any of the considerations discussed in this chapter account for those two experiences?
2. In what respects, if any, might the assessment of group discussion made in this chapter have to be altered if we were examining the question from the perspective of a society other than our American culture? In other words, might different judgments have to be made if we were writing in the context of an African tribal society, for example, or of contemporary Chinese culture? How so?

References

Ackerson, L. *Children's Behavior Problems: Relative Importance and Intercorrelation Among Traits.* Chicago: University of Chicago Press, 1942.

Addington, D. W. "The Relationship of Selected Vocal Characteristics to Personality Perception." *Speech Monographs* 35 (1968): 492–503.

Adler, M. J. "Teaching by Discussion." Mimeographed address, 9 September 1954.

Adorno, T. W.; E. Frenkel-Brunswik; D. J. Levinson; and R. N. Sanford. *The Authoritarian Personality.* New York: Harper & Row, 1950.

Allport, G. "The Open System in Personality Theory." *Journal of Abnormal and Social Psychology* 61 (1960).

Altman, I., and W. Haythorn. "The Ecology of Isolated Groups." *Behavioral Science* 12 (1967): 169–182.

Argyle, M. *The Psychology of Interpersonal Behaviour.* Harmondsworth, England: Penguin Books, 1967.

———. *Social Interaction.* Chicago: Aldine, 1969.

———, B. Bryant, and P. Trower. "Social Skills Training and Psychotherapy." *Psychological Medicine* 4 (1974): 435–443.

Aronson, E., and J. Mills. "Effect of Severity of Initiation on Liking for a Group." In *Group Dynamics: Research and Theory,* 3rd ed., edited by D. Cartwright and A. Zander, pp. 119–124. New York: Harper & Row, 1968.

Asch, S. E. "Effects of Group Pressure Upon the Modification and Distortion of

Judgments." In *Groups, Leadership and Men*, edited by H. Guetzkow, pp. 177–190. Pittsburgh: Carnegie Press, 1951.

Bach, G. R., and P. Wyden. *The Intimate Enemy*. New York: Avon, 1968.

Baird, J. E., Jr. "Sex Differences in Group Communication: A Review of Relevant Research," *Quarterly Journal of Speech* 62 (1976): 179–192.

Bales, R. F. *Interaction Process Analysis*. Reading, Mass.: Addison-Wesley, 1950.

―――. "The Equilibrium Problem in Small Groups." In *Small Groups*, by P. Hare; E. Borgatta, and R. F. Bales, pp. 444–457. New York: Knopf, 1955.

―――, and P. E. Slater, "Role Differentiation in Small Decision-Making Groups." In *Family, Socialization and Interaction Process*, edited by T. Parsons and R. F. Bales, pp. 259–306. New York: Free Press, 1955.

―――; F. L. Strodtbeck; T. M. Mills; and M. E. Rosenborough. "Channels of Communication in Small Groups." *American Sociological Review* 16 (1951): 461–468.

―――, and F. L. Strodtbeck. "Phases in Group Problem-Solving." *Journal of Abnormal and Social Psychology* 46 (1951): 485–495.

Barnard, C. *The Functions of the Executive*. Harvard: Harvard University Press, 1948.

Barnlund, D. C. "Experiments in Leadership Training for Decision-Making Groups." *Speech Monographs* 22 (1955): 1–14.

―――. "Comparative Study of Individual, Majority and Group Judgment." *Journal of Abnormal and Social Psychology* 60 (1959).

―――. "A Transactional Model of Communication." In *Foundations of Communication Research*, edited by K. Sereno and C. D. Mortensen, pp. 83–102. New York: Harper & Row, 1970.

―――. *Public and Private Self in Japan and the United States*. Tokyo: Simul Press, 1975.

―――, and F. S. Haiman. *The Dynamics of Discussion*, 1st ed. Boston: Houghton Mifflin, 1960.

Barton, W. A., Jr. "The Effect of Group Activity and Individual Effort in Developing Ability to Solve Problems in First-Year Algebra." *Journal of Educational Administration and Supervision* 12 (1926): 512–518.

Bass, B. M. "Mood Changes During a Management Training Laboratory." *Journal of Applied Psychology* 53 (1956): 296–299.

Bavelas, A. "Communication Patterns in Task-Oriented Groups." 1951, In *Group Dynamics: Research and Theory*, 3rd ed. edited by D. Cartwright and A. Zander, pp. 503–511. New York: Harper & Row, 1968.

Bayless, O. L. "An Alternative Pattern for Problem Solving Discussion." *Journal of Communication* 17 (1967): 188–197.

Bebout, J., and B. Gordon. "The Value of Encounter." In *New Perspectives on Encounter Groups*, by L. N. Solomon and B. Berzon, pp. 83–118. San Francisco: Jossey-Bass, 1972.

Bennis, W. G., and E. Schein. *Personal and Organizational Change Through Group Methods*. New York: Wiley, 1965.

Berger, C. R., and R. J. Calabrese. "Some Explorations in Initial Interaction and Beyond; Toward a Developmental Theory of Interpersonal Communication." *Human Communication Research* 1 (1975): 99–112.

Berkowitz, L. "Sharing Leadership in Small Decision-Making Groups." In *Small*

Groups, edited by A. P. Hare, E. Borgatta, and R. F. Bales, pp. 543–556. New York: Knopf, 1955.

————. "Personality and Group Position." *Sociometry* 19 (1956): 210–222.

Berne, E. *Games People Play: The Psychology of Human Relationships.* New York: Grove Press, 1967.

Beukenkamp, C., Jr. *Fortunate Strangers.* New York: Grove Press, 1958.

Bion, W. R. *Experiences in Groups.* New York: Basic Books, 1961.

Birnbaum, M. "Sense About Sensitivity Training." *Saturday Review* 52 (November 1969): 82–83ff.

Blanchard, W. H. "Ecstasy Without Agony Is Baloney." *Psychology Today,* 3 (January 1970): 8, 10, 64.

Borg, W. R. "Prediction of Small Group Role Behavior From Personality Variables." *Journal of Abnormal and Social Psychology* 60 (1960): 112–116.

Boulding, K. "Preface to a Special Issue." *Journal of Conflict Resolution* 12 (1968): 409–411.

Bradford, L. "Introduction." *Journal of Social Issues* 4, no. 2 (1948): 2–7.

Brewer, M. "We're Going to Tear You Down and Put You Back Together." *Psychology Today* 9 (July 1975): 35–36, 39–40, 82, 88–89.

Brilhart, J. K., and L. M. Jochem. "Effects of Different Patterns on Outcomes of Problem Solving Discussion." *Journal of Applied Psychology* 48 (1964): 175–179.

Bryant, B., and P. Trower. "Social Difficulty in a Student Population." *British Journal of Educational Psychology* 44 (1974): 13–21.

Bunker, D. R. "Individual Applications of Laboratory Training." *Journal of Applied Behavioral Science* 1 (1965): 131–148.

Burke, R. L., and W. G. Bennis. "Changes in Perception of Self and Others During Human Relations Training." *Human Relations* 14 (1961): 165–182.

Campbell, D. T.; W. H. Kruskal; and W. P. Wallace. "Seating Aggregation as an Index of Attitude." *Sociometry* 29 (1966): 1–15.

Cartwright, D., and A. Zander. *Group Dynamics: Research and Theory.* New York: Harper & Row, 1968.

Cathcart, D., and R. Cathcart. "The Japanese Social Experience and Concept of Groups." In *Intercultural Communication: A Reader* 2nd ed., by L. A. Samovar and R. E. Porter, pp. 58–66. Belmont, Calif.: Wadsworth, 1976.

Clark, R. D., III. "Group Induced Shift Toward Risk: A Critical Appraisal." *Psychological Bulletin* 76 (1971): 251–270.

Coch, L., and J. R. P. French, Jr. "Overcoming Resistance to Change." *Human Relations* 11 (1948): 512–532.

Condon, J. C., and F. Yousef. *An Introduction to Intercultural Communication.* Indianapolis: Bobbs-Merrill, 1975.

Condon, W. S., and W. D. Ogston. "Soundfilm Analysis of Normal and Pathological Behavior Patterns." *Journal of Nervous and Mental Disease* 143 (1966): 338–347.

Cortes, J. B., and F. M. Gatti. "Physique and Self-Description of Temperament." *Journal of Consulting Psychology* 29 (1965): 408–414.

Coser, L. A. *Continuities in the Study of Social Conflict.* New York: Free Press, 1967.

Costanzo, P. R., and M. E. Shaw. "Conformity as a Function of Age Level." *Child Development* 37 (1966): 967–975.

Cottle, T. J. "Let's Keep a Few Secrets: Our Soul-Baring Orgy Destroys the Private Self." *Psychology Today* 9 (October 1975): 22–23, 87.

Damusis, V. B. "Small Group Discussion Characteristics Influencing Perception of Group Consensus and Leader Behavior." *Dissertation Abstracts International* 33 (1972); 2493.

Deutsch, M. "An Experimental Study of the Effect of Co-operation and Competition upon Group Process." *Human Relations* 3 (1949): 199–232.

Deutsch, M., and M. E. Collins. *Interracial Housing: A Psychological Evaluation of a Social Experiment*. Minneapolis: The University of Minnesota Press, 1951.

Dewey, J. *How We Think*. Lexington, Mass.: Heath, 1910, 1933.

Duncan, S. "Some Signals and Rules for Taking Speaking Turns in Conversations." *Journal of Personality and Social Psychology* 23 (1972): 283–292.

Ekman, P., and W. V. Friesen. "Differential Communication of Affect by Head and Body Cues." *Journal of Personality and Social Psychology* 2 (1965): 725–735.

———. *Unmasking the Face*. Englewood Cliffs, N.J.: Prentice-Hall, 1975.

Ellis, D. G., and B. A. Fisher. "Phases of Conflict in Small Group Development: A Markov Analysis." *Human Communication Research* 1 (1975): 195–212.

Exline, R. V. "Visual Interaction: The Glances of Power and Preference." *Nebraska Symposium on Motivation*, (1971): 163–206.

Festinger, L. "Informal Social Communication." *Psychological Review* 57 (1950): 271–282.

———; S. Schachter; and K. Back. "The Spatial Ecology of Groups." In *Social Pressures in Informal Groups*, by L. Festinger, S. Schachter, and K. Back. Stanford, Calif.: Stanford University Press, 1950.

Fiedler, F. E. "Personality and Situational Determinants of Leadership Effectiveness." In *Group Dynamics: Research and Theory*, edited by D. Cartwright and A. Zander, pp. 362–380. New York: Harper & Row, 1968.

Fisher, B. A. "Decision Emergence: Phases in Group Decision Making." *Speech Monographs* 37 (1970a): 53–66.

———. "The Process of Decision Modification in Small Discussion Groups." *Journal of Communication* 20 (1970b); 51–64.

———. *Small Group Decision Making: Communication and the Group Process*. New York: McGraw-Hill, 1974.

Fleishmann, E., I. Harris; and H. Burtt. *Leadership and Supervision in Industry: An Evaluation of a Supervisory Training Program*. Columbus, Ohio: Ohio State Bureau of Educational Research, 1955.

Fromm, E. *Escape From Freedom*. New York: Holt, Rinehart and Winston, 1941.

Frost, J. H., and W. W. Wilmot. *Interpersonal Conflict*. Dubuque, Iowa: Brown, 1978.

Frye, R. L., and B. M. Bass. "Behavior in a Group Related to Tested Social Acquiescence." *Journal of Social Psychology* 61 (1963): 263–266.

Gardner, J. W. *No Easy Victories by John W. Gardner*, edited by H. Rowan. New York: Harper & Row, 1968.

Gassner, S. M.; J. Gold; and A. M. Snadowsky. "Changes in the Phenomenal Field as a Result of Human Relations Training." *Journal of Psychology* 58 (1964): 33–41.

Gergen, K. J. "Multiple Identity: The Healthy, Happy Human Being Wears Many

Masks." *Psychology Today* 5 (May 1972): 31–35, 64, 66.

Gitter, A. G.; H. Black; and J. E. Fishman. "Effect of Race, Sex, Nonverbal Communication, and Verbal Communication on Perception of Leadership." *Sociology and Social Research* 60 (1975): 46–57.

——; H. Black; and A. Goldman. "Role of Nonverbal Communication in the Perception of Leadership." *Perceptual and Motor Skills* 40 (1975): 463–466.

Goffman, E. *The Presentation of Self in Everyday Life.* Garden City, N.Y.: Doubleday (Anchor Books), 1959.

——. *Interaction Ritual: Essays on Face-to-Face Behavior.* Garden City, N.Y.: Anchor Books, 1967.

Goffman, E. *Relations in Public.* Allen Lane: The Penguin Press, 1971.

Goldhaber, M., and G. M. Goldhaber. "A Transactional Analysis of McGregor's Theory X-Y." In *Everybody Wins: Transactional Analysis Applied to Organizations,* edited by D. Jongeward, pp. 265–271. Reading, Mass.: Addison-Wesley, 1973.

Good, L. R., and D. A. Nelson. "Effects of Person-Group and Intragroup Attitude Similarity on Perceived Group Attractiveness and Cohesiveness." *Psychonomic Science* 25 (1971): 215–217.

Gordon, T. *Group-Centered Leadership.* Boston: Houghton Mifflin, 1955.

Gouran, D. S., and J. E. Baird, Jr. "An Analysis of Distributional and Sequential Structure in Problem-Solving and Informal Group Discussions." *Speech Monographs* 39 (1972): 16–22.

Haiman, F. S. "Concepts of Leadership." *Quarterly Journal of Speech,* 39 (1953): 317–322.

Hall, E. T. *The Hidden Dimension.* Garden City, N.Y.: Doubleday, 1966.

Hare, P. "Small Group Discussion With Participatory and Supervisory Leadership." *Small Groups,* by P. Hare, E. Borgatta, and R. F. Bales, pp. 556–560. New York: Knopf, 1955.

——, and R. F. Bales. "Seating Position and Small Group Interaction." *Sociometry* 26 (1963): 480–486.

Hawes, L. C., and D. H. Smith. "A Critique of Assumptions Underlying the Study of Communication in Conflict," *Quarterly Journal of Speech* 59 (1973): 423–435.

Haythorn, W. W. "The Composition of Groups: A Review of the Literature." *Acta Psychologica* 28 (1968): 97–128.

Haythorn, W. W.; A. Couch; D. Haefner; P. Langham; and L. F. Carter. "The Behavior of Authoritarian and Equalitarian Personalities in Groups." *Human Relations* 9 (1956): 57–74.

Hazlitt, W. "Characteristics." in *Selected Essays of William Hazlitt,* edited by G. Keynes. New York: Random House, 1930.

Herrold, K. F.; J. Davitz; D. Fox; and I. Lorge. "Difficulties Encountered in Group Decision Making." *Personnel and Guidance Journal* 31 (1953): 516–523.

Himber, C. "Evaluating Sensitivity Training for Teen-Agers." *Journal of Applied Behavioral Science* 6 (1970): 307–322.

Homans, G. C. *The Human Group.* New York: Harcourt Brace Jovanovich, 1950.

Horowitz, M. "The Recall of Interrupted Groups Tasks: An Experimental Study of Individual Motivation in Relation to Group Goals." *Human Relations* 7 (1954): 3–38.

Hoult, R. "Experimental Measure of Clothing as a Factor in Some Social Ratings of Selected American Men." *American Sociological Review* 19 (1954): 324–328.

Janis, I. L. *Victims of Groupthink: A Psychological Study of Foreign-Policy Decisions and Fiascoes.* Boston: Houghton Mifflin, 1972.

Johnson, A. "An Experimental Study in the Analysis and Measurement of Reflective Thinking." *Speech Monographs* 10 (1943): 83–96.

Kardush, M. M. "Status Congruence and Social Mobility as Determinants of Small Group Behavior." *Dissertation Abstracts International* 30 (1969): 1234.

Kelley, H. H., and J. W. Thibaut. "Group Problem Solving." In *The Handbook of Social Psychology*, edited by G. Lindzey and E. Aronson, pp. 1–101. Reading, Mass.: Addison-Wesley, 1969.

Kendon, A. "Some Functions of Gaze Direction in Social Interaction." *Acta Psychologica* 26 (1967): 22–63.

———, and A. Ferber. "A Description of Some Human Greetings." In *Comparative Ecology and Behaviour of Primates*, edited by R. P. Michael and J. H. Crook. New York: Academic Press, 1973.

Knapp, M. L. *Nonverbal Communication in Human Interaction.* 2nd ed. New York: Holt, Rinehart and Winston, 1978.

———; R. P. Hart; G. W. Friedrich; and G. M. Shulman. "The Rhetoric of Goodbye: Verbal and Nonverbal Correlates of Human Leave-Taking." *Speech Monographs* 40 (1973): 182–198.

Kohs, S. C., and K. W. Irle. "Prophesying Army Promotion." *Journal of Applied Psychology* 4 (1920): 73–87.

Krumboltz, J., and B. Potter. "Behavioral Techniques for Developing Trust, Cohesiveness, and Goal Accomplishment." *Educational Technology* 13 (1973): 26–30.

Larson, C. E. "Forms of Analysis and Small Group Problem-Solving." *Speech Monographs* 36 (1969): 452–455.

———, and R. D. Gratz. "Problem-Solving Discussion Training and t-Group Training: An Experimental Comparison." *Speech Teacher* 19 (1970): 54–57.

Lashbrook, V. J. "Leadership Emergence and Source Valence: Concepts in Support of Interaction Theory and Measurement." *Human Communication Research* 1 (1975): 308–315.

Leathers, D. G. "Process Disruption and Measurement." *Quarterly Journal of Speech* 55 (1969): 287–300.

Leonard, G. *The Man and Woman Thing and Other Provocations.* New York: Dell, 1970.

Levine, J., and J. Butler. "Lecture Versus Group Decision in Changing Behavior." *Journal of Applied Psychology* 36 (1952): 29–33.

Lewin, K. "Forces Behind Food Habits and Methods of Change." *Bulletin of the National Research Council* 108 (1943): 35–65.

———; R. Lippitt; and R. K. White. "Patterns of Aggressive Behavior in Experimentally Created 'Social Climates.'" *Journal of Social Psychology* 10 (1939): 271–299.

Lewis, S. A.; C. J. Langan; and E. P. Hollander. "Expectation of Future Interaction and the Choice of Less Desirable Alternatives in Conformity." *Sociometry* 35 (1972): 440–447.

Lieberman, M. A. "Behavior and Impact of Leaders." In *New Perspectives on*

Encounter Groups, by L. N. Solomon and G. Berzon, pp. 135–170. San Francisco: Jossey-Bass, 1972.

———; I. D. Yalom; and M. B. Miles. "Impact on Participants." In *New Perspectives on Encounter Groups*, by L. N. Solomon and G. Berzon, pp. 119–134. San Francisco: Jossey-Bass, 1972.

Lippitt, R. *Training in Community Relations*. New York: Harper & Row, 1949.

Maier, N. R. F., and A. R. Solem. "The Contribution of a Discussion Leader to the Quality of Group Thinking: The Effective Use of Minority Opinions." *Human Relations* (1952): 277–288.

Maltz, M. *Psycho-Cybernetics: A New Way to Get More Living Out of Life*. Hollywood, Calif.: Wilshire Book Co., 1971.

Mann, R. D. *Interpersonal Styles and Group Development*. New York: Wiley, 1967.

Marin, P. "The New Narcissism." *Harper's Magazine* 251 (October 1975): 45–50, 55–56.

Marsiglio of Padua, "Defensor Pacis." in *Readings in Political Philosophy*, edited by F. W. Coker, pp. 250–251. New York: Macmillan, 1938.

Maslow, A. H., and N. L. Mintz. "Effects of Esthetic Surroundings: I. Initial Effects of Three Esthetic Conditions Upon Perceiving 'Energy' and 'Well-Being' in Faces." *Journal of Psychology* 41 (1956): 247–254.

Massarik, F. "Standards for Group Leadership." In *New Perspectives on Encounter Groups*, by L. N. Solomon and B. Berzon, pp. 68–82. San Francisco: Jossey-Bass, 1972.

McCroskey, J. C. "The Implementation of a Large Scale Program of Systematic Desensitization for Communication Apprehension." *Speech Teacher* 21 (1972): 255–264.

McGregor, D. *The Human Side of Enterprise*. New York: McGraw-Hill, 1960.

McGuire, J. M. "Aggression and Sociometric Status with Preschool Children." *Sociometry* 36 (1973): 542–549.

Meadow, A.; S. J. Parnes; and H. Reese. "Influence of Brainstorming Instructions and Problem Sequence on a Creative Problem Solving Test." *Journal of Applied Psychology* 43 (1959): 413–416.

Mehrabian, A. "Inference of Attitudes from the Posture, Orientation and Distance of a Communicator." *Journal of Consulting and Clinical Psychology* 32 (1968): 296–308.

———. "Significance of Posture and Position in the Communication of Attitude and Status Relationships." *Psychological Bulletin* 71 (1969): 359–372.

Mill, J. S. *On Liberty*. New York: Henry Regnery, n.d.

Miller, H. "Is the Risky Shift the Result of a Rational Group Decision?" Proceedings of the 78th Annual Convention, APA, 1970, 333–334.

Mintz, N. L. "Effects of Esthetic Surroundings: II. Prolonged and Repeated Experience in a 'Beautiful' and 'Ugly' Room." *Journal of Psychology* 41 (1956): 459–466.

Moran, G. "Dyadic Attraction and Orientational Consensus." *Journal of Personality and Social Psychology* 4 (1966): 94–99.

Morse, N. C., and E. Reimer. "The Experimental Change of a Major Organizational Variable." *Journal of Abnormal and Social Psychology* 52 (1956): 120–129.

Newcomb, T. M. "An Approach to the Study of Communicative Acts." *Psychological Review* 60 (1953): 393–404.

———. *The Acquaintance Process*. New York: Holt, Rinehart and Winston 1961.

Nilsen, T. "The Communication Survey: A Study of Communication Problems in Three Office and Factory Units." Unpublished dissertation, Northwestern University, 1953.

O'Connor, J. R. "The Relationship of Kinesic and Verbal Communication to Leadership Perception in Small Group Discussion." *Dissertation Abstracts International* 32 (1972): 6589.

Parnes, S. J., and A. Meadow. "Effects of 'Brainstorming' Instructions on Creative Problem Solving by Trained and Untrained Subjects." *Journal of Educational Psychology* 50 (1959): 171–176.

Perlmutter, H. V., and G. De Montmollin. "Group Learning of Nonsense Syllables." *Journal of Abnormal and Social Psychology* 47 (1952): 762–769.

Postman, N., and C. Weingartner. *Teaching as a Subversive Activity*. New York: Dell (Delacorte Press), 1969.

Preston, M. G., and K. Heintz. "Effects of Participatory Versus Supervisory Leadership on Group Judgments." *Journal of Abnormal and Social Psychology* 44 (1949): 345–355.

Pyke, S. W., and C. A. Neely. "Evaluation of a Group Communication Training Program." *Journal of Communication* 20 (1970): 291–304.

Pyron, H. C., and H. Sharp, Jr. "A Quantitative Study of Reflective Thinking and Performance in Problem-Solving Discussion." *Journal of Communication* 13 (1963): 46–53.

Reddy, W. B. "Sensitivity Training or Group Psychotherapy: The Need for Adequate Screening." *International Journal of Group Psychotherapy* 20 (1970): 366–371.

Redl, Fritz. "Group Emotion and Leadership." In *Small Groups*, by P. Hare, E. Borgatta, and R. F. Bales, pp. 71–87. New York: Knopf, 1955.

Reese, M., and R. Whitman. "Expressive Movements, Warmth, and Verbal Reinforcement." *Journal of Abnormal and Social Psychology* 64 (1962): 234–236.

Reicken, H. W. "The Effect of Talkativeness on Ability to Influence Group Solutions to Problems." *Sociometry* 21 (1958): 309–321.

Report of the Proceedings of the Third Annual Creative Problem-Solving Institute, University of Buffalo, July 1957.

Rice, R. W., and M. M. Chemers. "Personality and Situational Determinants of Leader Behavior." *Journal of Applied Psychology* 60 (1975): 20–27.

Riesman, D. *The Lonely Crowd*. New Haven, Conn.: Yale University Press, 1950.

Roethlisberger, F. J., and W. J. Dickson. *Management and the Worker*. Cambridge, Mass.: Harvard University Press, 1939.

Rogers, C. R. *Client-Centered Therapy: Its Current Practice, Implications, and Theory*. Boston: Houghton Mifflin, 1951.

———. *On Becoming a Person: A Therapist's View of Psychotherapy*. Boston: Houghton Mifflin, 1961.

Rogers, W. T., and S. E. Jones. "Effects of Dominance Tendencies on Floor Holding and Interruption Behavior in Dyadic Interaction." *Human Communication Research* 1 (1975): 113–122.

Rokeach, M. *The Open and Closed Mind*. New York: Basic Books, 1960.

Rosenfeld, L. B., and G. D. Fowler. "Personality, Sex, and Leadership Style." *Communication Monographs* 43 (1976): 320–324.

Ruesch, J., and W. Kees. *Nonverbal Communication: Notes on the Visual Perception of Human Relations.* Berkeley, Calif.: University of California Press, 1956.

Russo, N. "Connotation of Seating Arrangement." *Cornell Journal of Social Relations* 2 (1967): 37–44.

Samuels, M., and N. Samuels. *Seeing with the Mind's Eye.* New York: Random House, 1975.

Sargent, J. F., and G. R. Miller. "Some Differences in Certain Communication Behaviors of Autocratic and Democratic Leaders." *Journal of Communication* 21 (1971): 233–252.

Schachter, S. "Deviation, Rejection, and Communication." *Journal of Abnormal and Social Psychology* 46 (1951): 190–207.

Scheflen, A. E. *How Behavior Means.* Garden City, N.Y.: Doubleday (Anchor Books), 1974.

Scheidel, T. M., and L. Crowell. "Idea Development in Small Discussion Groups." *Quarterly Journal of Speech* 50 (1964): 140–145.

———. "Feedback in Small Group Communication." *Quarterly Journal of Speech* 52 (1966): 273–278.

Schumacher, E. F. *Small Is Beautiful: Economics as if People Mattered.* New York: Harper & Row, 1973.

Schutz, W. C. *Joy: Expanding Human Awareness.* New York: Grove Press, 1967.

Secord, P. F.; W. Bevan, Jr.; and W. F. Dukes. "Occupational and Physiognomic Stereotypes in the Perception of Photographs." *Journal of Social Psychology* 37 (1953): 261–270.

———; W. F. Dukes; and W. Bevan, Jr. "Personalities in Faces: I. An Experiment in Social Perceiving." *Genetic Psychology Monographs* 49 (1954): 231–279.

Segall, M. H.; D. T. Campbell; and M. J. Herskovitz. *The Influence of Culture on Visual Perception.* Indianapolis: Bobbs-Merrill, 1966.

Seligman, M., and R. E. Desmond. "Leaderless Groups: A Review." *Counseling Psychologist* 4 (1973): 70–87.

Senn, D. J. "Attraction as a Function of Similarity-Dissimilarity in Task Performance," *Journal of Personality and Social Psychology* 18 (1971): 120–123.

Sharp, H. Jr., and J. Milliken. "Reflective Thinking Ability and the Product of Problem-Solving Discussion." *Speech Monographs* 31 (1964): 124–127.

Shaw, M. E. "A Comparison of Two Types of Leadership in Various Communication Nets." *Journal of Abnormal and Social Psychology* 50 (1955): 127–134.

Shaw, M. E. *Group Dynamics: The Psychology of Small Group Behavior.* 2nd ed. New York: McGraw-Hill, 1976.

———, and J. C. Gilchrist. "Repetitive Task Failure and Sociometric Choice." *Journal of Abnormal and Social Psychology* 50 (1955): 29–32.

Sheldon, W. H. *Atlas of Man: A Guide for Somatyping the Adult Male at All Ages.* New York: Harper & Row, 1954.

Sheridan, E. P.; J. Shack; R. E. Walker; K. Sheridan; G. Egan; and J. Lavigne. "A Training Program for Small Group Leaders. II. Evaluation," *Journal of Community Psychology* 1 (1973): 8–12.

Siegel, A. E., and S. Siegel. "Reference Groups, Membership Groups, and Attitude Change." *Journal of Abnormal and Social Psychology* 55 (1957): 360–364.

Simons, H. W. "Representative Versus Participative Patterns of Deliberation in Large Groups." *Quarterly Journal of Speech* 52 (1966): 164–171.

Slater, P. E. *The Pursuit of Loneliness: American Culture at the Breaking Point.* Boston: Beacon Press, 1976.

———, and W. G. Bennis. "Democracy Is Inevitable." *Harvard Business Review* (March-April 1964): 51–59.

Spitz, H., and B. Sadock. "Psychiatric Training of Graduate Nursing Students." *N.Y. State Journal of Medicine* (June 1973): 1334–1338.

Steinzor, B. "The Spatial Factor in Face-to-Face Discussion Groups." *Journal of Abnormal and Social Psychology* 45 (1950): 552–555.

Stogdill, R. M. "Personal Factors Associated With Leadership: A Survey of the Literature." *Journal of Psychology* 25 (1948): 35–71.

———. "Group Productivity, Drive, and Cohesiveness." *Organizational Behavior and Human Performance* 8 (1972): 26–43.

Stone, W. N., and M. E. Tieger. "Screening for t-Groups: The Myth of Healthy Candidates." Paper read at the American Psychiatric Association Meeting, San Francisco, 1970.

Strodtbeck. F., and L. Hook. "The Social Dimensions of a Twelve Man Jury Table." *Sociometry* 24 (1961): 397–415.

Strongman, K. T., and C. J. Hart. "Stereotyped Reactions to Body Build." *Psychological Reports* 23 (1968): 1175–1178.

Thibaut, J. W., and H. H. Kelley. *The Social Psychology of Groups.* New York: Wiley 1959.

Torrance, E. P. "Some Consequences of Power Differences on Decision Making in Permanent and Temporary Three-Man Groups." *Research Studies, Washington State College* 22 (1954): 130–140.

Tuckerman, B. W. "Developmental Sequence in Small Groups." *Psychological Bulletin* 63 (1965): 384–399.

———, and M. A. C. Jensen. "Stages of Small-Group Development Revisited." *Group and Organization Studies* 2 (1977): 419–427.

Uesugi, T. T., and W. E. Vinacke. "Strategy in a Feminine Game." *Sociometry* 26 (1963): 75–88.

Valiquet, M. I. "Individual Change in a Management Development Program." *Journal of Applied Behavioral Science* 4 (1968): 313–325.

Van Zelst, R. H. "Sociometrically Selected Work Teams Increase Production." *Personnel Psychology* 5 (1952): 175–186.

Vargiu, J. G. "Subpersonalities." *Psychosynthesis Workbook* in *Synthesis* 1, no. 1 (1974): WB9–WB47.

Walker, R. N. "Body Build and Behavior in Young Children: II. Body Build and Parents' Ratings." *Child Development* 34 (1963): 1–23.

Weigel, R. H.; P. L. Wiser; and S. W. Cook. "The Impact of Cooperative Learning Experiences on Cross-Ethnic Relations and Attitudes." *Journal of Social Issues* 31 (1975): 219–244.

Wells, W., and B. Siegel. "Stereotyped Somatypes." *Psychological Reports* 8 (1961): 77–78.

Wheatley, B. C. "The Effects of Four Styles of Leadership Upon Anxiety in Small Groups." Unpublished dissertation, University of California, 1966.

White, R., and R. Lippitt. *Autocracy and Democracy*. New York: Harper & Row, 1960.

———, and ———. "Leader Behavior and Member Reaction in Three 'Social Climates.'" In *Group Dynamics: Research and Theory*, edited by D. Cartwright and A. Zander, pp. 318–361. New York: Harper & Row, 1968.

Whyte, W. H. *The Organization Man*. New York: Simon and Schuster, 1956.

Wiemann, J. M., and M. L. Knapp. "Turn-Taking in Conversations." *Journal of Communication* 25 (1975): 75–92.

Wilmot, W. W. *Dyadic Communication*. Reading, Mass.: Addison-Wesley, 1979.

Author Index

Subject Index